Say Uncle

...a memoir

Chris Voisard

ISBN: 1470161478
ISBN 13: 9781470161477

Secrets are like stars: They're hot, volatile concentrations of energy, and they have two ways of dying. Over time, small stars simply burn out and cool off, becoming what astronomers call white dwarfs. Massive stars collapse in on themselves, growing so dense that they create an immense gravitational vortex from which even light can't escape. They become black holes.

- Martha Beck

Part I

Chicago (blue)

CHAPTER 1

A Time to be Born (Out of the Hole)

I was in her, waiting to be born.

My mother, lying alone under a sweat-soaked sheet in the West Suburban Hospital outside of Chicago that Friday night, was probably thinking (like a lot of women do when they're in the grip-clutch of pain of childbirth) that she was having the longest, most agonizing labor ever to be experienced by any woman in history. She hoped, like all of us who have experienced that scary-torturous-awesome-surreal anticipation particular to a new person coming out of one's body, that it was all going to be worth it.

In the spirit of what was to become a family tradition, my mother spent her days before Christmas in a drug-induced fog, inhaling a pharmaceutical called "twilight sleep" from a tube at the side of the hospital bed. Everyone–the doctors, the nurses, and especially my mother–wanted me out; it was after all Christmas Eve, a fact that didn't faze me. I was staying right where I was, thank you. I already had that characteristic, the one that pisses some people off, of needing a little extra time. I hadn't quite come to terms with the Agreement I had made this time around, although it was a little late to be having second thoughts.

I was resting upside down in the watery, maroon uterus psyching myself up. If I could have breathed, I would have been puffing little breaths the way athletes do before their biggest challenge. After the contractions began, squeezing and urging me, I continued to resist for two whole days, giving myself, as I tend to do, that little extra time to reconsider, stubbornly clinging to my warm, dark, but now cramped home. There were easier tasks I could have taken on here on Earth, say triumphing over a fatal illness and then getting my smiling face plastered on every TV, showing the world that to Spirit a mere cancer cell is nothing, for example. Having my physical body filled full of Swiss cheese holes would have been easier for me to bear than being born with that one dark hole in my heart. Not the pulsing baby-beater inside my tiny chest, but rather my soul heart. The hole was a deep one passed on through generations. The one I promised to take on, with as much humor and grace as possible, and then fill it, in time to tell about it. A lifetime is so short, and I am so slow that I doubted my ability to do it. Then my resolve set in. I was ready. I was going in. Or rather out.

My grandmother, who I called Gogo as soon as I could talk, waited outside of my mother's hospital room. Gogo was sitting there with her long legs crossed, probably showing an expanse of creamy bare thigh despite the fact that the temperature outside was surely below freezing. She might have been smoking like she always did when she was nervous, forgetting to flick the ashes of her cigarette so that a long gray snake hung precariously from the lit end. She had a lot to be anxious about that night; although the least of it, I think, was caused by how well her daughter was holding up during the long labor.

My father Toni, spelled the Italian way, from An*toni*no, who I called Papa until I was five, was driving his bus route up and down Pulaski Road, while I was deciding whether to join this world or not. Fathers didn't coach their laboring wives how to breathe in those days, or offer ice chips, or videotape the water breaking. I'm sure that some of them paced back and forth in the waiting room, though; at least that's how they showed it on *I Love Lucy* or any other TV shows from those days. The fathers were always running around with crazy bulging eyes, grabbing the suitcase, spilling its contents, and knocking stuff over, as soon as their wives announced that they felt the slightest twinge of pain. Then there was the rushing to the hospital and smoking and pacing in the waiting room until a beaming doctor came out jubilantly proclaiming the gender, which of course was unknown in advance back then. Sometimes the dads would faint at that point. Toni wasn't There, though. He wasn't in the waiting room either.

Finally, I could hold back no longer, and fighting my instilled claustrophobia, went head first down the ridges of the birth canal and came into the startling brightness of this world just as all the church bells started ringing for the evening Christmas Eve Mass, and the snow had subsided to a steady, feathery fall. At least that's how Gogo romanticized that night whenever she told me about it. The doctor probably couldn't wait to untie his blood-splattered gown and rush out of the room, calling out a few obligatory holiday greetings over his shoulder. I was howling like crazy; it was before I lost my tongue in a dream I had a few years later.

It wasn't the doctor but the crackly voice of his dispatcher that told my father Toni he had a daughter. As he has told me countless times since, he changed the routing sign at the front of his bus to read "Out of Service" and raced through the wide, icy, tree-lined streets of Chicago at top speed until he got to the hospital. There, Gogo greeted him in the waiting room. Maybe she took an imperceptible step that blocked her son-in-law's entrance to the viewing room, maybe she started fingering the zipper on his woolen bus driver jacket; I'm not sure, but I bet Toni picked up her vibe. He knew Gogo wanted something and that most of the time she managed to get her way.

That night, my parents named me Margherita Christine Sottile, the Margherita after Toni's mother, although later we found out her real name was Michela, but it had been accidentally changed by Immigration. Michela would have been a cool name to have, but it was not to be. My middle name was Christine because of the Christmas connection. No one called me Margherita for even a minute; I was Christine from that day on, by Gogo's insistence.

Even though she had to spend the holiday in the hospital, my mother told me she didn't mind; she was too excited with the thought of having a new baby girl. The next day was Christmas morning, and I was around half a day old, fresh from the Source. Of course I can't remember what went down that day, but maybe I was new enough to be omniscient still, and that first Christmas is stamped squarely somewhere in my soul.

* * *

Gogo came into the room, her high heels making a click-click sound on the linoleum. She was there very early, even before my Papa arrived.

"Good morning, Duckies. Happy Christmas to you," Gogo said to my still-groggy mother lying in the hospital bed. "Oh, the sweetheart. Look at her. She'll be a Miss America some day; see if she isn't. Duckie, be careful, now. Look, you're smothering her. Here, give her to me," Gogo said, and she tugged on my small arm. I rolled my eyes back in my head and took a blurry look at my grandmother upside down, and thought, *No Way.*

I felt my mother's belly tighten beneath me when her mother came into the room, and the tension radiated up through me. Not even a day old is too young to be feeling the first pangs of worry, but the apprehension went up my spine quickly and started to settle in the blank slates of my brain cells. My mom gently took me off her breast, and I belted out a fresh wail of protest. This didn't deter Gogo, who started rocking me back and forth, cooing, "There, there now, Duckie, it's all right. *I'm* here now."

My mother stared from her prone position at my grandmother holding me.

"Duckie," Gogo said to my mother over my head. "Now I know you and Toni haven't been getting on well, have you? He told me that he really wasn't ready to be a father and was actually thinking of, well, moving on. I'm sure he's said that to you, too." Gogo stared directly at my mother, the two sets of blue-gray eyes locking.

My mother wriggled up in her bed and winced a little before she spoke. "Well, he's a little frightened of the situation, but I'm sure once I get Christine home, he'll see that everything will be fine. He saw her last night and seemed very fond of her immediately. He even held her for a minute or two." My mother squirmed to change position. "She's so small. He'll hardly notice her in our apartment."

"Zbyczek and I, on the other hand," Gogo said, ignoring my mother, "are desperate for a baby. You know that, Duckie. He's barely over the disappointment of the miscarriage last month."

My mother rolled her eyes a little at this.

"Haven't you thought you were pregnant the last three months?" my mother murmured, low enough for me to hear, but apparently not loud enough for Gogo who went on.

"Zbyczek might not have enough manhood in him, you know; I'm sure that's the problem," Gogo said in a low voice, like she was telling us a secret.

"So, Duckie, I was thinking…now you needn't answer right away, mind…but why don't you give the baby to me? You and Toni would be free to separate, if that's what the both of you want, and having a baby would make me and Zbyczek ever so happy. I know it would. I wouldn't do wrong by her, Duckie. You know that I'd love her as my own. I mentioned this to Toni a few months back, and he wasn't adverse to the idea." Gogo was talking very fast now.

I started howling anew at this. Even at one day old, I knew I didn't want to be given away. My mother's mouth was a straight line. Much to my relief, she shook her head 'no,' making her short curls bounce.

"Yes, but he's seen her now, and he's very pleased. I shan't. I want her." I noticed my mother's voice trembled as she said this.

Gogo looked at my mother without blinking. From my vantage point in Gogo's arms, I could see my mom scooching down farther under the covers. Her face and neck were red.

"Duckie, Toni already *agreed*," Gogo said in a softer tone, and her face changed from mad to sad in a second. At this I started crying harder, as loud as I could. I started kicking my legs for the first time ever. Gogo switched me over to her other arm.

"I don't care what Toni said. I had her; this baby is mine! Hand her back to me! Look, she's miserable."

"You never wanted a baby before!" Gogo said, half- real and half- fake crying now. "You know how much I've wanted one! Oh, Dorothy, let me have her now! You can have as many babies as you like, and with Zbyczek's problem... I might not ever have another one!"

Gogo started crying in sync with my own howls. She jiggled me up and down, boo-hooing into the top of my bald head.

My mother watched Gogo and me from her bed, her face turning even redder; little drops of water formed on her top lip. She seemed to be thinking hard. I held my baby breath, waiting for her decision.

"Well," she said slowly, "maybe, I could have another for you. I don't know..." She said this last part all in a big whoosh.

Gogo and I both stopped crying and the room was suddenly very quiet.

I looked at my mother with a surprised hiccup.

"Yes, perhaps. That's right, Duckie." Gogo's hysterics stopped as suddenly as they had begun. "You could get pregnant again easily enough, now couldn't you? You can have as many babies as you like, and I'm only asking for one. Here, take Christine." She handed me quickly back to my mother, where I nuzzled my nose into the smell of her skin. "I'll go over to your flat and see if Toni needs a bit of supper. I'm afraid we don't have much of a Christmas dinner this year, what with all the excitement. I do have the pud, thank goodness; I'll make some custard and take that to him. I'll be back later with some for you, too, Duckie. Now get some rest."

I felt the air in my mother's lungs whoosh out again the minute she heard the last clicking of my grandmother's heels down the hallway. Feeling her steady breathing, I fell fast asleep on her chest.

I have often wondered what would make a woman behave so outrageously as to demand her only daughter hand over her firstborn. It's not that surprising when you think about it, really. Through time women have done all sorts of unconscionable things to keep a man, and of course men have done the same to keep women, all in the name of love.

Gogo had seen what had happened to her mother, Mum Mum as she called her, when her husband, Gogo's father, left her for another woman. I've seen pictures of my great-grandmother, May. She was a very large woman, with a scowl on her face in every single photo. She had those dark rings under her eyes like a lot of people seemed to have back then, but her eyes looked like the lights had gone out—dead. Gogo must have felt a wicked-cold thread of fear go through her when she failed to make Zbyczek "smile as easily as she did at first." She used these words on their divorce papers. The cold thread I'm sure turned into a thick rope when he lunged across the table and throttled her neck just because she'd made an off-colored joke. I'm sure Gogo was desperate to do whatever it took to keep this good-looking Polish guy, sixteen years her junior. A baby was the logical answer, but Gogo's reasoning seemed to stop there. It seems that she never considered that the baby would one day grow up to be a thinking, feeling, questioning adult.

* * *

Now here's the part to this story where Gogo had to convince my father Toni to give up his next child to her. Yes, Gogo was a master manipulator, but this was a pretty big task, even for her. Of course, I wasn't there; I was a day old in West Suburban Hospital when this little exchange took place. It probably went something like this, from what my father has told me, mixed in with what I know about Gogo:

"Toni, Darling," Gogo said, as she took the cloth off of the Christmas pudding. She had put the Bird's custard in a separate jar covered in tinfoil to stay warm.

"Yes, Dorothy, what is it?" Papa eyed the pudding suspiciously. It didn't look anything like the *panettone* he was used to eating on Christmas night. He was sitting at the wooden table in the small apartment he rented with my mother. The overhead light fixture glared down on him, casting shadows under his eyes. My parents hadn't bothered putting up any Christmas decorations that year.

"You certainly got my daughter pregnant very quickly," Gogo started, casting her eyes down modestly. After all, she was talking to her son-in-law about his sex life, more specifically his virility, and she felt this required a certain amount of modesty on her part.

"Well, yes," Papa said, uncertainly. He wasn't sure if this was a subject to discuss with his mother-in-law.

"You must be a very potent young man," Gogo went on boldly. "Why, I can tell just looking at you, with your muscles and all that dark curly hair." She reached over and tousled the top of his head.

"Well..." Papa was warming up to this conversation.

"Why, I bet you and Little Dorothy could have dozens of babies if you wanted to."

"Yes, I suppose we could," Papa said, tentatively forking in a mouthful of the black raisiny cake.

"I think you could get a woman pregnant just looking at her. Or walking by her," Gogo said, wiping a drip of the custard off Toni's chin with a dishtowel she had grabbed off the sink.

Papa blushed.

"I probably would have to get a little closer than that."

"Well, Toni, Darling. Would it be so much just to give up one little seed for Zbysiu and me? Just one. Poor Zbyczek, he has a low sperm count you know," Gogo said, lowering her eyes and her voice.

"How old are you, Dorothy?" Toni asked, chewing thoughtfully.

"Really! I never! How dare you? Surely you must know, Darling, that you never ask a lady her age." Gogo temporarily lost her calculated cool at being asked the question she had dodged her whole life.

Toni remained silent, scraping the last of the pudding off of the yellow Melmac saucer.

"You can have plenty more children. Oodles more. Just one. Please, say you'll have one for us. I know you said before you'd consider giving Christine to me, but I've just been at the hospital and Dorothy won't hear of it."

"Well, I suppose I can have as many as I want," my Papa said, puffing out his chest a little.

Gogo clapped her hands. She let out a whoop and jumped up from her chair. She held Toni's face and kissed him on both his cheeks.

"Oh, thank you, Duckie. This means the world to me. You are a lovely man!" Tears were streaming down her face.

"I didn't say–" Toni began.

"No need to say anything, Darling. I will be forever grateful to you. You don't know the tremendousness of the gift you've just promised us. I must go and tell Zbysiu right away. Oh, thank you, thank you!"

* * *

I'm sure that my Papa sat at the table for a good while after my grandmother left, thinking, mulling, as he tends to do, as I tend to do. The enormity of what she was asking of him I'm sure did not pass him by, and he has told me how he justified it. He thought that the way things were done in this country was just different than they were done in Italy. He was confused and in culture shock. He thought that maybe having a baby for your mother-in-law was accepted here. It didn't seem much more strange to him than only having a half an hour off of work for lunch. He was more surprised that unmarried girls were allowed to go out on dates without a chaperone. He was used to doing as he had been told, especially by his parents, the parental relationship being the most revered of all in Italy. Coming from a fascist country, obedience was branded into his soul, he said. I guess you have to have a lot of rationalizations when you do something like he was contemplating doing.

Eleven months later when my mother became pregnant again, however, Toni said that he had second thoughts. As my mother's stomach grew, he came to the senses he was born with. America or no America, he knew that this was not right. The guys at the office where he worked knew his wife was pregnant, and he worried what he was going to say when he didn't keep the baby. Far worse, something he hadn't considered before, and something that he has a little trouble admitting to me, was the possibility of this second child being a boy. Giving a daughter to his mother-in-law was one thing, but his first son?

* * *

Toni has told me countless times that he tried to talk my mother and my grandmother out of this verbal agreement that had been made. An agreement that didn't seem like such a big deal at the time, but the hugeness of it was growing along with my mother's stomach. By now I was almost a year old, too young to remember anything, of course, but maybe I was still fresh enough from the Universe to Know what was Going On....

* * *

"Dorothy," Papa said one night after they thought I had fallen asleep. My parents were snuggling together on the couch, listening to music from the huge Grundig console that was the centerpiece of our living room.

"Hmmm?" my mother said, half-asleep. My mom was tired and very swollen. Papa rubbed his hand around and around her big, round tummy.

"Do you feel this baby's sex? Can you tell if there is a man or a female growing inside of you?"

"No, darling. Not really. I don't have much intuition–you know that, sweetheart. But if I had to guess, I'd say it was a boy." My mother said this without opening her eyes, slowly like she was half asleep.

At the word "boy," Toni stopped rubbing my mother's stomach with his one hand and instead placed both hands down on her belly protectively.

"Dorothy. This isn't right. I've changed my mind about giving up this baby."

At this my mother's eyes popped open. "Why, because I said it was a boy? I'm sure if it was another girl you'd have no problem." She brushed Toni's hands off of her stomach, and with great effort, turned onto her side, facing away from him.

"No, not just that. Even if it was another girl. It isn't right this business of giving our baby away to your mother. She lives right across the street. We see her every day. How are we supposed to behave when we see our baby with your mother and Zbyczek?"

"Maybe you should have thought of that before you agreed to this then. It's too late now."

"I don't think so. We haven't signed anything. All we have to do is tell your mother that we've changed our minds."

"Toni. I can't. I can't do that to my mother. You see how she's been carrying on, buying the bassinet and sewing the quilts. I can't tell her I've changed my mind now."

"Fine. You can't tell her. I can." With that, Toni climbed over my mother's body on the couch, and went into the bedroom, almost, but not quite, slamming the door behind him.

Toni has told me this story so many times, I feel as though I had been there.

* * *

He ran up the three concrete steps of Gogo's apartment in the middle of the afternoon, taking a fifteen-minute break from his bus route. He stubbed out the cigarette he'd been smoking on the handrail of the stoop, and knocked on the door. He squinted against the low, slanting sun, glancing back over his shoulder to make sure the idling bus was parked okay. Gogo opened the door a crack with the chain still on, peeking out with one eye. When she saw Toni standing there, she unhooked the catch and opened the door wide, smiling. "Hello, darling. What brings you here in the afternoon, you big, good-looking chap?"

"Dorothy, hello." He hesitated a minute, thrown off by Gogo's charms, but then because of the time constraint decided to come straight to the point. "Look. I've been thinking. It would not be right for Dorothy and me to give you this next baby. It's our baby, and we all live close by. It would be too difficult. I'm sorry I've changed my mind. I'm not going to give you our next child." He stared directly into her eyes.

He wasn't prepared for what came next. Gogo clutched the doorknob with one hand, clawed at her heart with her other, and promptly fell onto the Persian carpet, her dress flying up around her hips, showing a little of her white panties. Her bare legs kicked in wide arcs. Her eyes rolled back so that Toni could only see the whites, and she started convulsing and writhing on the floor as if in an epileptic fit. She made a low, moaning guttural sound that seemed to come from deep down inside of her. Toni, standing frozen in the doorway, didn't catch Gogo observing him coolly with one eye that was under the arm she had flung across her face. Then the shaking abruptly stopped, and she lay still on the floor, her breathing so shallow that Toni questioned if she were alive.

He crouched down next to her. "Dorothy. Dorothy!" he said. He put his face close to hers to detect if she was breathing. He could smell the faint aroma of cigarette smoke mixed with Lipton tea, but couldn't feel any breath. There was a little foamy spit dribbling out of the corner of her mouth. He looked down at her chest, sweat glistening in the cleavage. There was no heaving there, as there should have been after that kind of exertion.

Toni backed slowly out of the room. He pressed the lock button on the inside doorknob then went outside, pulling the door shut with a hard jerk. He jumped from the stoop to the sidewalk without touching any of the steps. He climbed into his bus, and cranking hard on the steering wheel, careened down the street.

* * *

Even though I wasn't there for this particular display of histrionics by Gogo, I saw plenty of others later, so I really don't think I exaggerated her fit. Toni didn't tell anyone what he had seen. He's told me that he hadn't felt this kind of fear in his life before, except for the time he had run away by jumping out of his small bedroom window in Sicily when he was four or five, and got lost. When Gogo didn't call for three days, instead of every three hours as she normally did, Toni came to the conclusion that she was dead, and that he had killed her with the shock of his request to keep his baby instead of giving it away. He even considered praying, that's how desperate he was, but was still too repulsed by Catholicism to count on God at this point. He did make a promise to himself that he would do anything, even give away his next child, if he hadn't killed her.

* * *

On a hot humid day in August, on the twenty-fourth just like when I was born, my mother gave birth to a chubby, round, already-smiling boy. Toni got a call from the doctor at the insurance company where he was now working, telling him that he had a son. He drove to the hospital, and almost exactly as when he came to see me, was again blocked by Gogo at the door, only this time she was with her young husband, Zbyczek, or Beba as he had become to me, since I couldn't pronounce his Polish name. Hardly anyone could. The guys at Hotpoint called him John at Beba's request.

I was there at the hospital. At a year and a half, I could walk, and I could talk, and I could understand. Even though the memory is in me somewhere, I can't access those ancient files.

"Papa!" I said when I saw him, and ran towards him on wobbly legs. Toni scooped me up and tried to walk past Gogo and Beba.

"You're not to go in there," Gogo said coldly.

Beba nodded in agreement, though he darted his eyes to the left and right, settling with staring at the ground. Gogo took a handkerchief out of her purse and dabbed at Beba's sweating brow. He said nothing.

"Excuse me, Dorothy, I'd like to see my first son." Papa took a step forward the door.

"You can look at him, Toni, but you're not to touch him. He's ours." Gogo and Beba were holding hands, which I kind of liked, since usually all I saw them do was yell at each other. Beba's blue eyes seemed like they were looking at something over Papa's head. They stood staring at each other for a long time, then Papa pushed past them, carrying me on one of his hips the way I liked him to do. He and I walked into the hospital room, where Mummy lay with her eyes closed. She had thick white tape around her bosom. I could see the small dark head of the baby asleep in a little bassinet beside her.

Papa looked at his son in silence, while I got my first glimpse of my baby brother.

"Dorothy, I don't want to give away my first son," Papa said, trying one last time.

"I'm not terribly happy about it, either." Mummy didn't open her eyes.

"I say we go out there and tell your mother and Zbyczek that we've changed our minds."

My mother opened her eyes and stared at Papa, her mouth in a straight line. I was reaching out to her, saying "mumumumum" but she ignored me. "It's a little late for that now, isn't it? The only reason you want to change your mind is because he's your precious son. A boy. You didn't seem to care so much about giving away Christine when she was born."

I didn't want to think too much about what she meant by that remark, and I really didn't understand all the words yet, but ribbons of the essence of the meaning shot out like arrows, making my whole body feel heavy, doubling the small hole in my soul heart.

My brother, even though asleep, was feeling those arrows too. I was quiet after that.

"The only reason you married me anyway was to get into this country..." my mother went on.

"Dorothy, that's not true..." They went over and stood on either side of the bassinet.

"Toni, that's enough now..." Gogo said. "It's time for you to leave."

Papa looked around the room. It was very hot in there. He stared at Gogo and Beba, at Mummy and the baby. He let out a big breath, and shook his head. He handed me over to Gogo and walked out the door, slamming it hard behind him. He didn't even kiss me goodbye.

* * *

Toni told me how embarrassed he felt when all the guys at the office asked why he wasn't handing out blue cellophane-wrapped cigars. When his coworkers found out that he had given up his son, a rumor started around the office that the new Cris-Craft boat Toni had saved for was actually a bribe from his mother-in-law in exchange for the baby.

Gogo and Beba named my brother George Stefan Golda; the George after Beba's brother Jurek, which is Polish for George, who died in a concentration camp, and the Stefan after Beba's twin.

* * *

Would you like to look inside one of my family photo albums? Yes, all these are still in black and white with scalloped edges and the little triangle dealies to put in the corners to hold them in place. So old-fashioned looking, isn't it? Here's Gogo and Beba leaving the hospital as proud parents of a newborn boy. There's Gogo all dressed up and skinny in a straight-skirted tweed suit, with a little pill box hat, Beba in a jacket and tie, looking kind of solemn, George, all in white, with a big Georgie smile, the way he still smiles when he's not too stressed out, in the old-fashioned bassinet stroller they called the perambulator. There's Gogo and Beba looking down lovingly at the new bundle of white they hold between them. Beba cradling George, Gogo tucking his blankie up around him. A shot of both of them with one hand on the stroller, kissing each other on the mouth. Both Gogo and Beba kissing George on either cheek, mugging for the camera, the photographer unknown to me. Snap. Snap. Snap.

The day my mother gave away her son, she somehow managed to cut all her heartstrings, and she began practicing The Lie, the pathology passed through generations, that I resolved to try to end before entering this world. I'm not sure how she did this, but I know people separate their heart from reality all the time when it gets too painful; I've done it myself. I do know that the truth can be buried, but it's always there, not far from the surface, trying to come up like a clover in the crack in the sidewalk. Cut it, smush it, poison it. It will find another opening—or at least that's what I've observed so far in this life.

And my two-year-old heart was absorbing all that was going on around me. My soul, though still feeling wise and fresh, was already starting to wilt a little around the edges.

CHAPTER 2

After the Goodbye (Round Peg Square Hole)

"Christina, I'm going to California," he said again that morning. Actually, he said *"Vado a California,"* and my stomach squeezed tight like it did every time he said it. I was standing on the toilet so I could watch his face in the mirror as he scraped the shaving cream off with the razor.

"Pa-*PA*!" I said, drawing out the second 'pa,' with a tone that was scolding and flirty; "Domani, per favore!" I would only speak with him in Italian back then, and I tried to sound cheerful and playful, worried that if I was whiny, it might drive him away even faster. He took a few more swipes with his razor, making dark paths in the white cream on his face. I thought, by the faraway look in his eyes, that he was considering my request for him to wait another day.

"Okay, tomorrow," he said, after what seemed like forever, and our mutual brown eyes met for a moment in the steamy medicine cabinet mirror. Too soon, he went back to gazing at the image of himself. He was wearing a white sleeveless undershirt, and his big muscular arms, the ones he always told me to squeeze to see how hard they were, glistened with the moisture of the bathroom. A lock of black curly hair fell onto his forehead. I let out the breath I didn't know I was holding, so glad that I'd talked him out of it again. This was a big job for me, a four-year-old, this daily cajoling my father out of his plan to go to California, and even though I'd held the job for only a week or two, it seemed like an eternity in my short life.

And the life, so far, had been pretty good. I can only remember shimmery blue images (all my Chicago memories are painted blue) and snatches of conversation before the time I was four, but I remember clearly how I felt: Safe. Probably because it was the last time I was to feel that way for a very long time to come.

It was just me and my mom and my dad, a traditional family unit, living in a basement flat on a tree-lined street of redbrick triple-story apartment buildings in the suburbs of Chicago. I have dreamy blue and gray images of the people's feet and ankles as they walked by our sidewalk-level window. I remember lines of clothes and white diapers fluttering in the wind against the blue-gray sky, and how those lines zigzagged and were intercepted between the apartment buildings across the street. I remember piles of sooty indigo snow piled up in clumps along the sidewalk with footprints crunched in it.

I had my own room and it was painted blue. There were anchors on my bedspread, and I had a red upholstered rocker where I liked to sit and play my harmonica or look at my Little Golden Books. Sometimes, if I was quiet too long, Papa would call out from the next room, "Christina?" and I'd answer, "Sí?" expecting him to ask me something, but he was usually just checking to see if I was all right. I liked when he did that.

I felt brave then. I explored fearlessly.

I climbed on the counter and chugged vinegar straight out of the bottle, just because I loved the taste of it on tomatoes. I took bendy paper straws out to the backyard to see if I could suck up dirt. I didn't care that both of these antics led to instant vomiting, it was exciting to find out what would go down and what wouldn't. Once I pulled on the cord of a heavy radio just to see what would happen, and toppled the whole shelf of encyclopedias on top of me. I'd leap and jump and fall and hardly ever cry, even when I got hurt. Well, physically hurt. I only cried when I felt disrespected by adults. I felt serious and wise back then, still fresh from the Source, and a little embarrassed to be a kid, or maybe even a human. I hated when grown-ups talked down to me, or tried to make me laugh with silly faces—I thought it was so demeaning and insulting.

So I was more mad than afraid when Papa threw me over the side of our CrisCraft powerboat into the coldness of Lake Michigan. It didn't take me long to realize that I wasn't going to drown because the puffy orange life jacket I had on kept me bobbing on top like a cork; yet I cried over the indignity of being thrown in by surprise, especially after I had said, very clearly I thought, that I didn't want to go swimming. I kept up the howling long after my mom came in after me, her glasses off, the water flattening her dark curly hair. She held me in the water, comforted me, and said it was okay; but I went on crying long after I had recovered from the shock. When I looked up at Papa on the boat to make sure he understood how mad I was, I saw something in his face that brought my tears to an abrupt halt. It was something like disgust. What scared me more than the cold water was that look on his face.

Besides that time on the boat, I don't remember ever being scared in my very young life, but all that changed when Papa started telling me he was leaving for California. Then a wispy dark thread of fear started wrapping itself around my young heart, finding its way to The Hole that was already there, and The Fear started doing its dirty work.

Once, in my blue room, I thought I had awoken in the middle of the night and saw a fly on the top of my sheet, near my face. I sat up to knock it off with my hand, and when I did, I saw that there were flies all over my blue bedspread, completely covering up the anchors embroidered on it, moving slightly and buzzing, so my bedspread seemed alive. I threw back the covers in horror, and saw that more flies were teeming between my sheets, all around where my bare feet were. Swinging my legs around to get out, I stopped short because my rug was also moving. Then I realized I couldn't see my rug at all; it was all flies. The room was silent except for that low buzz.

I started screaming. Not just a little.

I wouldn't stop, not even after my mom and Papa came in, and turned on the lights. I kept blubbering and crying and saying "the flies" over and over, trying to make them understand the depth of my terror. Both of them moved around the room with quick, uneven movements, furrowed brows, brushing their hands over my furniture, throwing my covers off of my bed, saying, "there are no flies, Christine!" I screamed for a long time after I knew that they were right, but a small part of me still thought that what I had seen was real.

My mom told me later that my hysterics made her think something was wrong with me. But there was something wrong with her. And my father. And their marriage. Plans, secrets, agreements, betrayals, and flies, I mean lies, were swirling around our house and I could feel it, that's all.

Papa and I had had that little exchange about his trip to California daily, for a couple of weeks or so, but I'm not sure, time is so stretchy when you're four. Sometimes, I'd see that same look of disgust on his face when he was shaving, the same one that I saw that day on the boat. As kids tend to do, I thought he was leaving because of me, since he offered me no other explanation, and I was too scared to ask for one. I tried to be extra good and do everything he said. Every time Papa said he'd wait another day to leave, I felt as though I'd bought myself all the time in the world, and the weight was gone, at least until the next day, when the routine would start all over again. I was pretty proud of myself; sort of smug actually, each time I talked him into staying another day. That first taste of power through manipulation went down nice and easy. Too bad I didn't throw that up, like the vinegar and the backyard dirt.

* * *

I knew about this place, California, since we had already been there not long before when Papa had driven us there in his red and white Nash. The trip was *so* long, I couldn't believe he wanted to drive there again. I had sat in the back seat for what seemed like a million days, though it was only four or five, and in the front were my parents with Gogo appropriately sitting in the middle, her golden head of curls towering above my parents' shorter, darker heads. We hung around with Gogo and Beba and George a lot since they lived across the street from us, so they seemed like family, though I didn't know they were actually related to us.

"Oooh, Duckie! Look at all that gorgeous white sand! We must be getting close to California!" Gogo said, turning around and giving me a big smile. I thought it was funny how my mom and Gogo called each other Duckie, even though they were both really named Dorothy.

"Don't be daft, we're only in Utah. That is *salt* you see there." My mom alway spoke as if it was hard for Gogo to understand her.

"I think I know sand when I see it, Duckie!" Gogo sniffed and pushed her glasses up on her nose.

I peeled myself off of the sticky back seat where I had been laying, and peered out the window at the gleaming, sparkling white stretch of land, the endless blue sky. I was hot and bored and didn't care if it was sand or salt, and couldn't see why they did either. I could see Papa gripping the steering wheel very tightly with both hands, not his usual position of one hand on the steering wheel, and the other elbow hanging out the window.

"Duckie, please. It's salt. This is Salt Lake City. Don't you understand the whole city was named after this ... salt?" My mom spoke slowly and carefully as if she were talking to a very little child. The very way I hated when grown ups talked to me.

"DON'T Duckie me!" Gogo shrugged her shoulders and turned away from my mom the best she could in the cramped front seat of the car. "Toni, darling, why don't you tell her then?" she appealed to Toni, who glanced over at his wife and mother-in-law with his eyes squinted as if he had a bad headache. He didn't answer.

"Well, I never! At least I deserve the common DECENCY OF AN ANSWER!"

All three of them lit up cigarettes.

Gogo's voice was reaching the hysterical pitch. I wondered if there was going to be one of those big arguments. I sort of wanted one; at least it would break the monotony. Suddenly Papa slammed on the brakes, toppling me to the floor, and pulled up hard on the handle of the emergency brake. He leaped out of the car, slamming the door behind him. I scrambled back on the seat so I could watch him walk purposefully toward the sparkling white substance in question, his muscled brown calves showing beneath his shorts. He scooped some of the stuff up with one hand, and licking two fingers of his other hand, put some in his mouth. He smacked his lips a few times while looking out over the pale blue horizon wavy with heat. His eyebrows furrowed in concentration, and he seemed to be looking at something far away. He stayed out there longer than he needed to, I thought. The car was quiet the whole time. Finally he brushed his hands together, and walked back toward the silent car. He started the car without saying anything and we started driving.

After a very long, quiet time, he said:

"Salt."

* * *

We made it all the way to San Francisco, where I was thrilled to go in the underwater tank at Playland at the Beach. A round capsule holding about a dozen people was plunged into the gray- green ocean, and we could see the silvery fish swimming all around us. I was creeped out (probably because my mom was) by the huge grotesque Laughing Sal, a lady mannequin with red hair and a freckled clown face who shook and gyrated as she laughed in this maniacal, out-of-control way. That's about all I remembered of the trip, that and the crayons I brought melting all over the back dash of the car. We must have stayed in San Francisco all of one day. Then we turned around and drove all the way back to Chicago.

Playland was fun and all, I thought, but California didn't seem to be *that* great. I didn't understand why Papa thought it was so important to go back there. After all, *I* wasn't there.

* * *

Papa didn't kiss me goodbye the day he left. When I got up he was gone.

I came out of my blue bedroom in my pajamas. I peeked into the bathroom, but the light was out; it was dark. It was still steamy and smelled like soap, though. I already Knew, but I asked anyway.

"Mummy? Where's Papa?" I was hoping against hope that the feeling in my tummy was wrong.

"He told you, didn't he? He went to California today."

I was so mad at myself for sleeping too long. I should have been up earlier to talk him out of it. I hated myself, maybe for the first, but certainly not the last time. This was all my fault. I started crying.

"There, there," my mom said, picking me up and swaying me back and forth. "He'll be home soon, it won't be very long at all."

The smell of my mom's neck comforted me a little.

"How long?" I said, and cried a little more even though I wanted to be brave.

"Oh, I'm not sure..." my mom said, rocking me back and forth.

That thread of fear that had been winding around my heart ever since the fly dream turned into a curtain of lingering darkness that day. I felt lonely for the first time.

A couple of days later I heard my mother on the phone. I knew she was talking to Gogo by the crease between her eyebrows, and the way she wanted to hurry up with what she was saying. I could tell she didn't want me to hear by the way she turned her back to me and tried to whisper.

"They came knocking on the door in the night. Three of them. Yes, uniformed policemen. Of course it frightened me terribly, wouldn't it you? Yes, all right. Yes, it probably would be better. Goodbye."

My mother replaced the black receiver carefully down in the cradle and turned to me.

"We're going across the street to stay with Gogo and Beba and George. Won't that be fun?"

"Why did policemen come to our house in the night?" I vaguely remembered a red flashing light shining through my window, but thought it was a dream.

"Oh, nothing really darling. I guess your Papa left and didn't pay some tickets, that's all."

"So why can't we stay here? What if Papa doesn't know where we are when he comes back?"

"I don't want any more policemen knocking on the door. Who knows what other tickets he didn't pay."

I thought it would be fun to have some extra company, but the three of them would not even begin to take the place of my Papa.

We only took our clothes and a few of my toys across the street to the one bedroom apartment, since it was going to be crowded with the five of us. I didn't like leaving my blue room and my red rocker behind, and I couldn't take very many of my Golden Books. I hated that there wouldn't be a little place just for me. I wished we could stay and wait for Papa to come back.

* * *

"Come in, come in, close the door quickly now, don't let the heat in, I had a fly in here this morning already, and it took me ever so long to kill the bugger. I hate a fly," Gogo said, as soon as we arrived at her front door. I thought that I hated flies too.

"Here Duckie, take that hot jersey off. Arms up like a soldier!" Gogo said to me, while I obediently put my hands up in the air. Pulling my T-shirt up over my head in one motion, she gave me a kiss on my tummy when it became bare. It only took a couple of minutes for Gogo to give me a slice of suet pudding with treacle to eat in front of the television, where George was already sitting, sucking his thumb.

After being there a few days, I concluded that Gogo's husband Beba seemed nice, but musky and aloof, although he was always friendly with me. He spoke in a thick accent that I didn't know was Polish yet. I liked Beba, and he was handsome like my Papa, but so different.

I could feel a vibration from him that I didn't understand. One hot afternoon, not long after we moved in, I walked into the bedroom and saw Beba lying asleep on top of a tangle of white sheets, his brown body naked. I was shocked at seeing his penis. It looked huge, and foreign, the way it flopped to one side. I'd seen George in the bathtub a lot of times, but his three-year-old button on his boy-body didn't prepare me for this. I knew somehow that I shouldn't be looking, but stared a second longer, and then backed out of the bedroom slowly, quietly closing the door with a click. No, this man could never take the place of my Papa; it only made me miss him more.

George and I started playing together right away, even though he was barely three years old. We were soon pulling faces in the mirror, laughing at how identically we could contort our faces. I thought it was amazing how this other person, a boy no less, looked exactly like me. Sometimes, the way he would lift only his left eyebrow, contorting it into an 'S' shape when he didn't understand something would remind me of Papa with a swift short pain in my heart. It would pass though, and sometimes hours could go by when I was playing with Georgie that I didn't think about Papa at all. Even though I could see the top of our house from the second story window of the apartment, it seemed like we were far away.

I was curious about Gogo. She had curly hair, glasses, and an accent like my mom, but Gogo's spirit always seemed to be floating around in the sky and I could tell that my mother tried to keep hers on the ground. One day, I was perched on one of the arms of the big sofa chair in the living room, with my mom in the chair. She was showing me an irresistible miniature sewing kit that had three different pairs of tiny ornate scissors. Gogo had brought me this gift on her last trip to England, but had saved it until now, when she thought I was old enough to use it properly.

"Mummy, why does Gogo bring me presents if she's not my mum?" I asked then. At the time I must have thought that presents only came from your parents.

"Well, she's not your mum, but she is related to you, of course," my mom answered.

"She is? How?" I was puzzled as to how this could be true.

"Don't you know?" my mother asked, squinting at the needle she was trying to thread with the tiny threader in the kit, by holding it up to the lamp.

I thought for a moment. "No. I don't."

"She's my mother, silly." My mother said this without looking at me.

"*That's* your mother?" I said, shocked. I hadn't considered she even had a mother. Looking at the two of them then, I saw a resemblance in how they looked. Both had very curly hair, my mom dark and Gogo blonder, and they both wore glasses and had English accents.

"Why don't you call her Mum, then?"

"Oh, I don't know..." her voice trailed off.

I looked steadily at my mother, waiting for more explanation, but the needle was threaded and she was making the knot on the end by licking her thumb and forefinger and rubbing the thread in between. She was done talking, so I did what I did whenever my mother's voice petered out to a non-conclusion; I made the answer up. My first thought was that it was a Secret, but I didn't like that, so I changed it in my mind, deciding that once you grew up you stopped calling your mother Mum. This also sent a little wave of uneasiness through me, imagining that I would have to call my mother something else someday. I shook my head to get rid of the circular thoughts that were already looping through my psyche on a regular basis, and concentrated on the sewing task at hand.

I still didn't realize Gogo was my grandmother, though. I didn't yet put it together that grandparents are your parents' parents. Gogo didn't let me call her any kind of grandmother name; she had tried to make me say 'Dorothy' but it came out Gogo.

* * *

Every day I'd stare out the window of the apartment looking at the house across the street where we used to live, hoping maybe my Papa would come back that day. I was afraid he might be worried if he came home to the house and we weren't there. Maybe he didn't know we were staying across the street. So I spent a lot of time looking out the window for him, fiddling with the ring that pulled down the shade, picking the paint off the window sill, working on a hole in the paint that got bigger and bigger as the weeks went by, like the one in my heart. I was standing guard, so that I could let my mom know the moment he came back, and we could go home.

The Window Patrol was my new almost-full-time job, taking the place of the Talking-Papa-Out-of-California job. Before that, before the flies, I never needed a job; I could just Be.

My inner fantasy life was born at that window. Sometimes, standing there, looking out over what seemed like my old life, I would imagine my Papa coming home. I could picture him driving up in the little mint-green Rambler, and jumping out fast like he always did, like he couldn't wait to get out. In my mind's eye, I would start waving like crazy, knocking on the glass even though I knew he wouldn't be able to hear me from way over there, but then I imagined he would look up and see me in the window, and I'd be jumping up and down, and he would wave and smile and blow me kisses. Other days, I lost hope, and just wound the shade string around my finger, then unwound it again, over and over.

(My first blue painting was that window, with the small panes of pain. Only I painted my ex-boyfriend, who was appropriately named Tom, peeping in with that crazy look in his eyes.)

Even though I missed my Papa terribly, I'd never say anything to anyone. But I thought about it all day. I missed the way he'd make me espresso and French bread for breakfast, and tuna and tomato for lunch. The eggs and chips Gogo made me were okay, but it wasn't the same. I missed singing opera with him in the car. I missed talking to him in Italian, our own language together that only we shared.

* * *

In the few months since he'd been gone, I noticed my mom's tummy getting very big. It pushed against my back when she snuggled in bed with me. When I asked her about it, she told me that there was a baby in there, and that soon I would have a baby brother or sister, wouldn't that be nice?

I considered this. A baby would be fun; I thought we could maybe name it Swee'Pea after the baby in Popeye.

"Are you still going to love me the most though?" I asked her.

"Of course darling, I'll love you just as much as I do now," she reassured me. I wasn't sure if I wanted to share my mom; I clung to her more now that Papa was gone.

At my daily post at the window the next day, it occurred to me that Papa probably didn't even know that Mommy's tummy was huge, and that a baby was going to come out of it pretty soon now. Looking across into the sidewalk-level window of our old house, I suddenly saw a light flick on. I wasn't imagining it like I had so many times before. My heart raced a little bit. Was Papa over there? I stared at the tiny, faraway window, seeing if I could detect anything, but it was too low to the ground for me to see anything. A few minutes later, the phone rang. My mom said someone wanted to talk to me, and I fairly skipped over to the phone, *I Knew*, and she handed the heavy black receiver to me.

"Christina! *Come stai?*" my Papa's familiar voice came through the phone.

"Papa! *Dove sei?*" I squealed back.

"Across the street from you at our house," he answered.

"I knew it! I saw the light on!" I said this into the phone in Italian, then aside in English, "Mummy! Papa is home! Let's go!"

"Papa, we're coming right now. I'm so glad you're home!" I was jumping up and down on the hardwood floor on my tippy toes in my socks. "What took you so long?"

My mom and I walked across the street to our old house, my mom walking slowly because of her huge stomach. I was holding her hand and walking fast, almost tugging on her arm. I hadn't been in my house since the day we left. I walked past my blue room, looking in and seeing the anchors on the bedspread. Papa was standing in the living room, looking exactly the same, except his face was a hard mask void of any emotion I could decipher. I ran up and hugged him, and he picked me up and kissed me, but only lightly on the forehead. "Papa, we've been across the street with Gogo and Beba, and it's fun playing with George, but there's not enough room and did you know that Mommy's having a baby and why'd you stay away so long, are you home for good *are we moving???*"

He put his fingers up to my lips. "Christina, I can't stay long."

"What, why?" My heart was deflating quickly after being puffed up so big.

"I'm going back to California." I looked over at my mom to see if this surprised her, but she just stood there looking down, rubbing her stomach.

"Are we coming with you?"

He waited a long time before he answered. He didn't look at me; he looked far away. Then his face got mad, and he said, "No."

I didn't ask how long he was going to be gone this time. I didn't ask him why he was leaving. No one told me. The three of us stood around awkwardly. I could feel my tummy was jittering, and my mouth was so dry I couldn't speak. I felt the dark curtain of acceptance close over my heart, covering the hole that was almost full-sized now. I felt the pain in my chest when I breathed. I kissed him goodbye.

Okay, I guess I had to have kissed him, but really I don't remember that last kiss, though there must have been one. I can remember all of the details of that day from way back then, seeing the light across the street, talking to him on the phone, the thrill of hearing his voice, and going back home to see him, but that last goodbye, that last kiss, has been conveniently deleted from my memory bank, put into a separate file in my brain titled "Things Too Painful to Remember."

It could have been different. The hole that grew in my heart that day, the one I lived with, dodged, and covered up for the first half of my life, could perhaps have been avoided. All my father had to say was something like, "Listen, Christina. I have to go. Later you'll see why I feel as if I have no choice. It's not because of you. I love you. Even if I don't see you for a while, remember that I am always thinking of you." But that isn't what happened. Of course, it really couldn't have. It was already fated. Like I said, I had agreed before I was born to accept the Hole and fill it up to tell about it. I wouldn't only be filling my own hole; I would simultaneously be filling Gogo's, and my mother's, and Reyna's, my daughter who was yet to be, and Reyna's daughter, who is still to be.

CHAPTER 3

Herstory

Before I go on with *my* story, maybe I should tell you a little bit about *her* story. The 'her' I am referring to is my grandmother Gogo, and also her daughter, my mother; both of them are confusingly named Dorothy. You may be wondering what events would shape Gogo's character into one who eventually demands that her daughter hand her firstborn baby over to her. Or what in my mother's background would prompt her to agree to have another baby for her mother, and lie about it. Although Gogo was a culprit in deepening The Hole in my heart, it is only fair to point out that she inherited this hole from *her* mother, and passed it down to my mother, who passed it on to me.

I know this history, because luckily, Gogo was a storyteller, and to a lesser degree my mother was too. I grew up hearing these stories. When Gogo told stories they were very dramatic. In the afternoons she would sometimes be moved to act out an anecdote, often getting down on the floor, or kicking up her legs in the air to illustrate a point; but my favorite time to hear Gogo's stories was after I was in bed. I could see her shadowy silhouette in the dark, sitting perfectly still, weaving the tales that I'd heard so many times before, while I painted pictures in my head.

It was from those ever-changing stories that I've gleaned fragments of Truth, and I've arranged and rearranged these rare jagged pieces until a clearer picture was formed; a picture clear enough to reflect like a mirror. And although this mirror is fractured and glued together, it is functional enough to startle me when I look into it and am able to see my own hazy image staring back at me.

I believe Gogo was born wild from a rare rogue seed. Nature and nurture both form a person, and I think Gogo had a good dollop of the somewhat crazy nature that runs through us all.

Once when I was about twelve, Gogo pulled out one of her grade-school photographs to show me what she looked like at my age. She handed me one of those large, cracked, sepia-tone photos that smelled musty from the album it had been hiding in for so long. I gazed at the faded image of rows of preteen girls all wearing identical flouncy skirts below the knee, and big white sailor collars on their blouses. They somberly stared at me from the past with those unsmiling faces and the characteristic dark circles under their eyes, like all the people in the photographs of the early 20s seemed to have. A huge bow was perched on each head of side-parted hair, identically cut in a bob just below the jaw line. The girls looked almost clone-like in their conformity, except for one girl who stuck out like a sore thumb. She was dressed like the others, but her hair was a gigantic, frizzy mop; almost cartoon-like in exaggeration. She was the only girl with a slightly mocking half-smile on her face.

"Which do you think is me, Duckie? Go on, look closely," Gogo said to me.

I scanned the rows of duplicate 1920s preteens. I really couldn't tell which one was her, I just hoped against hope it wasn't the weirdo, although by twelve, I already Knew.

"Is that you?" I pointed to a random girl, far away from the Frizz Head.

"No Duckie, look closely at her mouth, of course that's not me."

I wanted to, but I really couldn't ignore the obvious. I had to ask about that One Girl, although I was already feeling a queasy embarrassment creeping over me.

"What happened to her?" I asked casually, already Knowing.

"What do you mean?"

"I mean, her hair!"

"Curly isn't it?"

"It's more than curly...it's....it's..." I didn't know what to call it. Maybe freakish.

"Why, that's me, Duckie!" Gogo said, beaming so that the gap between her front teeth showed, telling me that she was *proud* to be that girl in the picture. I looked back at the photograph and studied Gogo's crooked smile. I could tell how she loved being noticed, unlike me; all I ever wanted was to blend in.

Those curls gave her away, as if they were the external manifestation of what was going on inside her head. The photograph spoke volumes. I stared closely at her face in the picture; into her eyes that were wide open and defiant.

At the time that this picture was taken, Gogo was a member of the Terrible Four. Many of Gogo's bedtime stories would revolve around how The Four would get into all kinds of trouble; like one story when they all cut school to go sliding down a brick wall on pieces of cardboard, and later getting caught because their 'knickers'— her word for underpants—had holes in them when they took them off for bed. She told me about how she and the other four would often have to "stand behind the screen" at school, the place of disgrace for misbehaving.

Gogo didn't obey the rules from the beginning. Not only was she unapologetic about it, she reveled in it, taking her punishments as badges of honor. She was a non-conformist and she was proud of it. Her hair gave her away.

You've gathered by now that Gogo left the father of my mother, my grandfather, and had instead married this young stud—a Polish soldier. I don't think she was ever madly in love with her first husband, but rather got married because she thought it was time. Why don't I let her tell you that story? Get in bed with me for a minute, here, I'll move over, and listen while Gogo (imagine a strong British accent with a Cockney twang) tells us the story of how she met my Grandfather, her first husband, Archibald, or as most people called him, Taff.

* * *

When I saw the piano they had given me to play in the pub, I took my hands and ran them up and down the yellowed keys. Never mind that it was slightly old and shabby, I was ever so pleased to have a paying job. Not many nineteen-year-olds in London had a job in those days, mind you, not with the General Strike going on. I had to squint my eyes a little to see the notes on the music they had put out for me, but I didn't want to put on my glasses.... I was rather vain when I was young.

You're vain now, I'd think in bed, but I wouldn't dare interrupt one of her stories. If she lost the momentum, sometimes she'd just leave, saying I'd have to wait until another night.

I was so pleased and grateful, Duckie, that Mum had made me take piano lessons. Good old Mum, bless her soul; how she found the money, I'll never know. I remember her rummaging around the bottom of her bag looking for shillings to pay the old piano teacher. Did I ever tell you he was an albino?

Oh yeah lots of times, I'd think. "I think so," I'd say.

His skin was white as snow, and his eyes were pink; he was blind, I dare say, but oh, could he play a piano! He could tune our old one by ear. Mum would go without stockings to pay him. At least when I started working I was able to give her a bit back.

She paused here, I figured to think about her Mum. Sometimes she'd cry when she talked about her, but thankfully not this time.

So, yes, my first job was in the pub. It was terribly noisy and smoky, and I wasn't certain when I was supposed to start playing, as the nasty old owner had led me to the piano, and then turned his back to the bar to pour his pints. Oh, Duckie, I wish you could have seen the dress I was wearing; I did feel smart. Navy with dainty white polka dots, it was; of course I had made it myself without pattern, you know, I copied it directly off of a magazine that I had seen in the sweet shop on High Street. When I sat down, I'll admit this to you Duckie, I didn't pull the dress down to cover my knee; I do have nice legs you know, and I never knew if a handsome bloke might show up at the pub.

It wasn't my first piano-playing job of course. Did I tell you I played the piano in the cinema on the Uxbridge High Street? The films didn't have sound in those days, Christine. It must be difficult for you to imagine no sound, let alone no color. I played along with the movement of the film, and I played anything I damn well pleased. I couldn't see the music you know, it was too dark; and the audience was none the wiser. I did have fun at that cinema...

But I liked this job better, Duckie, because I wasn't sitting in the dark. I like a bit of light you know. And, I had the chance to meet young men; after all, I was nineteen and ready to be married, as all the young girls were in those days. It was different then. If you weren't married by twenty-one you were considered a spinster, and only spinsters had jobs outside of the home. I didn't think I wanted to keep working.

Everyone in the pub was drinking bitters and getting tipsy, and I felt very daring that evening, so I ordered a lemon shandy when the bar maid passed. Only half a pint, mind you—I thought it might give me a bit of courage. When I started playing, it was pure magic; I wasn't moving my hands; the music was coming out of them, Duckie. When I'd finished, one good-looking bloke even gave me a wink.

"Was it Granddad?" I wasn't sure because she changed her stories a little every time she told them.

I'm getting to that… So presently, a young man with a shock of black hair and blue eyes walked toward me, carrying some music. He wasn't the most handsome man in the pub, but kind, I could tell by the crinkles around his eyes.

"Excuse me Miss, if you could be ever-so-kind," he said, holding the music out in front of him. He was trembling, you know, poor fellow. I could tell he was sweet on me already; I saw him glance at my bare knee; but I'd have none of it.

"Yes? What is it?" I said this quite brusquely.

"These are the songs that I will be singing tonight." And he held out the music papers again, and I almost snatched them out of his hand, rather rudely I'm afraid...

I started shouting at him, saying "I wasn't told that I was to accompany a singer! Why, I thought I was going to be able to play what I like. I'll have a word with the manager about this...." and I started to get up from the piano bench.

"Please don't," the young man said.

You mean Granddad?

Yes, it was your Granddad. He put his hand gingerly on my shoulder. He went on: "I'm sure you're pleased to have the work, the way things are now, and dare I say I felt lucky to land a paying job myself. I think we should both manage as best we can. My name is Archibald Morris. You can call me Taff if you like," and he held his big meaty hand out to me. I held my hand out limply. When I looked at the music he had, I was even more put off. It was all Welsh Hymn Tunes. I thought it was dreadfully boring, but I started to play anyway.

He looked almost frightened of me. He closed his eyes and when he opened his mouth, the most beautiful sound you've ever heard came from deep down inside of him, Christine. I looked at him again, this not-so-terribly handsome Welsh man with a lovely tenor voice. He seemed so sincere, so I gave him a smile, and he turned to me, and just as he was reaching the high note, he gave me a wink. Well, goodnight Christine.

"Gogo! Wait! What happened?"

Well, we got married of course. You know that. I'm dreadfully tired. Good night.

* * *

Gogo's mother, Mum Mum, had not talked to Gogo much about sex, and she told Gogo that she had had "absolutely no idea of what to expect" on her wedding night. When Mum Mum had to have—how would she have put it—*marital relations*, she said she would close her eyes and "think of the Queen," and she advised Gogo to do the same. Of course, Gogo was a lot more modern than that; after all this was the 20s. Girls were wearing short dresses, drinking, and nonchalantly sniffing cocaine; something my grandmother would indulge in every chance she could. She had kissed a couple of guys, and from the way Gogo talked, I think she probably thought sex was going to be good, maybe even great. From the slivers of truth in her stories, I gleaned disappointment with Arch. Gogo thought she was missing out on something, and she was going to find out what it was.

Regardless of my speculations about my grandparents' sex life, their union managed to produce a baby. Gogo named her only daughter, my mother, Dorothy, after herself. They called my mother Little Dorothy, and my grandmother Gogo, Big Dorothy. Gogo either had high hopes, or else a large dollop of narcissism to name her baby after herself. Maybe she thought she could start all over again, or live vicariously through her daughter. Perhaps she wanted a new Dorothy to reinvent, or else a Dorothy to act as a constant youthful mirror and companion.

I think the day my mother got her mother's name was the day she started hating her. That very day. Day One. The moment she realized that she carried the burden of being expected to follow in her mother's footsteps, was the moment she started the rebellion. The day my mother was named Dorothy was the day she decided to watch her mother carefully and do exactly the opposite.

My mother told me that she remembered at the age of four wishing her gay Aunt Jess were her mother. My mother was awarded a scholarship to a fancy high school, and Gogo pulled her out because she needed help with her sewing business, and this was when her hate started to gel. She hated everything about Gogo. She even hated *tea,* Gogo's constant companion.

"Why do you hate tea so much?" I'd probe.

"Just hate it, that's all, oooo-er." This answer was usually accompanied by a wrinkling of her nose, and some visible shuddering.

She'd never admit that she hated tea because of Gogo, but she would tell a story about Gogo giving her some cold tea in the middle of the night during an air raid in London, with bombs exploding all around them.

The War. I think that the war had more of an effect on both my mother and Gogo than they ever admitted. It must do something to your soul to have bombs going off all around you, tearing huge holes into the neighborhoods, not to mention people's hearts. I imagine that growing up in a war, when every day could be your last, must give a person a feeling of recklessness and survival by any means—which could explain a few things.

In the midst of the war, Gogo and my mother's flat was bombed, and they were left homeless. Gogo had had one of her premonitions, and decided that she and my preteen mother were going to go to the movies that night. While they were watching the show, the theater lobby was bombed, and the people poured out to the streets. When my mother and Gogo arrived at their house, only one smoky wall was left remaining.

Here's how my mother, a more rare and reluctant storyteller than Gogo, told me how it happened:

"'We're going to the pictures tonight Ducky,' Gogo said. 'Damn the air raid warnings. I can't bear another night of sitting in that shelter; not when it's been so warm outside. I need an outing.'

We walked down the High Street to the cinema. About halfway through the film there was one hell of a...BANG! Then another and another. The theater was being bombed. Of course the audience panicked and started to exit the way they came in, only to find the entrance to the cinema was ...GONE! Panic reigned! Everybody came back to get out through the side exits... it was a mess.

"Weren't you scared?" I always asked my mother this question, and she always answered no. The fear didn't register until much, much later when little things like a clogged toilet or throwing a dinner party would send her to her Valium bottle.

No, everyone was quite calm actually. When we finally got out, we slowly made our way home; it was only a few blocks away. There was smoke everywhere, and we could hear a rat-tat-tat like guns being fired. Of course by this time my mother was in hysterics...

She hated her mother's emotional excess, and I've witnessed her trying to talk Gogo down like a little kid countless times. And now that my mother's latent inherited anxiety has come into fruition, I try my best not to be condescending to her, as a safeguard against the Anxiety Karma. (Oh please don't let it get me.) She acted as if it was perfectly normal to walk home from the movies with bombs dropping all around you, and this "I'm perfectly fine" outer attitude amidst chaos and craziness followed her all of her life. Inside, the fear was doing its dirty work.

...but luckily my dad had left the Air Force base where he was stationed and came and found us. We had a corner apartment – but that had been demolished by one of the bombs. The air raid shelter we stayed in had been blown out of the ground! Luckily the people upstairs weren't in it either, and escaped with only a few scratches. The gunshots were coming from an army vehicle parked near our place, which was apparently full of ammunition.

Our bird, Charlie, was alive; his cage was the only thing left in the apartment, but he never talked again. Gogo's sister Daisy lived just down the road and was okay, and my Grandmother Ewer was staying with her at night, so she was okay as well.

"So where'd you guys go with no house?" I would ask this if I wanted to hear the details of her grandmother's house.

Since Mum Mum's house was empty, my parents and I went there to sleep. There was only one bedroom, and we all shared it that night. Needless to say we didn't get much sleep what with one thing and another! Did I tell you about Mum Mum's house?

"Yes," I'd think, "but please tell me again."

That's what my Grandmother wanted to be called – Mum Mum. I think it was some sort of low-income housing. It consisted of a kitchen, scullery, a "front" room or "lounge," and one bedroom upstairs. There was a little metal box with a door next to the open fire, which served as an oven. I wonder how she cooked in the summer... of course you don't get much of a summer in England anyway! There was no bath and the only toilet was a filthy shed at the bottom of the little garden. I was always scared to go there by myself. The "front" room opened directly onto the street. That's the door where Mum Mum had the vision of baby Ernie's coffin flying out of the house, right before he died. The room had a couch and two chairs and some photos and knickknacks, but NOBODY EVER sat in there!!! Not even at Christmas! Oh I forgot, there was no electricity; it was lit with a gaslight. After the bombing incident that night, Mum Mum moved in with Daisy full-time, and we slept in the "Haunted House" which is what I called it, until we were able to move into another apartment like the one that was demolished. We never slept in a shelter again. In fact, we used to look out of our bedroom window at night and watch London being bombed in the distance!

I never got tired of listening to all these details. My mother might as well have lived on another planet as strange and foreign as all this seemed to me. I didn't like it when she told the sad ending to that story, when her Dad left.

It was about that time, you know, that we started to see less and less of my Dad... Eventually my mother and father separated all together. No one ever really told me why. I guess they thought I was too young to know? And too stupid to ask?

But I have my theories on why they split up.

I can imagine the dreary sameness hitting Gogo the week they were settled into the new apartment, after all the excitement of the bombings. She still had the black market to dabble in for luxuries like stockings and butter, and, there were the "tablets" she started taking around that time. She told me she thought the pills were magic; they gave her enough energy to sew all night. But I think Gogo yearned for something more than could be found in a drug.

Gogo needed to put all that energy somewhere else besides sewing, which was how she made her living. Her husband was at the Air Force base every day and many nights. I can see Gogo waking up alone in the apartment day after day, giving my mother some tea and toast, and sitting down at her sewing machine to work on the alterations, popping a couple of tablets, and basically going crazy. Hadn't she once been making magic come out of the ivory keys?

She met her young Polish soldier in the Underground. He was twenty and she was thirty-five. Unlike Taff, Beba was tall, dark, and handsome, exuded testosterone, and spoke in a low, growly voice with a thick accent.

One day, toward the end of her life, Gogo said to me, "There can be lovemaking so powerful that you know that surely you and he are the only ones to ever experience such a thing; as if the two of you alone are unlocking a secret Universe."

Until this time, all the family called my mother Little Dorothy, and her mother, my grandmother Gogo, Big Dorothy. After Gogo met her new boyfriend, my mother wasn't called Little Dorothy too much anymore, because Gogo didn't want her lover to know she had a daughter.

When Little Dorothy was almost sixteen, she came home from school one day to find the front door locked, which was surprising to her, since the door was never locked when her mother was home. She tossed her leather school satchel on the steps and jiggled the iron doorknob back and forth, and tried banging the heavy iron knocker. She put her ear up to the door and listened, certain she could hear her mother's voice inside.

"Mum! Mummy! It's me, Little Dorothy! Let me in!" She pounded the door with her open palm. "MUM! Open up!"

But no one came to the door. After fifteen minutes of knocking and calling out, Little Dorothy sat down on her book bag, hugging her knees around her chest, trying to keep her plaid school skirt over her legs to keep them warm.

Knowing my mother, it's my guess that while she was waiting out there, her mind was superficial and smooth. Perhaps she was thinking idle thoughts, like wondering if the woman in the window across the street always put the kettle on before she took off her coat. It was easy and soothing for my mother to keep her mind on this level, a skill she would cultivate and use throughout her life. Already, she had learned not to dive beneath the surface of her feelings, the dark, seemingly endless depth was much too scary for her to deal with. That evening, beneath the safe, serene surface of her psyche were thoughts, I believe, something along the lines of, "Why the fuck is my mother locking me out of the house; am I really that unimportant to her?"

Would you like to witness when the hole in my mother's heart became permanent, irreparable? Why she felt she had no choice but to pass it to me? I imagine it went something like this:

Finally, after what seemed an interminable amount of time, when the weak sun was slanting low, Little Dorothy could hear the latch of the door sliding from the inside, and turned around to see her mother standing in the doorway in her best house dress; the newish one that was covered with purple violets and had no grease stains yet. Little Dorothy noticed that she was without a bra or stockings, which wasn't unusual, but her face was red and puffy; she wasn't wearing her glasses, and she was nervously fingering her curly hair at the temples.

"Mummy!" Little Dorothy wailed. "Didn't you hear me? Why didn't you open the door? Were you asleep in the middle of the day?"

"Shhh. Quiet, and don't call me Mummy," her mummy said, under her breath.

"What?" Before Little Dorothy had time to digest this last bizarre request from her mother she saw a tall, dark man standing in the back of the hall, adjusting the brass buttons on his military uniform in the hall mirror. The man took a few tentative steps toward the open front door, when Gogo reached back and pulled him forward by hooking her arm in his.

"Zbyczek, I'd like you to meet my..." Here there was only the very slightest of hesitations. "... my cousin, Maude. Maude, this is my gentleman friend, Zbyczek."

Little Dorothy was momentarily dumbstruck. Maude was her middle name. And cousin? What, had she gone crazy?

"Mum! What are you saying?"

Big Dorothy gave Little Dorothy, who was now Maude, a well-practiced look that sent a bolt of fear straight into her heart.

"You never mentioned a cousin to me, Dorothy," the man was saying. "Did I hear her call you Mum?" Zbyczek narrowed his eyes and his face turned dark.

Big Dorothy didn't skip a beat. "Oh, well, she calls me that sometimes, since I seem to take more care of her than her own Mum does. Isn't that right, Duckie? I do wish you'd stop calling me Mum though, since I'm not, after all. Why, I had no idea that you were sitting out here. Come in, you'll catch your death of cold."

Zbyczek looked back and forth between Little Dorothy and Big Dorothy. His face was scrutinizing. He couldn't have helped but notice the strong resemblance between the two. "Nice to meet you Maude. Dorothy, I must be going." Poor, confused Little Dorothy stared in disbelief as she saw the stranger bend down and kiss her mother lightly on the lips. He put his hat on, squared the brim, and mumbled a low "excuse me" as he stepped over Little Dorothy, who was still sitting on the steps with her mouth agape, and skipped quickly down the garden path. Big Dorothy stood in the doorway waving and calling out "Cheerio!" until his dark frame disappeared around the corner. That's when my grandmother roughly grabbed my mother's arm and pulled her up into the house, slamming the door behind her.

"What are you doing home so early? You silly cat, sitting on the steps and crying," Big Dorothy said, jerking the satchel away from my Little Dorothy. "Didn't you say you had O Levels to practice this afternoon?"

"Yes, Mum, but we finished early. Who was that...?"

"You're not to call me Mum anymore." My mother stared at the mouth uttering this amazing proclamation. The lips were thin and set in a straight hard line. There wasn't a trace of lipstick on them. My mother felt her stomach turn cold.

"What? Why?"

"Zbyczek doesn't know I have a daughter, let alone a teenaged one, or even that I've been married for that matter."

"Been married? Aren't you and Dad still married?"

"Yes, I suppose technically we are, but I divorced him in my heart ages ago. Zbyczek is my boyfriend now, and if I have my way, he'll marry me someday. He never will though, if he finds out that I'm old enough to have a daughter your age. You're never to speak of my age or your dad around him, do you understand me?

And stop calling me Mum when he's around. You do understand how important this man is to me, don't you Doll?"

Little Dorothy stared at her mother. She continued to stay on the surface of her thoughts, because if she didn't, she would have surely drowned. Maybe she thought that she didn't like the scent of the men's cologne she could detect coming from her mother. Or maybe she mused on how pink her mother's face was or how her gray-blue eyes were dancing with something in between rage and ecstasy.

What she said was,

"Yes.... Duckie."

My mother never called her mother Mum again. From that day on, it was 'Duckie.'

They actually kept up this charade of my mother being Gogo's cousin for close to a couple of years. This may have been when my mother became adept at lying and subterfuge, but it's my experience that lies never last forever. Somehow, some way, the truth wiggles up and through. As careful as Gogo and my mother were about keeping the secret from Beba, Gogo made the mistake of leaving her passport out on the table when she had taken it out to renew it.

Can you envision Beba opening the passport to the picture of a smiling Gogo, the gap between her front teeth showing through her wide smile? Next he probably saw her name: Dorothy May Morris. Morris? That's when the first dull realization of deceit probably set in. She had said her last name was Harrison. Can you imagine his eyes shoot open wide with alarm and then narrow to slits when he read her date of birth: April 4, 1908. That would make her, he probably quickly calculated in his head, thirty-six years old! Twenty-six, the age she said she was, was bad enough; he was already dating an older, obviously more experienced woman. But thirty-six? That meant she was fourteen years older than he was. He may have scanned through the growing Rolodex of thoughts in his head labeled '*Why I Should Stop Seeing Her.*' He may have forgiven her for lying to him, but the fact that she was married was inexcusable. He could never marry outside of the Church, and the Catholic Church would not marry a divorcée. He then realized that she was probably too old to have the children he always thought he would have. She was probably too old, period.

So he dumped her.

And she vowed to win him back.

I don't know exactly how she did it, but knowing Gogo's powers of manipulation, it probably didn't take much effort on her part. Maybe a little calling, a little begging, intermittent tears, some lacy underwear, some carefully applied lipstick, a little cajoling, a little more lying, a little withholding, perhaps some jealousy-inducing tactics like flirting with other men; the usual stuff. Whatever she did, it worked, and when Zbyczek was released from the Air Force he moved in with Gogo and my mother, but only temporarily, he'd said, just until he could get to Canada to join up with his twin brother Stephan. Gogo must have thought that there might be a God after all when Beba found out he could not get into Canada without being married to a Canadian or a Brit.

I've seen their wedding picture. Gogo is smiling broadly, wearing a white suit, holding a huge bunch of lilies in her arms, and maybe I just imagine it, but it seems as if there was a look of triumph on her face. Beba is in his uniform, hair slicked back, a mysterious half-smile on his baby face, but his body is solemn. Gogo's sister, Daisy, is grinning, looking rather dowdy compared to her luminous older sister. Richard, Daisy's curly-headed son, about eight years old, is wearing a proper little boy's suit with short pants and holding his mother's hand. The sepia tones of the photograph make it look like it was pretend, like they all got dressed up and posed at one of those booths at the carnival.

My mother moved to Canada with Zbyczek, leaving little old me behind, was the way my mother put it.

I had no intention of following Gogo to Canada; I was having too good of a time partying with my friends at The Linguist Club in London. My Dad was supposed to be keeping an eye on me, and I suppose he got a little worried about me after he threw me a huge twenty-first birthday party. Maybe I drank too much, I don't know, but he shipped me off in a boat (no one thought of flying much in those days) to Canada to visit my mother. I thought I'd be back in England after a short visit, but I never went back.

Gogo met me at the boat and took me to the apartment in Hamilton, Ontario she shared with Zbyczek. It was over a general store, and wasn't exactly luxurious. Gogo was already back in her dress-making business, and right away put me to work sewing; I was so bored! I needed some excitement like I was used to in London, so I got the courage to put on my best dress and go to a dance hall by myself one night. That's where I met Mike. I suppose he's technically your uncle."

I imagined a long, dimly lit room with a sort of eight-piece orchestra playing on one of those elevated, brightly lit stages at one end. Even though it was the time of Fats Domino and saddle shoes, I imagine instrumental versions of Perry Como and Mel Tome tunes. I could see my mother walking in nervously by herself in her best dress, not even noticing the music; she never paid attention to music much, but maybe unconsciously walked to the beat of the subtle brush symbols.

I'm sure my mother had applied her red lipstick, and maybe taken the care to put on those faux pearls she liked to wear. Maybe she let some of her "bosom," as she called it, show. Even though she can't see very well, she probably put her glasses in her purse along with her Camels. I bet she looked adorable, and vulnerable, and I don't think that it was surprising that a very good-looking Italian guy made his way over to ask my mother to dance. I'll bet she wasn't surprised either, since she had quite a bit of practice at attracting men at her Linguist Club in London.

When I imagine this scene, it's like an old, grainy, black-and-white movie. The stranger extends his hand with a *bon journo* and pulls my mother out onto the dance floor. I can see my mother melt into his arms, as if she had never been held by a man before, even though it must have only been a month or so since she had been.

"*Como se ciama?* My name is Mike," the short, swarthy man might have said in a heavily accented, broken English.

"My name is Dorothy; it's my pleasure to meet you," she might say, gazing into his eyes.

Mike would look confused at my mom's clipped British accent, since he hardly spoke a word of English. Of course my mom had just been hanging out in that Linguist Club, and could speak French and Italian fluently.

"*Il mio nome é Dorothy, esso é un piacere venirli a contatto*," I can imagine my mother saying, rolling it off her tongue as though she'd been speaking Italian her whole life.

They swirl and glide in my mind's eye. My mother is uncharacteristically Present; she gazes at Mike, time slows down, I can't imagine what they're saying anymore, but there is much laughing. Mike's hand is always on my mother's back, and I'll bet that sometimes it slipped down lower, but my mother probably pretended like she didn't notice.

I can hear the orchestra saying goodnight, and then Mike is helping my mother on with her winter coat. He might have taken one arm firmly with his hand and lead her out of the double doors under a lit Exit sign into the cool evening. Outside in the cold winter air, he might have pulled her toward him and kissed her for a long time on the mouth. My mother's eyes were probably closed, but his were probably open wide in shock and disbelief at his good luck. I wondered how he asked her for that fateful date.

"May I see you today? No, *como se dice,* tomorrow? No, the next evening," I imagine him saying, probably stumbling in halting English.

"I'd love to." My mother would have answered very quickly, before he had finished his slow sentence.

"*Grazie*, at seven? On the corner here?"

"I'll be waiting," I hear my mother saying, as she turns away to catch a cab. Inside my mother's chest, her heart was probably yelling, "YES!" Well, maybe my mother's heart never yelled "yes!" but she must have thought that it was a jolly good turn of events.

Then it was Day and Night again. I wonder if the burden of the sewing Gogo had given her might have seemed lighter knowing she had a date with a handsome Italian that night.

The next night, my mother is walking very fast up the street, bundled up against the cold. Snow sticks to the hood of her coat and to the curls that stick out from under it. She stands exactly where he left her, stamping her boots and clapping her gloved hands together. She looks carefully at the dark, hooded clumps of people passing by her. Finally, a man approaches her. His face is covered with a dark scarf, only his eyes show. He is wordlessly offering his elbow to my mother. She puts her arm in his and they start walking down the street in unison. "*Buena sera,*" is all he says. They are silent.

"It was a lovely dance last night, don't you agree?" my mother finally speaks.

"*Sî,*" he says.

"What did you think of the music?" my mother might have said in Italian. Or some other pleasantry. Whatever it was, he says nothing.

Now she's talking faster and faster, and he remains silent. Finally, she's yanking her arm out of his. The man is shaking now, like he's laughing, and pulls down the scarf he had wrapped around his face.

"Who are you?" my mother stutters in broken Italian. "You aren't Mike!"

The man is laughing harder; his breath shows in the cold night air.

"*Mi ciama* Toni. I am Mike's brother."

And so their rocky romance began. Mike apparently thought that his brother needed a girlfriend more than he did at the time, and let Toni have a try. It worked. I think my mother was smitten immediately. For his part, Toni couldn't believe how easily non-Italian women took off their clothes. My mother wanted to follow Gogo to Chicago, but Toni could not go with her if she did, because the immigration laws did not favor Italians at the time. And so my parents were married, a little bit for love, a little bit for logistics. They were going to America.

CHAPTER 4

Leaving on a Jet Plane (Mouth Hole)

I'm bounding noiselessly down the red-carpeted stairs in the hallway of Gogo's apartment building in Chicago. I'm wearing my favorite blue velvet pantsuit; the outfit I love because the pants have straps under the feet, and the coat has a hood. I am flying; I feel free; my feet aren't really touching the ground. I can see the entryway that is tiled in small octagonal black-and-white tessellating pieces at the bottom of the stairs. I know that this room echoes when a person speaks or when someone clomps across it in hard shoes. There, it is always cool and dim, even when it is hot outside. One wall holds our mailboxes, bronze squares we open with a small key. I am alone. Before I reach the bottom stair, I notice a small, bluish-maroon lump sitting in the middle of the tile. I'm not scared of being outside of the apartment without a grown-up, just curious as to what the lump is. Now I am standing in the hall; I walk up closer; I think maybe it's silly putty; then I crouch down to get a better look at it. I poke it with my index finger, and it's mushy. It's a tongue. I know it is mine. I open my mouth to scream, but nothing comes out. I run back up the stairs to the apartment, grab the gold hand-held mirror off of my dresser, open my mouth wide and gape into the glass. I can't see anything; it's too dark in the cavernous expanse. I struggle to stretch my mouth open wider, turning the mirror to get a better angle.

I woke up with my mouth open. I reached inside my mouth with my thumb and forefinger and felt my tongue. I was relieved that it was there, still firmly attached to the back of my throat. I knew that it was a dream, but like the fly dream, it seemed so real, so I wasn't entirely sure.

The feeling of losing my tongue lingered. I thought about it every day. Something in me got arrested then. I felt like I couldn't speak. Or I felt like I couldn't be heard. I went from being chatty to very quiet.

Maybe something did happen.

Maybe I asked, "When is Papa coming home?"

And maybe I was told not to ask.

But I don't know. I do know that this is when I first got the urge to write.

I wanted to write because I couldn't say what I needed to say. But more importantly, I wanted to get a hold of my Papa, and writing was the only way I thought I might be able to reach him. I knew about letters. I saw Gogo writing to her sister Daisy in England on the thin blue *ParAvion* paper. I saw the pale envelopes edged with red and darker blue stripes return; saw them come out of the bronze mailbox in the dim, tiled hallway. I knew this was a way to communicate with people far away, and no one seemed further away than my father.

During this, the beginning of my fifth year on earth, the only year my mother was home with me; the only year she was Present with me; I asked her every day to teach me how to write. She obliged me, writing out the alphabet in neat block letters for me to copy. I soon asked her to write whole words, to explain to me what sounds the different letters made. She did.

She also read to me. During that same year, she read *Alice in Wonderland* and *Through the Looking Glass* in its entirety; one chapter a day. Sitting perched on the arm of the big chair while my mother read was my favorite time of the day. George would sit on the other arm sometimes, but usually he would get bored and run around. I was always sad when the chapter ended, and invariably tried to talk her into reading one more, which she never did. (Except for one time when we got to chapter XI of *Through the Looking Glass*, entitled *Waking*, that consisted solely of ".... and it really was a kitten, after all." I remember feeling cheated and a little bit panicked that that was all I was going to get of the story that day, but that day, and that day only, she read one more chapter.)

I loved listening to my mother's lyrical British-accented voice—the words full of emotion and expression—even though I didn't understand them all. I used to look down at the printed page in wonder, trying to grasp how the letters on the page could evoke a whole world inside my head. I marveled and delighted in the *Mouse's Tale*, where the words were in the shape of a tail, and I asked my mother to read the tale over and over.

* * *

I started to write to Papa almost every day. "*HOW AR YOU?*" I painstakingly printed in all capital letters, aware of my tongue sticking out with concentration as I wrote. I realized that I was writing in English, and was worried if he'd mind. Already the Italian words were starting to fade from my memory. Even if I could remember some of the words, I couldn't write them; I was just learning how to write in English. I did write, 'TE AMO' at the end of each note, though, I could sound that out. And always at the end, "P.S. RITE BAK."

I wanted to write in cursive like I saw my mother and Gogo do, in what I called scribble writing. I thought it would look more grown up; somehow make my writing be taken more seriously; but my mom said I better start with block letters, which made me mad and impatient. I'd follow her around the apartment while she cooked or cleaned, asking her to teach me cursive. I practiced scribbling a row of curlicues. Finally she said that cursive was just joining the letters up with lines. I went back to one of my letters to Papa and made lines between the middle of all the block capitals, and showed it to her. She said the lines needed to be at the bottom of the letters. I wrote again, joining the letters at the bottom, but could see that it still didn't look like scribble writing. Little things like that would make me fume with anger that my mother either wasn't taking me seriously, or wasn't telling me the truth.

Every day, when I finished my letter, I'd ask for an envelope, and carefully seal it; licking the gummy part more than I needed to lick it. I'd write "Papa" on the envelope. When Gogo left for work in the morning, I'd ask to please mail the letter for me. She promised she would. When she came home from work, I'd ask her, "Did you mail my letter?"

"Yes, Duckie," she'd answer vaguely.

Every day, I wanted to go down the red-carpeted stairs of my dream, to the cool dim hallway with the octagonal black and white tiles on the floor. Unlike my dream, I had to wait for my mother to take me there, to unlock the small bronze box (that was too high for me to reach anyway) with the special tiny key that I loved. I waited impatiently below while she pulled out stacks of papers and envelopes, and sometimes, the thin blue airmail letters from England. She would shuffle through the stack while I asked if there was anything for me, while straining on my tippy-toes to see. Once in a while, after I asked a few times without an answer, my mom would say, "Oh, here's something for you!" and my heart would leap. Then she'd hand me a glossy advertisement with a picture she must have thought I would like; an ad for a Sonny Boy drink or something. I'd look at the picture, my heart sinking back down, and say, "This isn't for me!"

* * *

My mom went to the hospital several times on false alarms, thinking the baby was about to be born. More than once, I saw her lumbering back up the red-carpeted apartment steps, hand on the wooden banister to help hoist herself up, her stomach still huge, when I expected it to be flat. Finally she left and didn't come home all night. In the morning Gogo told me I had a baby sister named Catherine Anne. I felt different after she told me that. I twirled around on the Persian carpet in the living room; light with the knowledge that I now had a sister, and a baby was going to be in the apartment. I went to the mirror to see if I looked any different. I thought that maybe I detected a little bit more of a grown up look in my brown eyes, and I stared into them for a long time.

A couple of days later, on a windy May morning, Gogo, George, and I took a taxi to pick my mom up. She was standing on the stone steps outside of the hospital, holding a bundle of white hospital-issued blankets. She got in the car looking all breathless and happy. The four of us, well five actually, although I didn't think of Cathy as a person yet, squished in the back seat of the cab. I peeked into the piles of swaddling, and then pulled back abruptly. "What's wrong with her?" was all I could say, shocked at the look of her face, which was all red and rubbed raw by her hands. I couldn't have been more disappointed. This was my little sister? It looked like a small red lump of squirmy flesh.

"Nothing. Nothing's wrong with her darling," my mom beamed.

That's what you think, I thought.

That night I dreamed that Papa and my mom had run out of food, so they decided to cook the baby. We were back in our old house across the street.

They put her in a machine that resembled the popcorn maker at the movie theater. She moved through a series of glass tubes, modeled after a cartoon I had seen, and came out of a chute at the end looking like a roast turkey. My parents brought her to the kitchen table, carved her up, and dug in with gusto. I was crying and arguing with them that we shouldn't eat her. When I woke up I was relieved that we really didn't eat Cathy, but disappointed that Papa wasn't with us. It made me wonder if anyone even told him that there was a new baby; I thought that maybe he'd want to see her. Then I wondered if he would be her Papa if he came back, or would Beba be her Dad since he was the one living with us? I didn't ask though. I was talking about him less and less.

I dubbed the new baby Fat Chops because her cheeks hung below her chin. After a week or two, her face got better, and she was very cute with her brown eyes and blond curly fuzz on her head, and rolls of baby fat everywhere. I liked to watch my mom nurse her, and sometimes, afterward, she'd let me hold her in my lap until she fell asleep, and I would sit perfectly still, hardly breathing, so as not to disturb her. A few months later when she started eating, I delighted in the way my mom fed her orange juice with a tiny little spoon; the juice—in a shot glass on a tray—surrounded by other little delicacies, like mashed banana. Having a new person to love and help take care of helped ease the pain of Papa being gone, but it didn't take it away. In a letter I wrote, " WE HAV A BABY" hoping it might entice him to come back, if only out of curiosity.

It was crowded in that one bedroom apartment with the five of us, and after Cathy was born, making it six, it became almost stifling, especially with the playpen permanently set up in the living room, and the extra crib in the bedroom. Since there was no backyard, they wouldn't let George and me out of the apartment because there really wasn't anywhere to play. We had to content ourselves with riding our tricycles around and around the hardwood dining room floor, being careful to avoid the crack in the ceiling where George said the Goon-goonk lived; some sort of evil demon that could suck you into an abyss up above. I felt some perverse pleasure at pointing to the crack when George was caught unaware that he was standing in the danger zone directly underneath it. It gave me a little jolt of confidence to make someone more scared than me, because now I was starting to get really scared that Papa wasn't coming back at all. I felt shut up in the apartment, just the way I felt shut up in my dream.

* * *

We went out so rarely that the few times we did, the memories stand out clearly as blips of excitement in the middle of monotonous days. Like the day that Cathy got her thumb stuck in the smokestack of the metal Choochoo Train. My mother had tried to twist and tug the train off of a loudly screaming Cathy using copious amounts of Vaseline, to no avail, so soon my mom and us three kids were on another ride to the hospital in a taxi! Even though George and Cathy were both crying and my mother looked distraught, we were going somewhere!

I spent a lot of time in front of the full-length mirror, wondering how much I had grown, and looking inside my mouth; I would wiggle my tongue, watching how the tip could dip into the huge brown holes I saw growing daily in my back molars. I was aware of those holes, but I wasn't so aware, consciously anyway, of the hole that was getting bigger in the heart of my soul. It was still small when the flies came out, but now it grew in accordance with each passing day of Papa's absence; of each day without a word; without an explanation; without a return letter.

Many nights, I would fall asleep to the sound of Gogo and Beba yelling and arguing with each other in the living room. Sometimes, in a strange way, the sound felt mildly comforting; I was used to hearing my mom and Papa yelling in the other room at night. During one particularly loud argument, with banging and crying, Beba came into the bedroom where the three of us kids were sleeping and put the small 45 of *The Little Drummer Boy* on the toy record player in the bedroom; I think to drown out the noise of the shouting for George and me. He came in between bouts of yelling, and put the plastic arm of the phonograph down over and over, usually setting the needle back at the beginning, but sometimes missing and laying it haphazardly in the middle of the song with a little scratchy sound, while he held and rocked Georgie, who was crying.

Pa-rum-pa-pa-pum. I lay still in bed, the room dark, and watched Beba and George's swaying silhouette against the light of the open door. Gogo was sobbing in the other room. *Come they told me, Pa rum-pa-pa-pum. A newborn king to see...* The version of the song was slow, with high-pitched angel voices singing, and a predominant, deliberate thump-thump beat of the drum. *Pa-rum-pa-pa-pum, rum-pa-pa pum, rum-pa-pa-pum.* I felt a cold creepiness move up through my body so I curled myself into a ball and put my pillow over my head until, finally, I fell asleep.

The Fear stayed. In the silent calm light of the morning I felt no better. I stayed still and realized, maybe for the first time, how scared I was; but I still couldn't admit what I Knew deep down. *Papa was gone and he wasn't coming back.* The thought whooshed through my head so fast that it didn't register, but I shivered all over, trembling in terror. What was I so scared of? Then I remembered. That Song. That horrible whiny, churchy song about the boy on the drum that felt like something you would play if someone were dead.

I jumped out of bed and ran to the little record player on the dresser. The record was still on it. I stared at it. *That* was the horrible thing that was making me so scared. Even if I wanted to, I wouldn't break it. I didn't want to do anything wrong or maybe someone else would leave. I took a pencil and put a big black X on the label of the side that had that song, to make sure I would never play it again by mistake.

A week or two later, I was watching my mom cook in the kitchen when I felt Fear come in my head and up and down my spine. I stopped and listened. It was coming from the living room where George was playing. *Pa Rum Pa Pa Pum... Pa Rum PaPa.. Papa... Papa!* I covered both my ears, and put my head down between my knees, but I could still hear it. *Pa Rum Pa Pa Pum.* I ran into the narrow dark pantry and closed the door behind me. I sat on the far end in the dark, on a sack of potatoes, my hands tight over my ears. My mother opened the door a crack.

"What are you doing?" she asked.

"Turn it off!" I fairly screamed at her.

"Oh, don't be so silly. I'll turn it off. Come out of there."

But I stayed a long time; until I was sure the song was well over.

* * *

Then another dream started coming. All my dreams I had when I was four were clear and vivid. I think that sometimes your soul starts talking to you really loudly. Unlike the Fly Dream, or the Cathy is a Roast Turkey Dream, or the Tongue Dream, this dream was a recurring nightmare. I was being chased. I felt powerless. A mean Santa, an opposite kind of Santa was chasing me. He was wearing a green suit and had a black beard. He was in the driver's seat of a big cement mixer. One arm hung out the window, and in this hand he held a huge butterfly net. I was running down the dark gravel street as fast as I could go, and I could hear the swooshing sounds that the butterfly net was making behind me. I knew if he scooped me up he would throw me in the back of the cement mixer where I would be tossed in the turning drum.

* * *

I wasn't always scared and missing Papa though. Sometimes the feeling would leave me for hours at a time. Like on Thursday nights when we would watch *Quick Draw McGraw* and George and I would each get a chocolate hostess cupcake served on a yellow Melmac saucer, or when my mom would make us a plate of little triangle sandwiches, some with peanut butter, and others with liverwurst, for lunch. And I felt a wave of pleasant anticipation once a week when Beba would give George and me a coin to put in the blue pig piggy bank that still sits on my kitchen counter.

It seemed that as that hole started boring into my heart—or maybe it was my soul, I'm not sure of the exact location—the hole never stopped calling to be filled. Not only did I have a huge cavity where I could keep my pain, I also had a larger-than-normal capacity for joy.

One cold morning, I woke up early, before anyone else, and the apartment, for once, was quiet. The air inside my room felt hushed and muffled. I had a feeling of safety; of insulation. I felt full of energy. I got out of bed in my nightgown and bare feet, scuttled across the cold hardwood floor, and looked out the bedroom window to see The Day. My world, which at the time was the view from the windows, had been magically transformed in the night. What I saw were shades of pure sparkling white, with a steady vertical movement in the sky, as if the life force that is always there for a rare moment became visible. I felt my breath slow way down. I was aware of every part of my body. I stood and stared at the white morning, my forehead resting on the cold windowpane, and I felt a sense of calm and Knowing. Like it was really all okay; everything was really all right; and if it wasn't, there was nothing I could do about it anyway. The cold glass soothed my head. I stayed like that a long time, not moving, looking at the snow, and listening to myself breathe.

Finally, I slowly lifted my head off of the window, and walked out into the living room. I stood perfectly still and sucked my breath in. The room was full of Christmas! I had completely forgotten. I knew Christmas was coming because of the TV commercials, and a few things that Gogo said, but I didn't really understand what it was, or what day it was to occur. The same magical feeling I felt at the bedroom window had followed me into this room and swirled all around me. In the middle of the dining room floor was a tall tree that I thought must have magically appeared in the night. It was covered with big, colored lights and heavy strands of tinsel. The room smelled full of Tree, and out of the window where I stood guard looking for Papa, I could only see streams of sparkly white, with the sun barely shining through.

Under the tree there were piles of wrapped presents, but I didn't really care if they were for me or not. I was just amazed that I had felt the magic in the bedroom and it had followed me to the living room. I thought I might burst with happiness, but at the same time I felt very calm. I wanted the feeling to stay with me forever.

Soon the rest of the house woke up, and noise and shouts and laughing and arguing and paper ripping and *thank-yous* and candy and doorbells and phone rings and toys and music distracted and pulled me in all directions, wiping out the Knowing that I had when I woke up, as well as the constant longing for Papa. I fell asleep exhausted and happy that Christmas, hugging my new curly-haired Tiny Tears doll, the one with the tear duct holes that leaked real water.

* * *

Gogo had gotten a job, working at Carson's Piere and Scott department store. I heard her talk about Saving Money to my mom. I heard her say she had A Plan.

After Gogo had been working a while, she made an announcement.

"I'm moving to California!" she proclaimed to no one in particular one night.

California? Where Papa was? Everyone stopped what he or she was doing. Beba looked up from the end of the dining room table where he sat in his undershirt, a newspaper spread in front of him, and a can of

Schlitz poised inches from his lips. My mom looked up from what she was typing on her new typewriter at the other end of the table. George and I stopped riding our trikes around the hardwood floor, and it even seemed like Cathy stopped kicking and fussing and was still. The words hung in the air for several seconds while we all digested Gogo's declaration. Finally Beba broke the silence.

"Do*RO*thy, no! You are talking crazy again." With his Polish accent Beba always put the emphasis on the second syllable of her name. "NO!" he yelled, slamming down the beer can, not even bothering to ask about the logistics, ready for battle. Obviously I thought he had already heard about this scheme, and had made up his mind.

"I am— see if you can stop me, then. You shan't, you know!" Gogo countered in a dramatic, pouty bad-little-girl voice, walking to the window and talking with her back to the room. "If you want to come, well, I would love that Zbysiu, but if you won't, I shall go without you, see if I don't then!" At this last bit of the sentence, she turned theatrically, a defiant gleam in her gray-blue eyes.

Even at four and a half, I knew if Gogo said we were moving, it was inevitable; we were moving. What Gogo wanted, Gogo got.

"*DOR*othy," Beba said, patiently now, changing tactics. "My work at Hotpoint...I don't know if I could find work as a welder in California. We cannot pack up and move across the country. All my family is here in Chicago. Dorothy, please. Be reasonable."

Gogo shook her curly head all through what Beba was saying. "Zbyczek, California is full of opportunities! I'm sure you'd find a job making double your salary."

I thought she made a good point. Obviously Papa thought it was better there. I started feeling a little twirly happy feeling coming out of my stomach. We might be moving next to Papa? Plus, anywhere must be better than here. I looked over to my mother to see if I could tell what she thought, but there was a glare on her glasses and she didn't say anything.

"If you go, Jurek stays here with me," Beba said, using the Polish word for George, as he often did. With that bold proclamation, he walked over to George, plucked him off of his tricycle and held him protectively against his chest. George wiggled and squirmed. My mother watched; her face completely blank. Now I could see her eyes, but it did no good in helping me see what she thought; they were dull and vacant.

"If you don't want to go, fine, but I'm moving to California, and so is Georgie!" Gogo said, her voice rising up an octave. "How dare you! How DARE you think about taking my son away from me!" There was a break in her voice when she said 'son,' and her eyes started fluttering back in her head the way they did when she was threatening to faint.

I glanced over at my mom again, who went back to her typing, pushing her glasses up her nose. She seemed to be tuning the argument out. She offered no opinion. She barely looked up when Gogo said to Beba, "Little Dorothy and the girls are coming too! You stay if you LIKE."

Beba had lunged forward toward Gogo when it looked as if there may be a swooning incident, but now he looked resigned. He put the wiggly George down, walked over to his place at the end of the table, sat down and took a long swig off his beer. Gogo flounced out of the room. My mother continued typing.

Seeing that the show was over, I got off of my trike, and went to lie down on the white vinyl couch. I thought about California, and wondered if Gogo wanted to find Papa for me. I had no idea that she was running. For although I knew about The Secret she had created (in the part of me that knew everything, that still knows everything) it had already gone under the Surface.

* * *

The very next day, the atmosphere in the house had changed. There was a buzz in the air. We were moving. Although they were never answered, I continued to faithfully write letters to my Papa. Now I would add, "WE AR CUMING TO CALFORNA TO! SEE YOU SOON."

The fact that my mom, Cathy, and I were *flying* to California is what excited me. I felt bad for George who had to drive with Beba and Gogo. I fantasized and wondered about every detail; what the plane would look like on the inside; if the engines would be really loud. I knew what I was going to wear. Even though I was only five I had some fashion sense. It was going to be the turquoise cotton pantsuit that Gogo had made me, because it matched perfectly the sunglasses I wanted to wear. The sunglasses were only toy plastic ones, but I imagined myself looking very cool when I landed in California in my aqua pantsuit and matching sunglasses, the way Lucy looked when she went to Hollywood.

A couple of days before we left, late that August, on one of those rare walks outside of our apartment, I shuffled along kicking the big yellow maple leaves that were already starting to fall, and thought about flying. I thought about flying a lot, but not necessarily in a plane. I had seen airplanes on TV—the kind with propellers—but I had heard the grown-ups say that we were going on a jet—a plane with no propellers. A jet was supposed to go even faster than a regular plane. My mind went around and around, as it tends to do, trying to understand the possibility of that kind of speed. Suddenly the thought came to me that if flying was possible, and speeds faster than airplanes were possible, maybe *anything was possible*. Maybe *I* could do anything. Everything. Even fly.

I turned on the sidewalk and looked behind me at my mom who was pushing the big blue perambulator with Cathy inside, and George walking along, holding on to the outside. They were walking very slowly, and I was up ahead. I wanted to ask my mother Questions, important questions about Possibilities but she was so Very Far Behind me, and that feeling of not being able to make her understand me washed over my head making my throat tight and my tongue feel big in my mouth.

"Mum?" I turned around and yelled. "Mummy? Will you watch me?" And then, when she didn't seem to be paying attention, "Are you looking?"

"Yes, Christine, I'm watching you," she called.

I turned, and with one last glance over my shoulder, I ran as fast as I imaginably could down the sidewalk. Leaves were crunching under my *Buster Brown Mary Janes*, and the ones I didn't crunch were swirling out of the way with my velocity. I felt my lungs balloon and stretch, my heart thumping in my chest. My eyes were unblinking with the force of concentration, and I stared straight ahead at a distant point down the street. When I felt myself losing momentum, I stopped, turned around and called back to my mom, as best as I could, as I was pretty out of breath, "Is that how fast a jet plane goes?"

"Oh, I think they go a little faster than that, darling," my mom called back.

I considered this for a moment, while I was catching my breath. I couldn't imagine anything being faster than all my effort, but if it was possible that a faster speed existed, then I reasoned that I should be able to duplicate it.

So I turned, concentrated, and then with everything I had, I burst forward as fast as I could possibly go, for the second time. This time I held nothing back; any fear of falling wiped out with my focus on speed. I stopped suddenly and turned on my heel.

"As fast as that?" I huffed.

"Oh, faster," my mom said absently.

This irritated me. I wondered if she was paying attention as to how fast I was actually going. Could a jet *be* any faster? I felt that all I had to do was try a little harder, put in just a little more effort, and surely I could run as fast as a jet plane. The seed that I could do anything if I only put my mind to it was planted.

That seed was a blessing and a curse back then. Everything was in my power, which was wonderful, but then again, it meant the weight of the world was on my shoulders. It was all up to me. All that had ever gone wrong was, in some way, my fault. If I had tried just a little harder, been a better girl, done what I was told, maybe Papa wouldn't have left at all. I was determined to fix it, and was sure I could. After all, we were heading for California. I had imagined him coming home to us, but the other way around was just as good, maybe better.

* * *

The day we moved, I woke up with a queasy feeling in my stomach. The aqua pantsuit made me feel a little better but not much. I don't remember going down the red-carpeted stairs of the hallway that last time. I don't remember shuffling over the black-and-white tessellating tiles of the cool, dim hall for the last time. I do remember feeling no regret in leaving. California must be better than Chicago, I thought. Plus, Papa was there.

I thought about George and Beba and Gogo stuck in the big green Ford, driving the whole way. Driving out to California was still fresh in my memory, and I knew it was no fun.

It was very hot outside the day we left and I felt sweaty and sick. At the airport, Cathy was running ahead, her blond ringlets bobbing, wearing the harness leash my mother had purchased especially for the trip. There was rushing, rushing—everything seemed a little blurry and we were moving really fast. My mother's anxiety radiated out of her and into me, bouncing off the waves of nausea rolling up my stomach.

Suddenly, we were outside in the wet-hot sun, the white gleaming airplane on the runway, shimmering as if it was underwater. It felt like we were very late. We ran towards the plane; there was no one else around us; this running felt dreamy, as if we were running in Karo syrup, the roar of the planes blanketing out all of the sounds. We climbed up the metal stairs; it was noisy and hot and windy, and the lady in the gray skirt and jacket took our tickets when we reached the top. I stared at her red lipstick, and the way her hair was so perfectly in a bun. I thought she was beautiful. I heard my mom explaining to the stewardess that she thought that we both had the stomach flu. The perfectly groomed lady handed me a paper bag. I stared at her red, manicured nails. What was this for?

"That's in case you get sick," my mom whispered to me discretely. I thought I'd never throw up in a paper bag, but once we were up in the sky, that's exactly what I did; once I smelled the food aroma coming from the back of the plane.

My mom was sitting upright in her seat, staring straight ahead. She hardly paid attention to Cathy, who was entertaining herself by running up and down the aisle, tethered to the harness my mother held tightly in her hand. She was acting That Way. She would hardly talk, and she wouldn't answer my questions. She just smiled in a way I could tell wasn't real. The fear waves radiated out of her, and they enveloped me, making me feel even sicker than I already was. I felt it was my job to make her feel better. I never considered that it should be the other way around.

"Mummy, what's wrong?"

"Hmmm? Nothing, darling."

"Are you scared of the airplane?"

"Of course not."

"Well, what? Tell me!"

"Oh, nothing. I just hope we find Gogo once we get to California."

I never thought about not being able to find them once we got there, and secretly, I didn't really care that much. I liked it better just my mom and Cathy and me. And Papa of course, once we found him.

But since I could see my mother was so worried, I tried to take my mind off of my nausea by staring out the window, and looking carefully below for Beba's blue-green 1952 Ford. Maybe if I spotted them, she'd feel better. I pressed my nose against the airplane window—it was cold and small and round—just as I had in the apartment window looking for Papa. But the roads below were so far away that the cars looked like pin heads, when I could see any cars at all, and it was impossible to see what color they were, as much as I squinted.

My mind wandered as I watched the land change from vast amounts of brown to green patches again; perfect squares of lime butted up against creamy sea-foam green. Clouds floated by slowly and cast shadows. I wondered how they got the lines so straight. I turned around and was about to ask my mom, but when I saw her thin lips stretched in such a taught line, I didn't, and scolded myself for not looking hard enough for Beba.

When we landed, I carefully stepped down the metal mesh steps that led from the plane, a crisp breeze whipping my hair into my face. The air surprised me. I was used to hot sweet sickly muggy damp air, or freezing bitter air that froze your breath and hurt your lungs when you inhaled. This air was so clean, so fresh; I felt new life in me. Then I looked around and took in the panoramic view of California, and was shocked by the rolling golden-brown mountains. I didn't remember the mountains from our road trip, I didn't even remember seeing a mountain before, and it made me suck in my breath hard. *So this is what a mountain looks like*, I thought.

Right before we left Chicago, *Folgers* coffee had put out a big advertising campaign saying "We're bringing a mountain to Chicago!" The signs were everywhere, on billboards, on the television, and on flyers that were delivered to the common area where the bronze mailboxes were in our apartment. I kept asking my mom, "When is the mountain going to get here?" She'd laugh and say, "Soon, I should think." I'd look around the flat Midwestern landscape, wondering where they were going to put it. I was disappointed when it never came. Now, standing at the top of the airplane stairs, the reality of mountains far exceeded my expectations. The mountain I waited for never came to me, but I went to the mountains, just like Papa never came to me, so now I was going to him.

* * *

Our hotel was the most beautiful place I had ever seen in my short life. Now I know it was the St. Francis Hotel on Union Square in San Francisco, but back then I just thought it was some sort of royal palace. I was used to chipped porcelain and cracks in the plaster ceiling and a mishmash of furniture; but this room had stately velvet red curtains, a fluffy white bed, and shiny brown furniture. I felt bad throwing up in the sparkling white porcelain toilet bowl that was nothing like the ugly brown stained one we had in our apartment at home. I stepped out onto the balcony, and looked down at the square below and was amazed by all the pigeons. I liked California. I could stay there forever.

The next day, my mom saved a couple of pieces of bread from breakfast, and we took it to the square to feed the gray birds, who looked enormous. I felt like a benevolent queen, choosing which birds would eat, and which would go hungry. The first time one landed on my head, it scared me. I could feel the sharp claws against my scalp, but the amused look of my mother's face reassured me that it was okay. I needed that reassuring face, instead of the face creased in worry, the way hers was most of the time.

I looked forward to feeding the pigeons every day during the week we stayed in the hotel waiting for Gogo and Beba to arrive, and was always sad when my two pieces of bread were gone. My mom laughed when we were playing with the birds. The rest of the time, she was That Way. On the last day, she bought me an entire loaf of Wonder Bread, solely for the purpose of feeding. I couldn't believe her generosity, and my good fortune, and fed the birds until I was sick of them, no longer tearing the bread into little crumbs, but boldly throwing out half and then whole slices to see the birds fight in frenzy. My mom was laughing, and Cathy was running and trying to catch one. I wanted it to be that way forever. Just my mom and me and Cathy, living in a Palace with nothing to do all day but feed pigeons. My life would be perfect like that, I decided; well it would be, as soon as we found Papa. I kept an eye out for him, looking at the men in the square while I fed the birds.

* * *

A few days later, George and I were sitting on the warm sidewalk in the sun, watching Gogo and Beba pouring through newspapers and phonebooks trying to find us a place to live. My mom stood near by, jiggling the well-used stroller that Cathy was sitting in. I watched with mild disinterest as Gogo and Beba struggled for control of the heavy black payphone receiver.

"Oh, look Zbysiu, here's one!" Gogo said, peering over her glasses.

"Dorothy," Beba said patiently, pronouncing her name as he always did, Dor-OH-thy, "that is an apartment, and it is in San Mateo. We need a house in San Francisco, near the airport where I am working."

"Never mind, I'm calling. It says 'attached house.' We have no idea where San Mateo is; perhaps it will be close enough for you to drive to work."

"Dor*OH*thy, no!" Beba said, but he was weakening after an hour of dead-end phone calls. He looked at the change in his open palm, and Gogo handily plucked out a dime.

"Yes, hello, my name is Dorothy Golda, and I am making an inquiry about the apartment advertisement." I noticed her accent got heavier, and her tone more saccharine when she was talking on the phone. I thought to myself that it must be a man she must be speaking with; she never used that tone on women.

Hunched over and staring down at the gutter, absently flicking pebbles, listening to Gogo and Beba argue made me made me realize how peaceful it had been that past week without all that bickering going on all the time. I wondered if I could talk my mother into getting our own house, a nice one that Papa would want to come back to maybe. We could always visit George. I looked up at my mom, but her forehead was furrowed with the effort of trying to light a cigarette against the wind while jiggling the baby stroller at the same time. I watched her carefully. She offered no opinion as to where we were going to live. She said nothing. And as was happening more and more often, neither did I.

Part II

Sixtyeast-fortieth (yellow)

CHAPTER 5

Dodging the Elephant (But not the Fly.)

When I paint pictures of Chicago, in my mind or on a canvas, the images are in shades of blue. Not only because of my blue room with the blue bedspread, and the blue velvet pantsuit, but more to do with the color of my yearning. San Mateo, I paint in shades of yellow. We had a yellow car and a yellow house, the weather was sunny, and I laughed more during those five years, at least sometimes.

Our house, which we still refer to as the address, Sixtyeastfortieth, all one word, was sandwiched in between two rows of apartments. We were "House C" and the surrounding apartments were units A, B, D, and E. Gogo got huffy if anyone called our house an apartment. "That is house C, not apartment C," she'd correct a deliveryman in her clipped British accent.

Beba pulled the old green Ford into the wide driveway of our new home that first day, and the six of us fairly tumbled out of the cramped car. I inhaled a big breath of the sweet-honeysuckle, freshly-mowed-lawn smell of suburbia in August, and looked around at the carports filled with big-finned Buicks and Chevys. I could see that the entire street was lined in apartments, the same as in Chicago, but instead of three-story red brick castles, these apartments were short and spread out, the steps on the outside surrounded by curly iron handrails. They were different shades of pastel stucco—pink, light blue, mint green—like ice cream. Sprinklers swirled out of the neat squares of lawn in front of each of the apartments, and some of the patches of green had kids running through the water and laughing. As I took in the scene around me, I felt a buoyancy, maybe even a hope, as the all-enveloping cocoon of blue Chicago lint that had been shrouding my psyche blew away in the warm California sunshine. *No wonder Papa wanted to move here*, I thought. *It's so much lighter.*

There was only a short, single, terra-cotta tile step separating the outside world from the inside of our house, instead of the two flights of red-carpeted steps we had in Chicago. No dark, musty-smelling purgatory hallway with tessellating tiles that echoed with creepy tongue dreams either.

Inside, the house looked gigantic compared to the one bedroom apartment we had all shared in Chicago. We opened the doors and wooden-sash windows and let the sunshiny summer smell drift inside through the screens. Us three kids ran from room to room, and the grown-ups meandered. Our voices bounced off the bare walls and reverberated up through the hardwood floors. "This will be my room!" "No this!" "Oooh Zbysiu, look at the garden! Oh, my roses shall be lovely there." "It's a big basement." "A dining room AND a breakfast nook!" "What's that? A fireplace, silly!"

Our furniture was coming out separately by a moving van, so for about a week we rattled around in the empty house. George and I spent our time sliding on the shiny hardwood floors in our socks, or down the stairs on our butts; bump, bump, bumping all the way down. At night we camped out on pads on the floor.

I spent a lot of the day in the driveway looking up the street for the moving van to arrive, just as I used to look out the window for Papa. I was good at Waiting. Anything I thought half-resembled a vehicle big enough to carry all our furniture, would send me running into the house yelling, "The Moving Van is here!"

After quite a few false alarms, our things finally arrived in a truck that was much more massive than I'd imagined, and the men in gray jumpsuits started carting in the two households of furniture. There was Gogo and Beba's big, dark overstuffed furniture, and my mom and Papa's white, fake-leather, skinny furniture that had been in storage since Papa left, and we had moved in with Gogo. Seeing the shiny, old Grundig stereo being carted up the one terra-cotta step, I felt a wave of nostalgia for Papa; I remembered him playing opera on the turntable and singing with me. But I knew he was close now, and it would only be a matter of time until I saw him.

There was something else that was moved in that day, something besides the lamps and tables and boxes of dishes, and that was a large elephant. I didn't see it come down the ramp of the moving truck like the other stuff, and I didn't see the men place it right in the middle of the living room in front of the fireplace. In fact I couldn't see it at all, but I could feel it. Sometimes I'd feel the wiry hairs of its thick hide brush against me, and I could smell the hay and dung that surrounded it. The grown-ups were obviously stepping around it, practically backing up against the walls because the elephant took up so much room. It held the secret up high between its tusks, too high for me to see, but I sensed it was there.

(My first yellow painting was of an elephant. I painted it before I did the one of Cathy, George, and me standing in the wide driveway of Sixtyeastfortieth in front of the yellow Ford Fairlane. I didn't know why I painted the elephant until much later.)

I would try, and I would test, and I would look into the eyes of the three grown-ups in a vain attempt to figure it out, but I couldn't. I was suspicious of all kinds of things, but couldn't guess what was held in the elephant's tusks.

I tried to catch the grown-ups not telling me the truth in little things, hoping it would help me figure out the Bigger Thing that was parked in the living room. Like one morning, I noticed a big spot of blood on my mother's bed. The large brownish-red stain sent a shot of fear through me. Why was she bleeding? I mean, sometimes I had spots of blood on my bed, if I picked the perpetual scabs that were on my knees, but never anything like I saw that morning. I worked up my courage to ask her.

"Mummy, did you know there's blood in your bed?"

"Oh, that, that's not blood." she said in that vague way she had.

Now I may have only been five years old, but I certainly knew blood when I saw it.

"It is too, blood."

Right here she could have taken a couple of minutes to give me a little mini-talk about menstruation, which would have been a great relief to me, but she didn't.

"Don't worry darling, it's something else, I'm not bleeding."

Yes, you are, I thought, and wondered why she was lying to me. I thought it must be really bad. Little seeds of doubt about my mother's word were planted in my psyche with incidents like that. The seeds grew strong little roots that took hold of me and didn't let go.

As soon as I could get my hands on a pencil and paper, and I had a table to write on, I wrote a letter to Papa. "WE MOOVD TO CALFORNA." I was sure nobody had told him we were here. It was my job to let him know. "WE CAM ON A JET." I wondered how he had come out here, he never told me if he was going to fly or drive. "WE STAD AT A HO TEL." I wondered if he had to stay in a hotel too, when he first got here. Did he have a house now? "PLES COM OVR." I thought that was a reasonable enough request. I mean, we were in the same state and everything, although I had no clue how big the state was, or if he was within walking or driving distance. I was sure though, if he knew we were here, he'd come and visit. "TE AMO," I remembered how to say that, but realized that the rest of my Italian was just about gone.

I looked the note over with a critical eye. I wanted it to be perfect so that it would make Papa want to come back to me. An image of Papa's face floated onto the screen of my mind, the face had That Look, the look where his eyebrows crinkled together in the middle, and the sides of his mouth turned down; the look he had that time he tossed me off the boat and I was crying in the water; the look he wore as he slowly shook his head back and forth with his hands on his hips; the look that told me I was doing it wrong, that he didn't approve; the look that he had given me enough times to convince me that it was the reason he had left.

Halfway down the page, I saw a smudge I had made with the side of my hand. I didn't think twice—I crumpled the letter up and got a fresh piece of paper and started painstakingly writing the note again. The second time, I had to erase some words a few times which made the page look messy, so I mashed up the paper again, feeling frustrated, and started over for a third time. When I finished that one, I held it up, squinting at my wobbly letters. It was okay. I carefully folded the letter, and gave it to Gogo to mail.

Just like in Chicago, I was waiting for the mail. Here, I could watch for the mailman walking up the street wearing his blue uniform. I would eye him carefully as he pulled a stack of envelopes out of his leather satchel, shuffling through them and smiling down to me. I would look up to the mailman hopefully as he handed Gogo the letters. I'd ask Gogo to check carefully, was she sure that no letter had come for me? Every day I got the same absent reply as though she wasn't really listening— just a "No Duckie, not today," her voice trailing off. I wasn't mad or anything, yet; just disappointed. I didn't think Papa would ignore my letters, I just figured they must take a lot longer to reach their destination than I thought. But every day that I didn't get a reply, that Hole, that was taking on a life of its own, grew and spread, and left it's mark on my heart like that blood on the sheet.

I withdrew. I went inside, and lived in my head where I could still be with Papa. I took to sitting in Cathy's little eating chair in the kitchen, like a high chair only low, staring with my eyes open wide, fantasizing for hours. Once I discovered the Escape Into My Head, I used it constantly. Sometimes I thought about shopping with Papa. Other times I thought about him spanking me. After a while I couldn't stop, I wanted to do it all the time. Gogo must have thought it was strange seeing me sitting there gazing off into space day after day, and would say, "What are you doing, sitting there staring like that? Go outside and play. Go on then!"

I was so busy obsessing about Papa that I didn't even notice when my mother left. She didn't move out of the house, like Papa did. She didn't warn me or say goodbye. She quietly got a job. "They hired me because I speak French!" I heard her saying to Gogo. "I've always wanted to work in a bank you know."

I didn't realize that I wouldn't see her anymore, either. She left the house before I woke up to catch the train to San Francisco, and she usually got home after I was in bed. I was okay with it at first; I didn't know it would be like that from now on. I didn't take it personally though, like I did with Papa. We had a pretty big house, but it felt crowded with that elephant in there. Deep down I knew that's why she left, and I didn't blame her. I could feel her fear of that elephant whenever she was home with Gogo and Beba.

That didn't mean I didn't miss her. I asked my mom to wake me up before she left for work, no matter what time it was. I had to make my own time to see her. She complied, and would come to the top bunk where I was sleeping and whisper, "I haven't had my coffee yet. You needn't get up if you don't want to. " It was still very dark, and it was always tempting to keep sleeping, but I'd force myself awake, climb down the ladder, and pad down the hall to her room with my eyes still closed and get into her bed, still warm from her sleeping in it. She'd have the TV on, and bring the little aluminum pan into the bedroom filled with scrambled eggs and toast. Here I would slowly wake up, and drink in the few minutes of the day that I got to spend with my mother.

I loved to watch her get ready. After her shower, she'd walk around nude, casually tossing a dress on the bed, throwing down a scarf and a belt, cocking her head to one side to see how it looked together. Sometimes, but not often, she'd put on underpants, white practical ones high up to her waist, but usually she didn't bother with them. She'd bend way over when she put on her bra, so her bosom fell in properly, and clasped the hooks by reaching around her back. Then she'd get out panty hose, and gather them up until just the toe was showing, and pull them on. She'd put on a dress, nicely belted, and a matching beaded necklace. She didn't wear any makeup except Mocha lipstick, which she put on by making her mouth into a wide "oh" in the mirror. She'd kiss me, smelling like fresh lipstick and soap, and then she was gone, clicking down the hardwood stairs to walk to the train station, leaving me in bed with the TV on, feeling empty.

Papa was gone, and now, so was my mom. That left Gogo to take care of me. It never really hit me that Gogo was going to be the one in charge of me, the one to make the rules, the one to shape me, the one I would have to turn to, the one to give me guidance and affection until my first day of school. We had only been living in the house about a month when the yellow wall phone in the kitchen rang.

"Yes, hello? Yes, today? At what time shall we arrive?" Gogo started moving around papers that were piled on the ironing board, looking for a blank piece. Finding a pencil, she started jotting down notes on the back of an envelope. I was standing underneath the ironing board watching her. It seemed to be important.

"We'll be there, thank you very much," Gogo said in her British way. She hung up the phone, and looking down at me said, "Christine, you're starting school today!"

I was? I could hardly believe it. I'd always wanted to go to school. Playing school with my stuffed animals, putting them in rows and pretending to play "teacher", was one of my favorite games.

Gogo put me in a pretty dress that she had made for me just the day before, (cutting the fabric without using a pattern,) a light blue cotton sundress with white edging that tied at the shoulders. Gogo made me lots of pretty dresses. I loved the red wool plaid wraparound with the 'Ding Dong School' bell embroidered on it, and I thought that would be a good first day of school dress but it was too hot to wear that day.

I sat on Gogo's knees while she brushed my hair and pulled it back with a piece of blue sewing ribbon. I felt very important to be going to school. Cathy and George stood watching me get ready. "Why can't we go to school too?" George said. Gogo told him he wasn't old enough, and he was going to stay behind with Beba.

I felt pretty that afternoon walking down the sidewalk holding Gogo's hand, despite the wilting heat. There was that pervasive honeysuckle-summer smell outside, and a low buzz of insects. Gogo was only wearing a pair of light blue short shorts, and a white sleeveless cotton blouse. I wished my mom were taking me to school because she would never wear her shorts too short like Gogo did. That was the only reason I would allow myself for missing my mom at that moment—the rest of the reasons hurt too much.

When we arrived at George W. Hall School, (I could read the big sign over the hall) all was quiet. The metal merry-go-rounds stood still, shimmering in the heat. Inside the large plate glass windows, I could see kids were already sitting around in a circle on little chairs. Gogo had brought me late.

"We better hurry, it looks like they already started," I said, pulling Gogo's arm toward the classrooms.

"You're not going in there. We're going to talk to the headmaster." Gogo said, pulling me away from the classrooms toward the office. "You don't need kindergarten. That's for babies who don't know how to read. I'm going to see to it that you start in at least the second level." My heart started sinking. I wanted to start school in kindergarten, like everybody else did, and I didn't want to talk to any headmaster.

After we got past the secretary, we were ushered into the principal's office. She was an older woman with a kindly face and a dark blue suit despite the heat. She stood and smiled at us and said, "Hello, can I help you?"

"You sit there, Duckie." Gogo said to me, pointing at a chair. All my Mistrust plants stood up at attention, and I narrowed my eyes, but hopped onto the chair, my feet not touching the ground, and folded my hands in my lap. I waited, expectantly, obediently. I didn't want to make things worse.

"Christine can read anything you'd like. She is far too advanced for kindergarten, and should start in the second grade at the very least." Gogo got right to the point.

I squirmed with embarrassment, but I said nothing, concentrating on smoothing the blue cotton skirt on my lap.

The lady, still patient, continued smiling.

"Well, I'm sure that this is quite a smart young lady. And you are... is it Mrs. Golda? Are you Christine's... mother?"

I wanted to blurt out *no! That's not my mother, my mother would never do this,* but I said nothing.

"No, but I look after her for my daughter."

"Oh, so you're her grandmother?"

No one ever called Gogo my grandmother. She certainly didn't refer to herself that way. I looked up to see Gogo's cheeks get pink.

"She is my daughter's daughter. And she is far too advanced to start her schooling in kindergarten.

"I believe it would be in Christine's best interest if she went to school with her peers. She may be able to read, but her maturity level wouldn't be right for second grade. Besides, it is the school policy that..."

Gogo would have none of it; she cut the lady off saying, "Bring her a book to read, let me show you! Any book you like."

A book was produced, and I dutifully began to read. The letters were big and the words were easy, but my voice was quavering and my face felt hot.

"That one is too easy," Gogo said, scanning the shelves in the office. "Bring her a difficult book, one from your second level." The principal put another book in front of me. The writing looked very small and the words looked long, but I managed to stumble through some of it. I probably could have done better, but I started to pretend I couldn't read anymore. I wished I didn't know how to read. If no one else knew how to read in kindergarten, then I didn't want to either.

I tuned out the following argument that ensued between the principal and my grandmother. I was used to doing that, tuning out arguments, that is. I was also used to waiting patiently for them to be over. I watched as the brow on the principal's kindly face started to furrow. I idly thought how Gogo made a lot of people look mad.

Finally the principal was leading Gogo and me to my kindergarten class, very late. I thought how dumb that all was, how much time we wasted. They stopped what they were doing and all looked as me as I tried to blend in as inconspicuously as possible.

"This is Christine," the principal was saying, "and Christine, this is your teacher, Mrs. Pillow." I thought the name was funny, especially since she was big and lumpy like an old pillow. She smiled at me warmly.

Gogo blurted, "And she is a very good reader."

My face was burning hot.

"Well, that's wonderful..." Mrs. Pillow was saying. "Why don't you take a seat over there Christine?" I willed Gogo to leave, and after a few more agonizing minutes, she did.

* * *

So this was how it was going to be, I thought, trying to compose myself in the cool classroom. I was going to be dealing with Gogo full-time. No Papa, hardly any Mummy; Gogo. It was going to be Gogo, I could see now, who was going to be taking care of me, taking care of all three of us. I wondered how George could stand having her for a mother; it never seemed to bother him. I knew Gogo loved me, but I felt very sad and worried.

* * *

At first, life with Gogo being my mother was okay, except for the Guilt that was my constant companion. I knew Gogo was trying hard, but all I wanted, all I wished for every single day was my mother, completely taking over the longing I had for Papa. Gogo made me anything I wanted for breakfast in the morning, even if it was Wonder Bread and Kool-Aid. The lunches Gogo packed for me were big and wholesome, like thick roast beef sandwiches on country bread and a thermos of vegetable soup. Sometimes, feeling horrible, I threw away the beautiful lunches because they didn't look like the other kids' food that consisted of peanut butter and jelly sandwiches on puffy air bread, cut in triangles, and Granny Goose potato chips. Gogo walked me to school every day, George and Cathy in tow, while I guiltily wished I had a sign around my neck that said, "This is not my mother." When she dropped me off at my classroom, I would say to friends, "That's not my mom. My mom is young and cute," even though Gogo looked great for her age, which must have been in the fifties. Gogo told me I was beautiful all the time, that I would be Miss America someday, and that I was an Italian Contessa. She said she loved me (and George and Cathy) a thousand times a day, yelling it from the kitchen where she was cooking chips, and we would all yell it back. But she'd also surprise me by slapping me unexpectedly, but not too often at first. She snored most of the afternoon away sleeping in the armchair in the living room. She was overly protective, and wouldn't let us out of her sight, when all the other kids could roam the neighborhood freely.

I lived for Saturdays, the day I could be with my mom. I'd leave little notes on her pillow, saying "Three days 'til Saturday!" with pictures of the sun, because I always wanted it to be sunny that day, so we cold walk to the Hillsdale mall together, and have a lunch of peanut butter sandwiches and tomato soup at Moore's cafeteria. But Saturdays went by way too fast, and it seemed a very long time until the next one rolled around.

I didn't know the word for it yet, but even though my parents were gone, I was optimistic. Seeing my mom on Saturdays and a few early minutes in the morning was better than nothing, and I continued to write Papa, sure that any day now, I was going to get a letter in return. I was drowning a little bit though. I needed something to hold onto besides my over active imagination.

I found that something in school. I loved school. Things were orderly there. There were rules that I could follow. I was good at everything, and Mrs. Pillow loved me. I loved everything about kindergarten: laying down on the towels we kept in our cubbies for a nap, snack time with the graham crackers and a little carton of milk complete with a paper straw, singing around the piano, listening to fairy tales, playing in the doll house, learning to tie my shoes.

Before we ate our snack, we said a prayer in deadpan staccato unison: "Thank you for the food we eat, Thank you for the world so sweet, Thank you for the birds that sing, Thank you God, for EV-ry-thing..." This prayer puzzled and intrigued me. I had never said a prayer before. I knew what God looked like, from images TV or books, an old man with a long white beard, sitting in a throne in the clouds. But no one had ever talked to me about God. I wanted to know more. I sensed it could be something to hold onto, but I wasn't sure.

One day, during art time at school, I was painting on a easel, side by side with another smock-protected girl, both of us producing the same basic five-year-old standard landscape consisting of a house (a square with a triangle on top), grass, a tree or two, the sun, (a dot with lines spoking out around it), and a thin strip of blue across the top for the sky. Suddenly, impulsively it seemed, this girl reached over with her plump brush full of yellow paint and smeared a thick, diagonal line across the expanse of my large sheet of newsprint. The line extended from the strip of blue sky, to the strip of green grass. She lingered on my picture to make the line thicker. I was speechless by this invasion, but finally managed to come out with, "What's that?"

"That's for God to come down." The girl said, her face smooth and untroubled, as if she thought she was simply passing me some information I should know, not messing up my painting. I stared at the yellow swatch for some time, glancing occasionally at the girl. The yellow path didn't look good in my painting, and I tried to stay mad, but I was more fascinated. I was surprised that I felt a little happy feeling inside, a hazy, misty, lightness that was all over the room. I didn't want to forget the feeling.

* * *

For the next year or more, I would spend my weekdays concentrating on school, and looking forward to my Saturdays with my mom. I wrote to Papa regularly, always thinking the next letter would be the one to receive a reply. I worked on trying to be perfect and inconspicuous at the same time. Once in a while, I'd round a corner in the house, sliding on my socks on the hardwood floor, having fun, and I'd run smack into the elephant. Once, I looked deep into one of it's dark, round, sad, wrinkly eyes, and realized it looked exactly like that dumb hole in my heart that I was trying very hard to ignore.

* * *

Mrs. Lyon, my first grade teacher, didn't know that she helped me to Let Go. She didn't know that she had taken my small chubby hand in her long, red-finger nailed one, and pried my small fingers loose from what I was holding onto so tightly.

"Today, children, we are making Father's Day Cards!" she said.

I sat very still at my desk, trying to find out what the funny feeling inside of me meant. Something was different; something had changed. I didn't want to make Papa a card. I didn't want to write to him anymore. I didn't want to think about him anymore. I didn't want to miss him anymore.

I had written Papa faithfully, and I had been very patient waiting for him to return my letters. I still felt a little bit happy with hope when the postman came, but I had started getting tired of the hurt of my heart thumping down again when no letter came. I wrote less often, and finally stopped writing at all. Even though I still wanted to talk to him, it was better than being ignored. I realized I hadn't written him a letter in a long time.

Something in my heart had changed from missing him terribly, to not caring anymore. The numbness felt better than the pain. I even started feeling a little mad, and that gave me my first taste of power. If he didn't want to write me back, fine, I didn't need him.

I got out of my seat, and approached Mrs. Lyon's desk. She was very strict, but I wasn't afraid of her. I knew she liked me because I could read. I walked slowly, looking up at the windows, because I really didn't want to admit to myself what I was about to say.

"Mrs. Lyon? Can I tell you something?" I whispered so the rest of the class couldn't hear.

"Yes, Christine? What is it? By the way, do you take ballet?"

That threw me off base for the important thing I was about to tell her.

"No, why?"

"Your feet point out when you walk, like a dancer's," Mrs. Lyon said approvingly.

I was acutely aware of my feet pointing out, especially since Gogo made me promise to walk to school everyday pigeon-toed to correct the problem.

"Well, anyway." I said, losing my momentum, now my heart was pounding, she'd thrown me off base and it let the fear in. "I'm not going to make the Father's Day card." There, I'd said it.

"Why not?"

"Because I don't have a father." Once I said that, I felt a great relief. That was it. Done. I didn't have a father, and I didn't have to worry about it anymore. At the same time, I was surprised to feel the tears welling up in my eyes, and I swallowed hard. No way did I want to cry in front of Mrs. Lyon.

Mrs. Lyon smiled like it was no big deal. "Well, don't you have some man in your life?" she chuckled and winked like she'd just made a real funny joke. I didn't see what was so funny, but I thought for a minute.

"Well, I guess there's Beba. He's my grandmother's husband."

"Then it's...is it Beba? That's who you should make your card for." Mrs. Lyon said like it was perfectly normal to make a Father's Day card for your grandmother's husband instead of your father.

I shuffled back to my desk, trying to keep my toes straight. I didn't feel like making a Father's Day card for Beba, because he wasn't my father. I liked Beba though. He was nice to us, though sometimes he'd get mad, telling us to "smell the leather" of his belt, which made us laugh since he never hit us. I didn't see him a whole lot during the week, since he worked the graveyard shift at United and slept most of the day. Once in a while I saw him in the evening, but rarely. Sunday was Beba day, like Saturday was my mom's.

Beba would spend almost every Sunday with us three kids. Of course he was George's dad, and a lot of the activities were boy-centered for George, but he almost always took Cathy and me along. He would take us to church, and then to the Farmer's Market for chocolate éclairs afterward. He would work on making elaborate kites out of wood and plastic sheeting with George, and on Sundays we would try to fly them. He took us to the indoor roller rinks on rainy Sundays, and the Palo Alto Public pool on hot Sundays. He took us to schoolyards so we could ride our bikes around. My favorite Sundays were when Beba took us for a drive in his convertible. I considered all this as I stared at the blank piece of construction paper in front of me. I vacated into Fantasy, as I tended to do, and started thinking about the drive we had taken the last Sunday.

* * *

George and Cathy and I were huddled down low in the back seat of the convertible, trying our best to stay out of the wind. We could sort of talk with our mouths a few inches away from the vinyl seat, but if we sat up for a second we'd have to scream above the blast of cold wind that would sock us in the head.

We discovered a new game last week, and that was picking apart the car's upholstery. The creamy off-white vinyl seat, which we were very familiar with as our faces were stuck down by it half the time, had horizontal rows of piping, twisted black and white, like a very thin piece of two-tone licorice. We hardly had to touch the plastic cord at all for a little piece of it to come loose. Once a piece had started to come off, it was like a wiggly tooth, I couldn't leave it alone. I kept picking at it, then pick a little more, and then—I couldn't help myself—with a *riiiip*, like taking off a Band-Aid fast, I had boldly taken off a whole strand o the trim. George did it too. Cathy just contented herself with her thumb and her teddy bear, Wowo.

Beba would have been so mad if he knew we were abusing his car, his pride and joy, a two-tone yellow-on-white Ford Fairlane 500 convertible. We didn't mean to wreck his car, we just couldn't help ourselves. George was singing the little song he always sang about the car: "Ford—Fairlane—Con-ver-ti-ble, five huuuuuundred!" I told him, like I always told him, that he switched the order of the word 'convertible' and the number 500, and as always, he kept singing it the same old way anyway.

We didn't know where we were going. We never did. I don't think Beba did either, until we got there. The week before we had ended up in the Petrified Forest, and a few months before that we had driven to Santa's Village, my favorite. Today, I recognized the winding road, and knew we were heading to the Big Wave Beach.

Gogo came this Sunday, which wasn't always the case, so I had to wear my "mac," what Gogo called this big long coat that I had, with a hood and a belt and the plaid flannel inside. I thought it looked like something a spy would wear. I hated the coat, but I figured not too many people were going to see me hunched down in the back of the car, so I didn't put up too much fuss about wearing it.

We started fighting in the back seat, like we always do. Since I'm the oldest— seven—I tried not to join in. The fight started with George and Cathy pushing back and forth for more space on the seat. "Move over!" "No YOU!" They were getting louder and madder with each shove. I tried to ignore them as long as possible, busying myself with picking at the upholstery, but when one especially big push landed Cathy on my head, I got sucked in. All three of us were wrestling like crazy. It looked like George was going to win; that was happening a lot lately. I used to always be able to beat him up. He had me on the floor between the door and the middle hump, his knees poking me in my back. I was screaming my head off.

Gogo turned around and started flailing her hand toward the back seat, trying to slap anyone she could reach. That sent the other two diving for the floor too, which was just out of reach of Gogo's hand. We waited until the flailing hand stopped, then climbed back on the seat. It only took a minute or two before George started edging over toward me again, and I gave him a sharp bang with my hip, sending him sliding hard into Cathy as we made a sharp turn on the winding road. Cathy popped her thumb out of her mouth and gave a long, screechy, exaggerated, "OW!"

Now Beba turned around, glancing back and forth between the road, and us and with his right hand in pointed at us and said, "NO!" with that Polish accent which made it sound more like, "Nawh!" His finger was pointing at us, but at the same time his thumb was pointing straight up, so that it looked like a capital L, or like a kid pretending he had a gun. "Nawh," he yelled again, so hard that the veins in his temple jiggled like they do, making the short hairs growing there sort of stick out. When he turned back around, I made my hand into an L and mouthed *No,* which made Cathy and George start giggling. Then all three of us were doing it, making our hands into little guns and saying "No!" louder and louder, while laughing harder and harder. Then George pinched the hair next to his ears on his temple between his thumb and finger, and pulled straight out on his hair while saying "Nawh!" We were laughing so hard. That's when both Gogo and Beba's hands started hitting the air in the back seat at the same time, so all three of us all dove onto the floor again, but we were still laughing. I was actually getting too hot with that dumb mac on, even with the cold air blowing above us. We came up when we thought it was safe again, but we were still kind of giggling.

"Now that's better, Duckies!" Gogo said after a while, when we had calmed down, but soon she and Beba started their own kind of fighting.

"There is another way to get to the ocean, Dorothy, but it takes twice as long," Beba was explaining.

"Zbyczek, don't be daft, this is the only way to get to the seaside, unless we went up and over the Golden Gate Bridge...."

"Do*ROTH*y" Beba said that way he did when he was trying to be extra patient with Gogo. "There is another way..."

George and I started whispering "Do*RO*thy" to each other, copying Beba's Polish accent.

"Don't tell me; I'm not stuuuuuuuupid you know! Get out a map, I'll prove it to you," Gogo said, trying to open the glove compartment latch.

"You can't look at a map with the top down."

"Yes you can."

"Can NOT."

"Can, you know."

They'd always fight like that, so I stopped listening; it was boring. Then the wind seemed calmer, so I stuck my head up and could see we were over the top of the mountain, coming down the hill to the beach. I saw a few seagulls in the blue sky, and could smell that salty smell. The colors outside were bright. Gogo and Beba's argument stopped. Cathy's eyes were closed with her head leaning on Wowo, and George was looking out the other window. It was silent for a few minutes. All of a sudden, Gogo jumped like she had seen something. We all looked toward her to see what was up.

"I thought I saw a buttercup!" she said, with the same voice she would use if she saw an angel or something. George and I looked at each other. We were rolling our eyes and shrugging our shoulders, like "big deal."

"Oooooooooh!" Gogo screamed. "Look at the Pansies!"

I looked at George with my eyes opened wide, and we started laughing again, which woke Cathy up, who started laughing, but I don't think she knew why. We were saying it over and over; we said it so many times it turned into a joke. "I thought I saw a buttercup! Ooooooh!" "Look at the Pansies!" The "ooh" got longer every time we said it. We did this until we saw the ocean, laughing the whole way.

Gogo, this time anyway, took our teasing and laughed with us. "They are lovely, aren't they Duckies?" She said to us, each time we copied her, and played along with us.

* * *

I was smiling to myself at my desk, and let my mind come back into the classroom. I didn't know how long I had been gone. *Yeah, Beba is a pretty good guy*, I thought. *At least he's there, unlike Papa, who can't even be bothered to answer my letters*. Beba doesn't get too mad at us, and he puts up with Gogo. I started coloring the front of my card, which said: "Happy Father's Day Beba!"

* * *

And so I came to a place of Acceptance my seventh year. Papa was gone for good, and I would see my mother every once in a while. My new family was Gogo and Beba, their son George, my sister Cathy, and the elephant.

CHAPTER 6

God and Fairies (Down the Rabbit Hole)

My favorite part of those Sundays with Beba wasn't the wild, windy car rides over to the beach; it wasn't the doughnuts he bought for us at the food court; it wasn't when we were roller skating at the Rolladium or flying kites in the park. My favorite part—though I tried to keep it a secret—was going to church.

Every Sunday, Beba would cart the three of us kids over to St. Gregory's in the yellow Ford Fairlane, with the top *up*, since the three of us were wearing our Sunday Best. Cathy and I wore straw hats, white gloves, and sometimes matching frilly dresses with freshly whitened shoes; while George would be dressed in tweed dress slacks that Gogo had made him, a buttoned down shirt, and his hair slicked down with Vitalis.

I didn't let on to George and Cathy how much I looked forward to going to Sunday Mass. I complained to Beba about how long and boring the service was, in a sort of solidarity with the younger two, but my protests were half-hearted. As soon as I entered the building with the sun shining through the stained glass windows I felt a sense of order and decorum that I craved. I liked the clear tones of the gold bells ringing; the spicy smell of the incense; listening to all the Latin and letting it wash over me, although I didn't understand any of it. I could count on the mass being the same each week; the same repetitive—okay even boring—standing, sitting and kneeling; and I liked that.

Boring was starting to be preferable to Gogo's unpredictable mood swings that seemed to be getting wilder with each passing day. One day she'd be doing the can-can in the living room while singing "Knees Up

Mother Brown," and the next day she'd be throwing her fish and chips across the living room in some sort of rage.

"I don't see WHY the children have to be raised *RO*man Catholic!" Gogo suddenly spat out one Saturday afternoon while sitting in her big armchair. I looked up from the carpet where I was watching cartoons on TV, and wondered why she put such a big emphasis on the 'ro' of Roman like that, making it sound like a bad word. I turned to see how my mother would answer. As was often the case, there was no reaction from her.

"But why *Roman Catholic*?" Gogo repeated again. "I don't think Zbyczek has any right to dictate how we raise these three, do you Ducky?" Gogo called at my mom who was staring at the television. My mom finally shrugged her shoulders.

"Well, Christine and George are already baptized Catholic," she said vaguely.

"Yes, I know we had a christening. I'm not daft, you know."

I sat staring at the rug and wondered why Gogo didn't want us to go to church. My mother didn't seem to care. It didn't cross my mind to ask Gogo or my mom about church, or why they didn't go. I couldn't tell if they didn't want us to go to church, or if they didn't want us to believe in God.

Now that I was in second grade, I knew more about God than just thanking him for my graham crackers, or that feeling I had when that girl painted God's path on my picture. In spite of Gogo's feelings about the Catholic Church, Beba enrolled both George and me in Catechism class, which we both attended once a week after school.

Our teacher, Sister Mary Grace, wore a full black-and-white habit that showed only her face puffing up through the stiff white linen that tightly framed her features. She taught us the difference between a Mortal and Venial sin, how you could get stuck in purgatory, how you could get prayed out, and how you could burn forever in a fiery pit if you died with a mortal sin on your soul. But she never mentioned the word "hell," even though we knew that's what she meant.

We were given a little workbook to reinforce these concepts. I covered mine in gold foil which was left over from when Gogo made George's king crown for the Christmas play, because the gold seemed appropriately god-like and holy. For homework, George and I colored the pictures of Jesus and Mary, and people burning in pits of fire, and filled in the blanks in the workbook that taught us all The Rules.

There were a lot of rules, and they seemed stern and rigid, but at least they were spelled out clearly, unlike the rules we had at home, or rather the lack of rules. I could never guess what would make Gogo mad. Sometimes Gogo let us scream and fight for hours without saying anything; and other times she would come in and start hitting us for whispering in bed.

The workbook would quiz us: Not attending mass on Sunday. Is this a Mortal or Venial sin? I knew the answer was that it was mortal, but that seemed kind of harsh. Burning forever in hell just because you skipped church one Sunday without saying you're sorry? I wondered if God would give you a break if you didn't have a ride. It worried me how easy it was to slip up, and I felt even more pressure to be perfect than I already had. Not only could adults abandon you if you did things wrong, but later, after you died, you could suffer agony for eternity. George and I sometimes took breaks from our catechism homework to roll off the back of the couch, screaming and writhing in agony once we reached the pretend fires of hell below on the Persian carpet, and then laughing our heads off. It kind of relieved the pressure.

Gogo and my mom never asked what we were learning about in catechism, or even mentioned God. Gogo would faithfully wait for George and me outside of the church when catechism was over, holding onto Cathy in the stroller, and she would walk us the five or six blocks home, but never did she talk about what we were learning. Gogo said things like "God love her" or "God bless her soul," but that was about the extent of her talk of God. Gogo taught us faith, though. As surely as catechism taught us to believe in things we couldn't see or prove, so did Gogo. She communicated with the Other World regularly.

Gogo taught us about Santa Claus, who started visiting our house in November. She described to us in detail how Santa brought the chill air of the North Pole in with him when he came to our house to check up on us. Poltergeists lived in our house although they weren't welcome, and always did annoying things like take Gogo's sewing scissors, or her special chip spatula just when she needed them. "Damn those little buggers," was her usual comment to the poltergeists. She talked to her dead brother, Ron, all the time, giving us details of how she felt his cold presence, and the conversation they had. And someone else lived in our house beside Gogo, Beba, my mom, George, Cathy, the elephant, and the cat, Magic... and that was Joey.

* * *

"Oooh-ooh! Joey!" Gogo called up the fireplace the day that we first met him. She was bent over at the waist, making her powder blue short-shorts ride up a little higher. George and Cathy and I stood in a row in front of the brick hearth, eyes wide and expectant. Gogo stuck her head right inside the dark fireplace a little more, looking up.

"Joey are you there? Oooh-oooh!" Suddenly there was the thwack and crackle of cellophane hitting the grating on the fireplace floor. The three of us gasped in unison, but didn't dare to move.

"There now!" Gogo said, dusting the ash off the package. Into the dark void of the chimney she called, "I knew you were up there, you rascal you!" She winced a little as she straightened out, rubbing the small of her back.

"Here you are. Mind! Share this now; it's for all of you," Gogo said as she held out the package of multicolored blowout noisemakers. George snatched the package out of her hand and bit into the cellophane with his back teeth. The foil and tissue blowers fell to the floor, where Cathy and George scrambled to pick them up. They each put a plastic tip into their mouths and began to blow. A high-pitched, squeaky "Heeeeeeeeeeg!" came out, the curl of tissue filling with air as it uncurled straight out in front of them, and once deflated, curled back.

I was still too stunned to move. I didn't care nearly as much about getting a noisemaker as I cared about understanding what I had just seen. I saw it with my own eyes; it couldn't have been a trick; or could it have been? My eight-year-old mind struggled to make sense of what I had just seen.

Joey the Fairy lived in our fireplace, or so Gogo told us. "There are loads of girl fairies, you know that Duckies. We're lucky to have a boy. He has a fine tail; it's ever so long." I imagined it to look like a rat's. "He's big for a fairy, you know; he's at least this high..." Gogo said, as she spread her fingers wide. "And of course his wings are strong and sturdy." I had some skeptic in me already, but I really couldn't differentiate between fantasy and reality a lot of the time, though I struggled hard to do so. That day when Joey delivered the magic noisemakers, I stopped thinking so much, and joined in the spirit of the game.

"Did you see him, Gogo?" Cathy asked between blows on her noisemaker.

"Oh yes, darling, just a glimpse. He's very fast you know. He had on very dirty clothes which were covered in soot; they looked like rags, the poor little devil," Gogo said sitting down in her armchair and lighting a cigarette. "It certainly looked like he could use some new clothes."

That was all she needed to say. We got busy designing a new wardrobe for Joey. Cathy and George were using scraps of cloth from Gogo's remnant basket, but I thought it would be more practical to make his clothes out of paper. I had some stiff mint-green stationary that I thought would make a perfect suit. I asked Gogo to help me cut out the pants; I wanted to cut them out the way I saw Gogo make pants, with a half U for the crotch, so they wouldn't be flat. I then put them together with masking tape, so that the little trousers looked as if they were trimmed with tuxedo stripes of yellow piping. I was careful to cut out a hole for his tail in the appropriate place. Then I made the jacket, with yellow-trimmed masking tape lapels, coloring in the buttons with a brown crayon.

That night after I had put on my nightgown, I laid my little green outfit on the hearth of the fireplace along with Cathy and George's messy but sincere offerings. But I was careful to lay it out after Gogo had nodded off in her armchair so that she wouldn't see me doing it. "Mine is the only outfit wearable," I thought. " I hope it fits him." I worried it was too big.

I woke up early the next day and went straight to the fireplace, and sure enough all the new clothes for Joey were gone. Gogo was up and about, watering the plants with her slender metal canister. She ignored me as I stuck my head up the chimney, sniffing the ashy old-burned smell.

"Gogo, did you move the things we put here?"

"No Duckie...what things? I didn't notice anything. Why?" she said, looking with concentration at the plant she was watering.

"Oh, nothing."

After several minutes Gogo said, "Oh, I almost forgot to tell you, I saw Joey this morning. "

"Did you?" I asked holding my breath.

"Yes, I just saw the end of his tail going up the chimney. I think he saw me coming. I could only see his green trousers, with a bit of yellow, I believe. He looked quite nice for a change."

That feeling of deep joy and peace washed over me. Any doubts about Joey were gone after that, and I believed wholeheartedly in the fairy. I Knew inside that there was more to this world than we could see, and Joey was proof. I clung onto him for comfort. If Joey were possible, then anything was. I was a Believer.

* * *

And this Faith made it easy to transition into God, whoever He was; I could never really picture what He looked like, unlike Joey and Santa. It was a man, but I didn't relate to him being old with a beard anymore. I believed in God, even though Gogo and my Mom obviously didn't. God seemed scary and not nearly as fun as the fairies and the poltergeists. But He seemed more powerful too, and that's what I needed. Plus I liked the way his house—the church—was neat and clean and quiet, unlike our house that was a noisy mess most of the time.

George and Cathy brought some of the chaos of home into church with us, fighting violently under the pew during the mass, much to my humiliation. Just like everywhere else we went, it seemed to me that everyone was staring at us. No matter how much I vowed to stay above the fray, and sit and look ladylike as the other girls I observed in the church managed to do, I would end up getting pulled into the altercations, just like in the car, and then hating myself for it. I sunk down low in the pew when Cathy grabbed a handful of change out of the collection basket instead of putting her quarter in. At the end of mass when the priest would finally say, "Go, the Mass is ended," and the congregation would respond with, "Thanks be to God, " we kids would say "THANK GOD!" I would say it too, and I meant it - not for the same reason that I think George and Cathy did, but because the embarrassment would finally be over, for that week, anyway. None of this seemed to faze Beba though, who sat looking straight ahead, a serious expression on his face, his blue eyes far away.

* * *

Even though the dark confession booth scared me to death, I liked the idea that if I messed up, I could wipe the slate clean again just by going into the creepy dark closet and saying that I was sorry. I wished there were something like that for whatever I did to make Papa leave.

The sister at catechism tried to prepare us for our first confession, explaining what would happen, and walking the entire class over to the church, but she didn't prepare me for how frightened I would be. I sat waiting in the pews with the other kids, wondering what it would be like behind the mysterious door with the red or green light above it. When it was time for me to go in, I entered the dimly lit booth and knelt down, which triggered the light to go off and suddenly it was pitch black inside. My heart started thumping hard in my chest. The opaque amber window slid open, and I could see the shadowy silhouette of the priest, only inches away from me. I touched my forehead, chest, and shoulders in sign of the cross, a little shakily, as I had been instructed to do.

"Bless me father, for I have sinned, this is my first confession, these are my sins...." I stumbled and stopped. The sister had told us to speak from our hearts, but nothing came to me. I forgot about my heart and combed through my mind, looking for something I had done wrong. But I couldn't find anything; after all, I worked on being perfect every day. I had to, for survival.

"Yes?" came the low growly voice through the screen.

"I talked back to my mother. I hit my uncle, uh my brother, I lied." I threw in the one about the lie because I had just lied about the first two sins, especially the part about my uncle being my brother. It was just easier to call George my brother instead of always explaining to people that my uncle was younger than me.

"God has forgiven you; your penance is three *Hail Mary*s," the priest said, sounding kind of bored.

After saying my memorized Act of Contrition prayer to the priest, I walked out of the confessional and into the church, feeling like a fraud. As I knelt down to say my penance, I realized I was sort of mad. I said the three Hail Mary's, but I was thinking, *Why should I? I haven't done anything wrong*. I realized I had sort of the same feeling I used to have when Gogo, my mom, or Papa used to hit me. I hadn't done anything wrong; at least they never explained what it was if I had; and I certainly wouldn't have known what to confess if they had asked me. It seemed that just by existing I was bound to mess up no matter how hard I tried to be perfect.

The next Sunday following my First Confession I was to receive my First Holy Communion. My mother had taken me shopping for the requisite white dress, which turned out to be unlike the other girls' dresses, that looked like fluffy, gauzy, miniature bridal gowns. My dress was made of sturdy white cotton that could be converted to a school dress by sewing on colored trim, which my mom eventually did. She also bought me some special white silky socks that didn't stretch, and she glued some white netting onto one of my headbands to serve as a veil, along with some fake white rose buds. She said my school shoes would have to do, but she put fresh white shoe polish on them the night before.

My mother woke me up early that Sunday, and had all the clothes laid out on the bed for me. I had a special, excited feeling. She brushed my hair, and helped me get ready, but she never mentioned anything about the ceremony I was about to partake in. She didn't come to the church, but waved goodbye as I got in the car with Gogo, Beba, and George.

I clutched my new white bible with the 3D crucifix inside the front cover, and my white pearly rosary as I sat demurely in the back seat of the car. I felt holy. I also felt hungry, as I had to 'fast' by skipping breakfast in order to be pure when I received the "Body of Christ." Christ's body was to be delivered in the form of a thin wafer that I was told by the sister not to let touch my teeth, but rather to swallow it whole. Rumors had flown around the catechism class that someone had actually chewed one of the wafers once, and promptly fell down dead, which I didn't really believe, but decided not to chew it just in case. The whole idea of eating someone's body kind of grossed me out, even if it was Jesus's, but I thought that it might be good for me; at least it couldn't hurt.

I sat through the mass with all the other girls in white dresses, and when it was time, I got in line to receive the wafer. I knelt down, and the priest came by with the golden goblet. He put the special gold shield under my chin in case the holy wafer should fall, so it still wouldn't touch the ground. I stuck out my tongue as I had been instructed to do, and then let the wafer sit under the roof of my mouth as I walked back to my pew. I knelt down to pray, concentrating very hard on the powerful juju I held with my tongue.

After that, I enjoyed getting up in the middle of mass to get my communion; it broke things up a little bit. I was mad the time I had to skip it because I had chugged a couple of gulps of green Kool-Aid before we left for church, breaking my fast. I thought it wouldn't count, since water was allowed, and it was hardly more than water. I wasn't sure though, so I asked Beba in the car if it was alright that I had swigged the Kool-Aid, and Beba said he'd have to ask the priest, which he did, outside the church before mass began. The priest rubbed his chin, squinting into the sun, and said that anything besides water was considered breaking the fast. I was thinking, *A little green powder?* but had to go along with the priest's decision. There were those Rules again. Again, at least they were consistent. Not like at home, where joking about Gogo's accent would always send her into to peels of laughter, except for last week, when it earned me a hard smack across the face. That Sunday I had to stay back in the pews with Beba, George, and Cathy, who never went up for communion. I knew George and Cathy hadn't had their First Communion yet, but suddenly I wondered about Beba.

"Beba? Beba!" I said in a loud whisper. He looked over at me, eyebrows up in question. "How come you never go up for communion?"

He leaned toward me and said in his deep, low voice, "I haven't gone to confession."

"Why didn't you go in when you took me yesterday?" I realized he never went into confession either.

He looked at me directly for a moment, and I could see his light blue eyes were a little watery. He turned and stared straight ahead at the huge statue of Jesus on the cross with the blood all running out of the hands and feet, and the crown of thorns stuck into his head. I could see that he was swallowing hard, because his Adam's apple was moving up and down.

"Huh, Beba?" I said more quietly, not expecting him to answer.

He didn't.

I wondered about that a lot. What could he have to confess that would be so bad?

* * *

I started practicing all the Rules and observing the holy days. On Palm Sunday, Sister Mary Grace gave us each a palm leaf in catechism class, saying "Put this behind your Crucifixion in your house, and pray to it each night this week." To make up for the lack of a cross in our house, I dutifully made one out of orange construction paper, hung it on the wall by my top bunk bed, stuck the leaf behind it, and knelt down and prayed to it each night in my nightgown. Gogo caught me at this one evening, and said, "What on earth are you doing? Kneeling down and praying to a bit o' paper and a leaf?"

Suddenly my little shrine lost all its holy power and looked silly. I got the same feeling I had had a few weeks before, when I was kissing my

Tiny Tears Doll good night while tucking her in her crib. The doll's cheek suddenly felt cold, and the image of the yellow plastic tugboat with black mold on the bottom that I played with in the bathtub popped unexpectedly into my mind. I realized with a sickening feeling that "my baby" was made out of the same stuff as that boat. I hadn't kissed her since. My heart sunk the same way now that Gogo had debunked my crucifix. Okay, maybe the paper and the leaf didn't hold any power, but just because my cross was fake that didn't mean God was fake, did it? *No*, I decided, *it didn't*. God was real. I needed God to be real. Joey was real, and his clothes were made out of paper. Wasn't that the same thing?

My Faith took hold, and I started praying like crazy. Sometimes it was obsessive. I thought it was my job to pray as many people out of purgatory as possible, since Mary Grace said it only took one prayer sometimes to get people out of the horrible place that simulated hell, and on to Eternal Bliss. Other times I prayed the same way I would wish upon a star. "Dear God. Please make mom come home from work earlier so that I can talk to her. Just a little earlier, that's all. Dear God. I know it's been a long time since I've asked this, but do you think you could tell Papa to write me back? Dear God. Please make Gogo stop hitting me. Thank you, God. Amen." Even though I prayed a lot, and with a fierce intensity, most of my prayers didn't come true. I thought I must have been doing something wrong. Maybe I was breaking one of the Rules that I didn't know about. Maybe if I was a little better… I was sure I could be, I just had to try a little harder.

There was something else though. For want of a better word, I'll call it Knowing. Knowing was the real God deep down inside of me; not who I *thought* God was, the guy I prayed to in the sky. Deep down inside I Knew. I Knew everything. I knew Papa wasn't coming back, and my mom and Gogo weren't going to change. I didn't want to believe it though, so I prayed harder. I squished and buried the Knowing.

* * *

The Knowing wasn't always bad, though, and when I wasn't trying to squelch it, the Knowing could bubble up to tell me good news, like it did in Mrs. Graham's class one day.

Mrs. Graham was my second grade teacher, and my favorite teacher so far. She wore her bright red hair in a messy upsweep fixed with bobby pins, and had brown and tan saddle shoes. She still seemed old like Mrs. Lyon did, but the difference was that she knew how to talk to kids. She didn't care if we touched our hands to her face; she didn't need to manage us by putting names on the board; she kept us so interested in what we were doing that there was hardly a need for discipline.

Sitting in Mrs. Graham's class this one day, I had this feeling—this Knowing—for the first recognizable time. I Knew I was going to be a teacher when I grew up. Not, oh, maybe I want to be a teacher, or oh, it would be fun to be like Mrs. Graham. There was no need to pray for this; it wouldn't have made any difference if I had. I just Knew. This was an *Oh! I am going to be standing in front of a classroom one day; there is no doubt; how interesting.*

* * *

That same year in second grade, yet another Knowing came to pass in me. It was too big for me to swallow, or even look at, so I let it rest where it landed—a small seed in my psyche—and I carefully buried it along side of the other Knowings I couldn't look at.

What was weird about Mrs. Graham's class was that it was a first and second grade split. I had never heard of that being done before, and I was surprised that George was going to be in the same class as me.

On the first day of school Mrs. Graham told us, "Now, boys and girls, I'm going to let you in on a secret. I don't want you to tell any other children that are outside of this class. No one! If there's anyone who thinks they can't keep a secret please raise your hand." Heads turned about, but no hands were raised. She looked around sternly; well, as stern as Mrs. Graham could be, which wasn't too stern. "This class is special. The reason there are first and second graders mixed in here is because all of you are extra smart and good at reading and arithmetic, so we are going to be able to work a lot faster than maybe you've been used to before. You are very special, but remember, you're not to tell anyone."

I looked around the room, smoothing the pink tulle of the slip of my store-bought dress; the only store-bought dress I was ever to own my entire childhood. Huh. We were special. James Callan with his ears that stuck straight out was special. Plump Nina Steindorsen, who walked with her right arm crooked up, bobbing her hand rhythmically back and forth as she walked – was special. Laurie Brown, whose Bluebird hat was always on crooked, was special. Martin with the wheezing asthma was special. My best friend Roberta—and oh, George and I, were special too.

Mrs. Graham taught us about Japan so vividly that I wanted to go there. She let us have 'Fun Days' where all we did was art. She threw parties at her house, and it was unimaginable to go the teacher's house! She gave every one of us a Christmas present, my gift being a little gold Scottie dog pin with a green jewel eye. She took us on field trips to the back of the QFI supermarket, and to a dairy where I got to feel the warm, smooth cow's udder. I thought she was the best teacher anyone could possibly have. But why Mrs. Graham would tell us this thing about us being a special class, and then tell us to keep it a Secret was beyond me.

That very first recess after Mrs. Graham laid the Secret on us, I told Carol Hardy, a friend who lived on our street, that I had a secret—but I didn't think I'd tell anyone what it was. In a weird way I wanted to unload it, so it didn't take much for Carol to wear me down; just a few days of begging; which is what I secretly wanted. As soon as I saw her towhead coming toward me at recess, I'd try to hide, but she'd track me down. "Puh-leeeeeeeze tell me the secret," she'd wheedle. I tried to tell her it was no big deal, but she was relentless. Finally, I gave in, but made her swear not to tell anyone, and she bobbed her head *yes,* her wispy blond hair flying. *Yes*, she promised; my secret was good with her.

The next day Mrs. Graham said to the class, "I'm not going to say whom, but someone in here told the secret I told you had to stay within this class." A collective little gasp whooshed through the room. I looked around thinking someone else must have told besides me, since Carol Hardy had sworn not to say anything; but all the other faces looked genuinely shocked with a sort of wide-eyed innocence. Then I saw Mrs. Graham catch my eye for a split second, then flick her green eyes away. *Oh God*, I thought, *it was me*—and Mrs. Graham knew it. I felt horrible because I liked this teacher so much.

I sat still in my seat, trying to look innocent; but I could feel my face was hot and knew it must be red. *I hate secrets*, I thought; *I hate them.* It was something like lying, which I also hated. I remembered telling some kids in kindergarten that I had never told a lie yet, and them looking back at me like I was some kind of weirdo.... or liar. Now I had lied. I had sinned.

Then a little bit of a weird feeling came over me. It was almost like a Knowing, but I couldn't think what it was. It felt icky. Was there some other secret I knew and wasn't supposed to talk about? I thought back. I strained far back in my memory, but the feeling was too far away to grab onto. Then that tongue dream, that creepy, yucky dream where my tongue fell out, popped into my head. I remembered the image of the maroon lump sitting there on the tiles. I shook my head to clear it. That stupid dream was always popping into my mind. Ew.

My attention went back to Mrs. Graham, who was telling us to get our reading books out. I would just have to forget about it, I decided. The icky feeling I had would go away; I knew. I just hoped that no one would tell me any more secrets I had to keep inside. I wasn't good at it.

* * *

One rainy Tuesday, the class was quiet. The second grade kids, myself included, were coloring purple mimeographed pictures of pagodas while the first grade kids read out loud with Mrs. Graham. I felt happy and content to be inside the peaceful classroom while the storm raged outside, the rain pelting onto the large, plate-glass windows. I rested my head on my left arm while I colored, so that I was looking at the picture sideways, my preferred method, because it made the lines distort. Suddenly, there was a sharp rapping on the classroom door. A lot of kids jumped, including myself. No one ever knocked on the door during class. I was still absently coloring when I felt a burst of energy come through the door.

"Yoo-hoo! Hello Duckies!" came the familiar singsong British accent. I stared at the door wide-eyed, along with twenty-five pairs of eyes. Gogo appeared in the doorway like a mirage. She was soaking wet from the torrential downpour, and was dripping all over the gray linoleum. Drops of water dripped off of her clear plastic headscarf she had tied under her chin, and were running down the tip of her nose, where the water dripped steadily.

Gogo looked exhilarated yet calm after her walk through the storm. She was taking off the plastic headscarf, yanking at the bow under her chin, and then shaking it dry. She folded it carefully on the creases, and put it back in its pink plastic pouch, snapping it shut. This made my eyes grow even wider than they already were, since this gesture was giving me the feeling that Gogo had planned on staying a while. I noticed that she had two huge shopping bags in her hands; the kind with handles that said Sears on the side, which she put purposefully on the floor.

"I brought Christine and George their boots; you don't mind, do you Ducky?" Gogo was calling across the room to Mrs. Graham. Mrs. Graham smiled, and said, "Yes, please come in!"

"Hey, who's that? Is that your mom?" Theresa Kludt whispered to me.

"No!" I hissed back. The recurring annoyance that everyone thought she was my mom washed over me. I made a mental note to explain it to her at recess.

Gogo was making a loud racket with the paper bags and the tissue, which she was throwing willy-nilly on the classroom floor. First she pulled out two huge –square, not rectangular –shoeboxes.

"Ooo-oooh! George! Come here, darling." George got up from his desk, and obediently walked toward the side of the room where Gogo had set up camp.

"Hello, Mum," George said, and gave her a kiss on her temple when she bent down.

"I thought you said she wasn't your mother?" Theresa whispered again. I shook my head and waved my hand a little, indicating I'd explain later.

Gogo opened the first box, and took out a pair of brown rubber boots.

"Let me see if these fit now, I'll take them back if they don't. I thought they looked a bit small, but the bloke promised they'd fit; he did, you know," Gogo muttered, shaking her head and frowning at the boot she held in front of her.

George put his untied tennis shoe into the boot.

"There now, lovely! They fit perfectly." She reached into the other bag and pulled out a yellow rain slicker with black plastic buckles. "Try this on too; go on, then!" George good-naturedly let Gogo put on the hood, so that he looked like the Gorton Fisherman on the Fish Sticks box, with only his eyes peering out. He stood stiffly with his arms out, while Gogo scrutinized him, along with the rest of the class, which had come to a complete standstill. Finally, she nodded, satisfied, and undressed him.

"Oooh-OOh, Christine! C'mon, Ducky, look snappy; let's try yours on, then."

I got up slowly and reluctantly, scraping my chair loudly in the mesmerized room, and walked with heavy steps over to my grandmother. "Don't just stand there, look smart; knees up, Mother Brown!" I put my foot up as she scrambled in the mound of tissue for the identical pair of rain boots, only in white.

"Okay, they fit," I said, low and quiet, quickly kicking off the boot, and trying to scramble back to the relative safety of my desk.

"Christine! Stand still; don't be so fidgety! You haven't tried your coat on yet."

I saw that my raincoat wasn't in a Sears bag, the way George's had been. Gogo was fishing around in the bottom of a canvas satchel she carried when she walked to the grocery store for just a few things. Then she pulled out the raincoat, which was clear with giant purple violets all over it. I could tell that she had made it.

Now, as I've said, Gogo was a great seamstress, and I loved most of the things she made me, but God, this raincoat! I recognized it as the shower curtain that she and Beba had bought last week for the downstairs bathroom. It hadn't been used for showering purposes yet, but I was mortified. The purple thread Gogo had used, and how she had hand sewed the buttonholes softened my heart a little, but not enough to forgive her yet for the humiliation she was putting me through.

"C'mon, Christine! I haven't all day!" Gogo was holding the coat open at the shoulders. I reluctantly put my hand in the sleeve, and then quickly shrugged it off.

Satisfied, Gogo started gathering up the empty boxes and bags that were scattered around her. "Thank you, Mrs. Graham. Goodbye Duckie! Ooohooh! George! Cheerio! Mind the cars when you cross the street! Cheerio!"

I went back to my seat, hot-faced, and tried to read my book, but it took a good hour to recover from the embarrassment. By lunchtime, the incident was behind me—that is, until we were excused to line up at the door.

"Aren't you going to wear your nice new boots out to recess?" Mrs. Graham asked George and me, while we were standing next to each other near the head of the line. We simultaneously shook our heads *No*. "It certainly was nice of your mother to bring those things to you on such a blustery day," she said to George and me. "Wasn't it boys and girls?" she continued, beaming at the rest of the line.

George was solemnly nodding his serious face up and down, his long brown bangs falling into his brown eyes. I surprised myself by blurting out, "She's not my mother!" right in front of the whole class. Suddenly the children began asking a flurry of questions.

"That's not your mother?"

"Aren't you guys brother and sister?"

"You look exactly the same; what do you mean that's not your mother?"

I squirmed, but George's face remained serene.

"No, boys and girls, that is George's mother, and Christine's, is it, grandmother?" Mrs. Graham said. I nodded my head.

"So, what, are they cousins?" Nina Steindorsen asked from her place at the back of the line.

"Yeah, cousins," I answered quickly.

"Actually," Mrs. Graham continued, "that would make George Christine's uncle."

I heard some giggling in the line.

"Whoever heard of having an uncle younger than you are?" said James Callan. "My uncle is old like my Dad." I wondered if both their ears stuck out like his.

"Well, it is possible, and we have an example of that possibility right here in our class," Mrs. Graham said, as she swung open the heavy green door, securing it on the brass stop outside with a thud-clink. The smell of rainy day whooshed in the room, although the rain wasn't coming down at the moment. From my place at the head of the line, I heard Mrs. Graham say, quietly, so that only George and I could hear, "But I must say, it is one of the oddest things I've seen in my twenty-five years of teaching; my goodness, you two look like twins!"

I stared at George. He had on the sweet smile; the smile that came out less often the older he got. Looking into his eyes, a little cold recognition moved up my spine. Those were the eyes I looked at in the mirror every day.

Then there was a Knowing, which I immediately buried, and there was another Secret, even from myself, which I immediately hated. I felt all my seeds of mistrust. Instead of trusting the Knowing within, I looked out, and prayed to God to make the feeling go away.

CHAPTER 7

No Exit (Digging a Hole)

The long-awaited Popsicle man, driving the white truck that blared a tinny-sounding "Pop Goes the Weasel," had already come by that hot early-summer afternoon. My Missile was melting faster than I could eat it. I had to lick hard so that the sticky red and orange goo didn't drip all down my forearm. Finally, I held the dribbling thing up in the air and tilted my head back to let the drops fall onto my tongue. I pulled the last big chunk off the stick with my mouth and chewed it, grimacing at the shivers it sent through my teeth.

While I was sucking contentedly on the stick, I decided to sharpen it on the sidewalk of the shady alley at the side of the house. I sat down cross-legged and rubbed each side of the stick on the concrete until I had a nice pointed weapon. I poked my thigh with the sharp end to check out its effectiveness, but I didn't feel much. I wasn't feeling a lot in those days; I was kind of numb.

I jabbed at my leg a few more times, faster, harder, and with increasing vehemence. The release felt so good that the pain was on time-delay, about thirty seconds after I stopped. I said "Ow!" out loud without much conviction. *It never really hurts until later*, I realized mildly. I absently rubbed the red spots on my thigh.

I thought that the stick could be more useful as a tool, and decided to dig. Maybe I could dig my way out. With the same mixture of delusion, grandeur, faith, and determination I felt when I believed that if I tried hard enough I could run as fast as a jet, I was suddenly convinced that if I just kept at it, I could eventually get through the earth, and dig my way to China.

I knew I wasn't the first kid to come up with this idea, but in my fantasy world, a world that I sometimes had trouble differentiating from reality, I was positive that with my stamina, I would be the first one to actually pull it off. I knew from this past year in school, my fourth grade year, that China was on the other side of the globe. I also knew about the hot molten lava in the center of the earth called The Core, represented by a red rubber ball in the plastic model of the Earth that had been in my classroom. I figured I would worry about that problem when I got to it, maybe when the dirt started getting warmer. I had all the time in the world. A summer afternoon could be an eternity.

I was sitting in the dirt between the huge agapanthus that lined the fence. I thought the plants were ugly; all leaves with one ridiculous shooting stalk of purple-blue flowers, but then again, everything was sort of ugly. I was alone, and I was digging.

On the other side of the gate I could hear the *pwack... pwack* of Gogo throwing snails against the fence with a vehemence matching that of my own during my leg jabbing, muttering "bloody rubbish" after each snail death by fence-smashing.

I dug harder, breaking through the top crust of dry earth. I wanted to escape. I had no other means of doing so but to dig straight down. I didn't have the guts to run away. I left notes on my mom's pillow, almost every night, telling her of new atrocities Gogo would pull, and begging her to get us a house of our own. I didn't care where this new house was going to be. China would be fine. I didn't care about California anymore. I didn't even know if Papa was still here. I started fantasizing how I would feel if we moved.

I wouldn't miss this neighborhood, I thought. I wouldn't miss the shabby apartments that, unbelievably, looked so fresh and colorful to me five years ago. I wouldn't miss the noise, the accents, the fried fish smell, the televisions blaring, the arguing, the millions of kids, the diapers, and the overabundance of babies on this block of East 40th.

I wouldn't miss our house, with Gogo snoring in the living room every afternoon on the big brown armchair, her legs covered with the old chenille bedspread, the TV perpetually on. I wouldn't miss the mess, or the mismatched furniture, or the cigarette smell mixed with the smell of old lard. I wouldn't miss the fighting and yelling all the time.

I wanted to live somewhere manicured. Somewhere void of personality or conflict, like my friends from school did; like the houses on TV. A neighborhood that was nice and quiet and neutral. I craved beige.

Okay, I would miss the people, I had to admit. I'd miss Dora and Virginia, newly arrived from Cuba, who lived across the street, with a house worse than ours, dead empty except for two nylon lawn chairs with metal frames and a huge color console television. I would miss their mother, Mrs. Garcia, who served us watermelon drinks wrapped with paper towels while we played Parcheesi, and would carefully polish the one piece of furniture every day with Pledge. I'd miss Jenny and Kevin, the two little Chinese kids who lived below the Garcias, whose parents grossed us out by serving frog legs at a birthday party, which we ate anyway, chewing gingerly on the rubbery parts and trying not to laugh. I'd miss Bonnie, the sixth grader in the other upstairs apartment, who seemed to have no parents, always listening to her 45s on a portable record player and trying to talk to me about sex.

I didn't want to think too hard about leaving George and Beba. Especially George. Even though we fought like crazy, and I hated him because Gogo and Beba favored him so blatantly, he was still the closest person to me. We didn't even need to talk—most of the time we communicated through our eyes.

Maybe it wasn't the neighborhood, or even our house that I wanted to get away from so much, I thought, as I got into a better position to dig lower, smelling the richness of the deeper soil, and seeing my first worm. *It was Her*. I heard a few more snails smash against the fence, and then one came flying over the top and landed only a few inches away from my hole.

* * *

Gogo still laughed occasionally, and told us stories once in a while, but most of the time she was either sleeping in her chair or screaming at us—but especially at me. When Gogo woke up from her daily nap, the first thing she would do was reach for the end table next to her chair and take a swig of cold tea out of her chipped china cup along with a handful of Bayer aspirin from a huge bottle she kept there. Then she lit up a cigarette, and put it down in the overflowing ashtray until it burned away. Her end table also had dozens of small brown bottles of her medicine.

I knew the doctor prescribed all this medicine for the vague illness she always complained about. I didn't understand it, but Gogo felt the fog somehow brought on her malaise. "Oh, the fog, I can feel the bitter cold in my bones!" she said, almost every day. If I pointed out that there wasn't a cloud in the blue sky, she said there was fog lurking somewhere, and I shouldn't be such a little cat.

I dug a little slower when I considered how all that medicine she took could have something to do with the weird way she acted now. I never would have suspected that medicine from a doctor could be bad for you, if I hadn't heard that tape.

I usually didn't listen too carefully to the tapes that Gogo's sister Daisy sent her from England. It was hard to keep my mind on what Daisy was saying; it was so boring. Things like, *"Well, Ducky, I'm about to put the kettle on for my afternoon tea, I shall enjoy that, you know, I'm tired to the bone. On my feet all day I was, never a break in the shop today. Let me see if I have the energy to peel the spuds and get those on, or Richard will be complaining about his supper being late again. There now, where's that spud peeler? Oh, never mind, I'll use the knife, though it's dull. I hate a dull knife, don't you Ducky?"* And on and on, like Gogo was in the room with her.

But on that last tape I caught something I couldn't forget. The familiar monologue was droning out of the Grundig, and Gogo was smoking a cigarette, squinting her eyes while she listened to Daisy's familiar, high, warbly, almost bird-like voice, thick with her British accent. Suddenly, I don't know why, I tuned in and caught this advice from Gogo's sister: *"Please be careful Ducks, I'm so sorry you have the burden of the three children, it must be dreadfully hard, I don't know how you do it, really, without any help at all. But please try to stay away from those tablets; they can't be good for you, you know. I can see every once in a while how you might need a little boost, what with all you have to do, but I'd try not to take them much, Ducks. See what the doctor says."*

I was shocked. She took those pills to help with the "burden" of taking care of us? I glanced over at Gogo, who sat smoking; she was oblivious to what I was hearing, or what conclusions I was drawing, and said nothing.

* * *

Maybe she wouldn't need to take those drugs if Cathy and I left, I thought, as I dug harder. Then she'd just have George—I'm sure that HE wouldn't be a burden to her, since George could do no wrong in her eyes.

Beba had escaped for a while, I mused, as I flicked a large clump of dirt toward the fence, countering Gogo's latest snail-pwack. He was back now, but he had been gone for a long time, close to a year. No one had mentioned that he was leaving, or why, but it happened after one of those big fights he and Gogo had all the time. Poor George tried to make jokes to attempt to get them to stop, and when he couldn't, he threw up. That last fight started because Beba told George to sit on the sofa for ten minutes as punishment for something he had done wrong. George started crying and yelling that he didn't want to sit there, and ran to Gogo. Beba started threatening to use his belt on him if he didn't mind, but George started yelling back at Beba, saying, "You're not going to hit me with that!" Since Beba always threatened, but never actually hit us with the belt, I was shocked when he struck at the back of the chair between Gogo and George, narrowly missing both of them, though Gogo screamed as though she had been hit.

When Beba left, George acted nervous and jittery all the time, but especially after they pulled him out of class to talk to the lawyer. The lawyer asked him who he'd rather live with, his mother or his father. George told me he was crying and refused to choose, but finally said he'd rather live with his mother, just because he was afraid what her reaction would be if he didn't. That's when George started thinking that color could rub off on his face, and he'd ask me the same questions over and over. "Do I have any color all over my face?" Gogo had George sleep in bed with her after Beba left, and George told me that Gogo slept flat on her back, with the sheet clenched in her teeth, because she couldn't bear to be uncovered.

Then, as suddenly as he left, Beba came back. One day I saw Gogo fluffing her hair around the temples with her fingertips in the medicine cabinet mirror, and putting on some pink lipstick, and I knew something was up. Beba came over a little while later, formally ringing the doorbell, and Gogo swung open the door expansively, saying, "Why Zbysiu!" Like she was surprised, she's such a fake.

When I leave, I never want to come back, I thought, using my fingernails to pull out a rock I had hit in my digging conquest.

I couldn't stand to see my mother cower in front of Gogo. I didn't want the only person in this world who was in my corner to be weak. I picked up a handful of moist dirt and squeezed it hard in my hand and watched it ooze out from between my fingers.

The gooey dirt reminded me of my mom. She loved playing with clay, especially Play-Doh. She made heads with different expressions when she was watching TV. One head would be fed up and sick of things, while another head would be coy and sly. She usually squished the heads as soon as she'd make them, putting the dough back in the cardboard container, but one night, she made a blue head with droopy eyes and a hauntingly wistful expression, and I begged her to save it, telling her how good it was. So she left it out on the white Formica end table to dry and harden under the lamp.

The next day, after my mom left for work and I was already lonely for her, I went to the table and the head was gone. I felt some iciness inside.

"Gogo, did you see the little Play-Doh head that was here last night?" I called to her in the kitchen.

Gogo came around the corner, shuddered, and crossed her bare arms over her thin blouse that she was wearing without a bra, as if to keep out the cold. "I smashed it!" she snapped. Her voice was mean, but her eyes looked scared.

I looked inside the Play-Doh can still on the table, and sure enough, I could make out part of the haunting eye, now all misshapen and looking up at me. A wave of anger washed over me. On one of the rare nights that I was hanging out with my mom, this head was created, and now Gogo wrecked it, just like she wrecked a lot of stuff."Why?" This was all I could get out.

"Well, Ducky, in the middle of the night, a bright light shining into my bedroom woke me up. At first I thought perhaps it was a policeman, shining his spotlight into our room, so I shot straight up and went to the window and peered out of the blinds. There was nothing there, I tell you. Nothing. I swung around, but the light was still on the wall, a huge glowing circle it was. I went up to it, and you know, Christine, it was the strangest thing. I could not make a shadow on the light! I tried with my hands all over..." At this point Gogo was patting at the air to demonstrate how she tried to make a shadow.... "And when that didn't work, I laid on the bed, and swung my leg..." Gogo was on the floor on her back, swinging her bare leg in a huge arc. "Nothing would make a shadow. Then suddenly I saw that there was a shadow already in the light, it was a bloomin' huge head, and directly, I saw that it was the exact profile of the head your mother had made. George saw it too; ask him. I ran into the living room and smashed the head with a good wallop that took all my might. When I went back into the bedroom the light and the shadow were gone, thank God."

I threw some rocks out of my hole and against the fence, the pings a little louder than the ones made by Gogo's snails. One I threw over the top, not exactly on purpose, but I wasn't trying to be too accurate either. I held my breath until I was sure it hadn't hit Gogo. Gogo was always mean to my mom, and it made me furious.

My mother had been dating a man named Ray for the past few months. I hardly ever saw my mother anyway, but since she started seeing this man, it was pretty much never, since she usually spent three nights a week at his place in San Francisco. The first time she'd spent the night at his house was New Year's Eve, and Gogo called the police.

"How old is your daughter, ma'am?" the cop asked, as I peered around the door at him. He had taken his hat off and put it under his arm, and had a pen poised over a little notebook.

"Thirty-four." Gogo said without humor, pronouncing it "thuh-ty foh."

"Uh, ma'am, it was New Year's Eve last night. Perhaps your daughter was, uh, just having a good time." The cop winked, scratching the back of his crew-cut head. I thought, *Yeah*.

"Nonsense! She's never stayed out all night! I want to report her missing immediately."

"Sorry ma'am, no can do. Adults need to be missing over three days to report them, not a few hours. She'll be along soon enough, I'm sure of it. If not, give us a call," the officer said, handing Gogo a card. She slammed the door in his face. When Mom came home later that day, there was a lot of screaming and yelling, mostly coming from Gogo.

Since I never saw my mom anymore, I was surprised when I looked out of the window one afternoon to see her breezing up the front steps. I jumped off the couch and ran to the hall to greet her.

"Hi Mom," I said, through the screen door. The air was warm outside and smelled like our peach tree. My mom looked especially nice in her orange cotton dress cinched in at the waist with a belt, with a matching orange beaded necklace.

"Hi, darling!" she said, bending down to kiss me on the lips lightly.

"What are you doing home?"

"Oh, I'm going to have some company for dinner tonight," she said, like it was nothing.

This little piece of information took a second to digest. Company for dinner? Had we ever had anyone over to our house for dinner? Not that I could remember.

Gogo yelled out, "What did you say, Duckie?"

I saw my mom's jaw set a little, but she strode into the living room where Gogo lay in her usual position, on the armchair in front of the television.

"I hope I didn't hear you say anything about *company* over for dinner," Gogo said, over the top of her glasses. "Because I shan't have it, not tonight Duckie, I don't feel well." She spit out the word company like it was a swear word.

My gaze went from my mom, back to Gogo, and now fixed on my mom again. I wanted this company to come to dinner, even if it was Ray. I'd only seen him a couple of times, and thought he was all right, even though I was mad and shocked when I saw him kiss my mother on the mouth that time.

"Duckie, listen. I've already asked Ray, and he's coming straight from work in San Francisco; there's no way to reach him now. He makes me dinner practically every night at his place, and he thought it would be nice for a change to come over here. It would give him a chance to get to know the girls better too," my mother said, with control.

Gogo pulled the ugly blanket around her, and I could see that one of her legs had creases in it from when she was sleeping. She lit a cigarette. "There's fog over the mountain. I can feel it in my bones today. I feel bitter cold, despite this heat, and I already have the chip pot on for supper," she said, like the conversation was over.

"You can still have your chips—we won't be a bother to you at all. I'm going to make some spaghetti, it's Ray's favorite, and we won't..."

"I shan't have it!" Gogo said, her voice rising, her sick act suddenly gone. "I'm not in the mood. If you want to have someone to supper, you need to give me some notice. You don't just come waltzing in here at five in the evening and expect me to be prepared for company!" She snuffed out the cigarette for emphasis, and standing up started pacing around the living room.

"Duckie, please be reasonable," my mom wheedled, following a few steps behind her.

"Stop Duckie-ing me!" Gogo snapped, turning suddenly around. "I said no, and that's that!"

My gaze had been going back and forth like I was looking at a tennis match. *C'mon Mom*, I thought. *Stand up for yourself. Tell her off like I never can—without being smacked anyway.*

Just then, my mother stopped following Gogo, and planted her white pumps squarely, saying slowly, "I pay rent here, you know. I pay for the girls' groceries, and our share of the electricity. This is my house too, and if I want to have someone come to dinner once in a while, I should damn well be able to!" Her gray eyes were fierce behind her glasses.

I was thinking, *Go Mom, go! Tell her a thing or two. Let's have company over for dinner and sit around a table and talk like normal people do, like people on TV.* Suddenly Gogo screamed over the blaring TV, "How *dare* you!" The 'dare' was long and drawn out, and in a low, gravelly, threatening voice from deep down inside her. I felt myself grow cold inside. "How *dare* you speak to me in that tone, you ungrateful little... after all I do for you Dorothy. I take care of your children, I do the laundry for them, and I feed them while you're out gallivanting with your new man until all hours of the night. How daaaaaaaaare you! You should bloody well be thankful you have a place to live at all. Why if it wasn't for me...."

I was quaking with fear for my own safety at this unexpected outburst. I drew my knees up to my chest. Just then, my mom started clutching her neck and slumped down heavily on the couch. She doubled over in what appeared to be severe pain, her head hanging between her knees, which were spread apart with the orange cloth of her dress, draped in a sort of a hammock that was supporting her head. I jumped off the couch, ran across the room, and held my mom's curls.

"What's a matter?" I asked, bending around upside down to meet her face.

"Oh, ooow, OOOOOWWWWW!" my mom howled. I jumped back, I glanced over at Gogo, who definitely had some of the rage knocked out of her, though she was still breathing hard. Reluctantly, I could tell, she said, "Dorothy. What is it?"

My mom was clutching her neck, and rocking back and forth.

"Is it your neck, then?" Gogo's voice softened a little.

My mom managed to squeak out a "Yes" of some sort, and my feelings switched along with her tactic. Is she doing this just to get Gogo to feel sorry for her? I looked down at her. She seemed to be in genuine pain. Gogo stood rooted for a second, and then went into the kitchen. I didn't like to see my mother crumble like this, I was ashamed that I felt a little disgusted with this neck thing, not really sorry for her at all anymore.

I heard the oven door slam in the kitchen. A few minutes later Gogo came back with a frayed blue tea towel, slightly singed brown where she had left it in the oven too long.

"Here Duckie, put this on it." She held the warm blue peace offering in front of her.

My mother weakly took the towel, never lifting her head up, and held it to her neck, still rocking a little on the couch. She was crying softly, and wiped her eyes under her glasses.

All three of us were quiet for a while, staring at the television. Cathy wandered in from the bedroom where she had been sleeping, her thumb in her mouth, dragging Wowo, her teddy bear, by one ear, only wearing a t-shirt and underpants.

"Hi Mommy!" she said, happily, snuggling into her lap, oblivious to the tension in the room.

"I still won't have him tonight," Gogo muttered, starting things up again.

My mom clutched the towel and whimpered a little louder.

Suddenly, my mom started scratching her legs furiously through her nylons. She stood up, and pulling down her panty hose, started scratching viciously at the back of her bare thighs.

"Look!" she yelled at Gogo. Gogo came over and peered at my mom's legs over her glasses that were perched on her nose. Huge red welts, the size of the palm of her hand, were popping up all over her legs. My mom started scratching at her stomach, too. I looked at her with horror. I thought that maybe she was faking the neck thing, but these giant mosquito bites spreading over her body were real because I could see them.

"Hives," Gogo said. "Let me get you a tablet to calm you down." She went to her side table and took a pill out of a prescription bottle and handed it to my mom. I ran and got a glass of water out of the kitchen, seeing the chip pot still bubbling away. Gogo had no intention of turning it off; I knew she was going to win, no matter how pathetic my mother acted.

I heard a car engine in the driveway. I went to the screen door, and saw Ray getting out of his green Karmann Ghia, wearing an olive-colored corduroy jacket with leather patches on the elbows that almost matched his car. *Maybe that's what artists wear*, I thought. He had a bottle of red wine under his arm, something I had never seen before.

I turned back to look at my mom, who had thrown the towel down, and was smoothing out the skirt of her dress and then running her fingers through her short curls. She walked quickly out of the door, intercepting Ray in the driveway. Through the window, I could see them talking face to face. A few minutes later, they both came in.

"Hello!" Ray said, cheerfully, to Cathy and me.

We both said a demure "Hi" in unison.

"Dorothy, how are you?" he said to Gogo who was back to sitting in her armchair, a little depleted. *Why did Gogo have to give my mother the same name as hers*, I thought disgustedly.

"Very well, thank you very much," she said, her accent a little stronger than normal, running her fingers through her own short curly hair, and crossing one leg over the other so that a large expanse of her thigh showed.

"Put your shoes on girls, we're going out to dinner," my mom said.

I couldn't believe this unexpected turn of events. Going out to dinner? I had never gone out to dinner in my life. Maybe this Ray guy wasn't going to be so bad to hang around with after all. I ran and grabbed my black Keds, then helped Cathy lace up her little tennis shoes. We walked out into the warm evening without even saying bye to Gogo. George was coming in from playing right as we left, filthy, his pants ripped, dirt smeared with sweat on his face.

"Where are you guys going?" he said, out of breath.

"Out to dinner!" I said, with superiority. "And YOU'RE not!" For once I got to do something and George didn't.

We got to the car, and I noted there was no back seat.

"Just climb back there; you girls can fit, you're not too big," Ray said.

We sat hunched over about two inches away from my mom and Ray. I studied my mom up close, since I had no choice. She was chatting away happily, looking at Ray with adoring eyes like she had forgotten about what had just happened. She did periodically rub her neck, and scratch her legs a little.

* * *

I re-sharpened the pointed end of my Popsicle stick. It was easier to be mad at Gogo for the way she treated my mother than it was to be mad for the way she treated me. When I thought about that stuff — The Letters, the hitting, the name calling — a hot rumbling would rise from the pit of my stomach, crossing my heart and causing it to pound hard, and then end up in my throat, where I had to cry or scream for relief. I was afraid of this feeling. It was so huge; I thought if I let it go, unthinkable things could happen. I started digging furiously with my stick as I thought about The Letters.

One recent afternoon, Gogo called me into the living room. "Christine, come in here, I have a surprise for you." I ran around the corner of the dining room, and skipped up onto the couch and down again in my stocking feet. I loved surprises, especially magical ones to do with Joey. I was hoping it was going to be a fairy kind of surprise, although those were happening less and less lately. When I landed on the other side of the couch, Gogo was standing in the center of the Persian carpet, her hands behind her back.

"What do you have?" I asked, peering around her back; first one side, and then the other. Gogo smiled and then dramatically put her hands in front of her, revealing a little bundle of papers, neatly tied with a piece of maroon colored sewing ribbon. She held the little package out in front of her, and said, "Go on, take it."

I was staring at it, and deep inside, my heart instantly registered what it was, but my mind took a couple more beats to recognize it. I could make out my own baby writing, on the top piece of blue paper. My throat closed up, and I didn't move. She stepped forward and handed me the little stack of letters saying, "Look how sweet your writing was then, Christine." She was smiling as she watched me stare at the letters through the tears that were welling in my eyes, in disbelief. I wouldn't cry in front of her though, I wouldn't give her the satisfaction.

I snatched the package out of her hands and ran to the upstairs bathroom leaving Gogo standing there. I closed and locked the bathroom door, leaning against it for a minute before I slumped down. Sitting on the cool green tile, I pulled the maroon ribbon and it came untied easily, the letters spilling onto the ground. I glanced at a couple of the brittle pages—it was all suddenly too pathetic. I saw the envelopes addressed in my baby writing to "Papa Sottile," the phrases, "I mis you," "rit bak soon" and "*te amo*" on each sheet. I had hardly thought about Papa for the past couple of years. No one mentioned him. It felt like I wasn't supposed to.

I burst into full sobs, putting my cheek against the cool edge of the tub, when I realized why he had never written back. Gogo had never even sent them. I cried until I couldn't cry anymore, and then I felt a hard coating forming around my heart. I looked at the letters surrounding me on the bathroom floor, and I calmly and systematically started ripping each page into little pieces. I flushed them down the toilet, taking five or six flushes to complete the task.

Afterward, I didn't feel sad anymore. I felt a cool, blue hatred toward Gogo, an anger so deep that I had made sure it was contained before I left the bathroom. She was a liar. She was not to be trusted. I needed to protect myself. I vowed to never ask her why she didn't send the letters. I would never let her know how deeply she had affected me. I vowed to be guarded and closed.

* * *

I let that mad feeling come up while I was digging. It kind of felt good sometimes to indulge in it, if I didn't let it get too out of control. Then I felt powerful. My mind danced to the next subject that I knew from experience would fuel the rage a little more. I was really letting it go now, I had experienced this obsessive mind swirl a bunch of times. I started shaking a little with the rage I felt when I thought about Gogo hitting me, things like a slap across the face for talking back, or a "good hiding," as she called a spanking, for walking on the sidewalk to take the garbage out, instead of through the garage as she instructed. Lately the violence was starting to amp up a notch. Now I noticed she started hitting me whenever George and Cathy were quarreling or fighting, saying it was my job to keep them quiet.

The notes on my mom's pillow were becoming more frantic, begging her to get us a house of our own. By the time Saturday rolled around and I actually saw my mother, the incidents weren't so fresh, and she never mentioned the content of the notes I left for her on almost a nightly basis. I'd say, "Did you get the notes I wrote you, Mom?" and she'd answer, "Yes, I got them sweetheart, thanks for leaving them for me." End of conversation. I was too scared to say more.

Then there was The Incident. I squeezed my eyes shut tight. I had gone through it in my head a few times, and I really didn't want to again. Sitting on the floor of my closet with the door closed and using a flashlight for privacy, I had written about it in my little blue leather-covered diary. The act of writing it down had comforted me for a while, but then I started reliving the scene over in my head again, and I stared doing so again, as I dug deeper and deeper into the cool moist earth.

* * *

Gogo came into the living room one morning while I was watching TV in the big comfy, ugly chair Gogo always sat in to take her naps. She noticed that I had left my tennis shoes in the kitchen when I had gone to take a swig out of the milk carton, and was now carrying them in one hand.

"What are these?"

I told her they were my shoes.

"Why did you leave them in the kitchen?"

"Because that's where I took them off."

"Because that's where *you took them off*? Is that where you leave them when you take them off, in the kitchen?" She held the tennis shoes close to my face, blocking my view of the television. I could plainly see the blue Keds label on the heels, and the flower I had doodled in black ink along the white rubber edging.

"I guess this time it was," I said. "I can't see the TV."

"Did I ask you if you could see the television?"

I said *No*, but she was blocking my way just the same, and I was missing the best part.

"I almost tripped on these!" she said, and pushed the shoes closer against my eye. When I jerked away, she grabbed the back of my head and shoved my face back down toward the shoes. "I almost fell on these shoes because they were in the kitchen. Is that where they belong?"

I didn't answer.

"Is it?"

"Gogo!" I yelled.

She asked me again if the kitchen was the place to leave my tennis shoes. They were hurting my eye, so I said no; it wasn't the place to leave them. She let go of my head. "Put them away," she said. She shoved the shoes toward me. I started to untie the laces to tie them together, while she watched. After a time, she sat down across from me on the coffee table. I was still fiddling with the laces, stalling to see the last part of the cartoon. Gogo was growing impatient. She said, "Don't think you're fooling me, Christine. You think you're so clever wasting my time? You're not clever at all, you're just a misery."

I didn't pay much attention to what she was saying. I knew it was her mood of the moment. It wasn't the mood where she said I was clever, beautiful, an Italian contessa, and surely going to be Miss America some day. This was one of those ever more frequent times, when she was in one of her crazy moods, where she would call me miserable and stupid. I noticed she was doing this only to me, and especially when no one else was in the house. I usually tried to just ignore her until it passed.

I finished tying the laces, keeping my eyes on the television set.

"All right," Gogo said. "Now, are you going to take those shoes to the bedroom?"

"No," I said. "When the show's over."

She jumped up from where she was sitting on the coffee table and slapped my face. She swung hard, but I managed to duck a little, so she only got me partially on my head and a little on the shoulder. I started yelling at her, and when she started yelling back, I immediately knew she was out of control, so I started looking around to see how to escape the chair I was sitting in. Then she was hitting me over and over again, her arms swinging wildly, while I blocked my face. When I dove over the back of the armchair, her nails made a long scratch in my arm. I scampered behind the furniture and ran into the bedroom, and flung myself down on the bed, breathing hard, quaking. She burst through the door again, her face contorted in rage; she started whaling on me with both her hands, slapping anywhere she could. She had caught me unaware, in a full prone position on my back, and I wasn't ready. She got quite a few good hits in before I rolled off the bed and scurried down the hall.

I decided to hide behind the door that swung into the dining room from the kitchen. I could hear her tramping out of the bedroom, going from room to room. She started calling out my name, but I didn't answer, I just tried to keep my breathing quiet behind the door. Judging by the tone of her calls, she wasn't sorry yet, oh no, she was ready for more. I wasn't sure what to think. The other times she hit me it was always a short-lived anger, one or two hits and then it was over. This was different; she was in a rage. I'd also seen her hysterical before, like when she'd her throw her dinner into the air when she was upset, or yell loudly at Beba, but this particular combo of rage and hitting, and no one else in the house except for me, made me start thinking about my survival. I licked my arm where a little blood was coming out from one of the scratches. I could hear her in the kitchen, then stomping at running speed through the breakfast room toward the door I was hiding behind. I acted on instinct. I rolled out from behind the door, and, making myself into a little fetal-position ball, I stationed myself in the doorway at the precise second Gogo was running through blind mad.

She tripped right over me, and landed on her side.

I leaped up and straddled her, pinning her shoulders down with my knees, just as I had done many times before when I was wrestling with George. My ten-year-old body was stocky and strong, and big for my age, but Gogo outweighed me. She threw me off. I started kicking with all my might. I don't know what part of her I got, I kicked her hard a couple of times. I was an eggbeater of flailing arms and legs. My rage matched hers, and she was not going to touch me again, that much I knew.

After a bit, I realized that she was gone, and I was flailing away at nothing. I lay still for a moment, breathing hard, listening for where she might be in the house, but I couldn't hear anything except for the sound of the television that was still on in the living room. I wandered around the house a little, feeling sorry for myself. I took a swig of milk out of the fridge. I saw my tennis shoes still in the living room when I walked by. I left them there, and went upstairs to my bed and fell asleep.

When I woke up, it was twilight, and sleep had left me temporarily blissfully unaware of what had happened. I wondered why I was asleep on the bed in the middle of the day, but rolling over onto one of the many bruises covering my body, I remembered. I could hear my mom and Gogo talking downstairs. Gogo sounded normal, like nothing even happened. A minute later, I could hear my mom coming up the stairs. She poked her head in my bedroom; I could sense her freshness, her innocence of the scene that had happened that day. She was all smiles, and her cheeks were still cold from being outside.

"What are you doing, asleep in the day?" she said, kissing my cheek. "Are you all right? You feel a little warm." She said putting her hand to my forehead.

"I'm fine," I said. I was so glad she was home.

"Would you like to take a bath, darling? I'll get one ready for you, and get you some of that cream of celery soup you like. Would that be nice?"

I shook my head yes, feeling my throat close. She got up and left the room. A minute later, I could hear the bath running.

"Go on in anytime, sweetheart. I put the heat lamp on," she said from down the hall.

I went slowly into the green-tiled bathroom and started peeling off my t-shirt and pants. I was a little shaky. It felt good under the red heat lamp in the ceiling. The red light with the green tile always turned the bathroom into an eerie, yet not entirely unpleasant, light. Naked, I could see the bruises on my arms and legs had already turned color. There was a big scratch on my arm. I thankfully sank into the warm tub, and turned off the water. I ducked down, so just my eyeballs poked out, holding my breath as long as I could, then slowly blowing bubbles in the water. A few minutes later, my mom came in.

"What are you doing, silly, under the water like that? Sit up then, let me wash your hair for you."

I sat up in the tub. My mom squeezed the Prell shampoo in her hand, and began vigorously rubbing my head. After a moment she slowed down. I knew she could see the bruises, and I was glad. She rubbed the lather a little more slowly, and then stopped all together.

"What happened?" she asked, at last, touching the tip of her index finger to the scratch on my arm.

I tried to answer her, but the words got stuck in my throat. Every time I tried to speak I seized up again. It wasn't self-pity; it was hearing my mother's voice, feeling her *I've been out in the world* presence, and for the first time in a long time, someone asking me about what was going on. But I couldn't explain any of it. My mom kept asking me what happened, and when I found my voice, I squeaked out that Gogo had hit me.

"She hit you! What do you mean, she hit you?"

It took me a while to get the story out. The words 'tennis shoes' just didn't sound that serious, and as I described what had happened I began to fear that my mom would simply dismiss the episode as ridiculous, so I stopped trying to explain all together, and simply sat there, splashing the water a little with one finger.

My mom waited a moment to see if I was going to say any more. Once she realized that I wasn't, she said, "Let me understand this, darling—it's important. She hit you because you left your shoes in the kitchen?"

I said that she had.

"Where were George and Beba and Cathy?"

"At Uncle Steve's."

My mom was quiet for a moment.

"She had no right to hit you like that. Has she ever done this before?"

I said that she had, but not like that.

"That's it then," my mom said. "I'll be right back."

I asked if she we were going to move now.

"No, " she said. "That wouldn't be possible right now."

She marched out of the room with determination. I felt vindicated. Finally she knew that all the complaining I did about Gogo was valid. It was horrible being stuck at home with a crazy woman all day with no one to protect me. Now, finally Mom could see just how bad it was; I was sure that she was going to do something about it. If we didn't get our own house right away, at least she was going to do something about the beating I had received that day. I sat waiting in the tub, while the water turned lukewarm.

She came back in, kneeled down, and said nothing. She gently tipped my head back so she could rinse my hair. I got out of the tub, and she gave me a towel she had put over the heater so that it was warm.

When she was getting my pajamas, I imagined what I wanted her to say.

"Christine! This is not acceptable. I will not allow my child to be treated this way by any one. How many times did she hit you?"

" I dunno. Twenty?"

"Twenty. Jesus. What have I been subjecting you to?"

I start listing some of the other, lesser annoyances of living with Gogo. I can't leave the yard, I can't have my friends over, she sleeps in her chair all day, she calls me names, hits me if the other kids are bad. During this litany, my mom is making unhappy, sympathetic sounds. She asks me if I would mind changing schools if we moved, I say not at all. "That's good, " she would say. "That gives me something to go on. You've obviously been doing as well as you can under the circumstances, but now I'm going to make sure you won't have to deal with this kind of thing again." Then she tells me her plan about moving into a house of our own.

But none of that conversation took place. I saw her mouth was set in a straight line, and I couldn't tell if it was mad, determined, or just defeated. It didn't matter. She didn't say anything. Nothing. Zip. Neither did I. She combed my hair through, put a hot water bottle in my cold sheets, and tucked me into bed.

"Goodnight, sweetheart," she said, kissing me on the forehead. "I'll leave the door open a crack for you." And she quickly walked out.

* * *

When the streetlights went on, it was time to go in, and I reluctantly abandoned my hole, which was only about a foot and a half deep, promising myself to start again first thing in the morning, but I had lost my momentum.

I said my prayers that night, and asked God if he could find us a new house so that Cathy, my mom, and I could have our own life, away from the craziness of Gogo. I didn't bother asking God about Papa anymore. Obviously the answer to that one was *No*.

* * *

A few days later, on Saturday, my prayer actually came true. We were walking along the sidewalk toward Hillsdale mall when my mom broke the news to me.

"Well, sweetheart, I know you've been unhappy living in this house, and I've decided that it's time we got a place of our own."

My eyes widened, and the sparkles in the sidewalk became more brilliant and sharp. I took in a quick breath. I was overwhelmed with hope and surprise.

"Really? When? Where?" I was skipping a little now.

"We can move into a little house I've found in Moss Beach on July 1st."

"Moss Beach? Where's that?" I asked.

"Oh, you know darling. It's right next to Montara, where Ray lives."

Now my hope and joy had a little gray cloud over it. Cathy and I had been to Montara a few times with our mother to visit Ray in the tiny studio house he had built. The little one-room house was in the middle of rolling brown hills leading to the ocean, with hardly another house in sight. The streets were unpaved, gray gravel, devoid of children. The sky was misty and gray every time we had ever been there. I thought it was the most backwards, uncivilized, and desolate place in the world. There weren't even sidewalks to skate or play hopscotch on. Now we were going to move over there. It seemed so far away, over the winding road. Still, I tried to keep my optimism. I had wished to move anywhere, after all. It wasn't China.

"What kind of house? Is it nice? Can we get new furniture? Do I get my own room now?" Maybe there was hope. I pictured a spacious, tastefully decorated home with a cheery fireplace. There would be beige wall-to-wall carpeting, thriving plants on simple stands, and quiet, no TV on, maybe some classical music playing softly in the background. We could sit around a dining room table for dinner, and set it with matching cloth napkins, I thought.

"Oh, it's fairly nice. I can't afford much, you know. You and Cathy will have to share a room still, but it's a nice big one. We'll go over and look at it if you like."

For the next few weeks, my troll dolls and Beatles records and Girl Scout badges were somewhat abandoned as I pored through magazines, cutting out little ideas of how we could decorate our new house. I'd show my mother the glossy pictures of shiny wood tables with cream-colored place settings and airy white flower arrangements, and ask her, "Can we have our house look like this when we move?" She'd smile vaguely, and say, "Mmmm, maybe something like that.... I'm not sure, don't get too excited, we'll have to start with what we've got."

I was hopeful when my mom bought the blue and white gingham fabric to make curtains for our new kitchen. She said she might make matching cloth napkins when I asked her to, which gave me a happy feeling inside, as I imagined setting the table for our dinners in the new house without the TV on. Just the three of us.

At least that's what I thought.

Part III

Moss Beach (gray)

CHAPTER 8

Fog and Union (Hole New World)

My mom, Cathy, and I drove the old Borgward over snaky Highway 92, the front seat piled high with boxes of our stuff, clothes and books and spatulas all sticking out, Cathy and me in the back seat singing Beatles songs along with the radio. As we left the warm peninsula sunshine, I turned and looked through the back window and said a silent goodbye to the life I had known. The sun-drenched suburban skyline got further and further away as more trees whizzed by my periphery.

Facing ahead, I saw that we were driving straight into a blanket of fog hovering above the mountain like a thin layer of cotton candy. At the top of the hill we had to stop for a few minutes while my mom added water to the radiator from a big mayonnaise jar she kept in the trunk just for that purpose. Soon enough we were back on the road and drove deeper and deeper onto the other side of the mountain, the sky darkening and the scenery changing from cheery pastel stucco to thick, soggy cypress trees.

I can only describe the late June day we arrived in Moss Beach as dismal. I didn't know that summer days on the coast were always foggy. If Chicago was blue, and San Mateo yellow, Moss Beach was definitely a swirly, drippy gray, a black-and-white Van Gogh sky.

After a lot of curves and turns and vegetable stands, there was a wide, light, slate-colored opening in the sky with seagulls swirling around in it. I could see the thin, darker gray line of the ocean horizon ahead. We turned right, driving North along Highway 1, the ocean on our left and seemingly endless fields of artichokes and Brussels sprouts on our right. Not too many houses, I thought, and I figured the funky, rotting odor must be the sprouts, which mingled with the salty, fishy sea air. I heard the foghorn in the distance, with its distinctive *aaaaaaaaw-oh*, *aw-oh*, a deep repetitive sound I could feel reverberating in my chest. When we got near the little airport, I saw how the lighthouse cut a rhythmic pie of blue light in the fog. We turned up a dirt road, void of any houses, and into the gravel driveway of what was to be our new home.

I was a little shocked when I first saw the old rental my mother had found for us for only sixty dollars a month. It was a small gray house, to match the sky, in the middle of nowhere. Artichoke fields were all around, with one neighbor to the right, and another house down the street, if you could call it a street; it was more of a wide gravel path. My mother pulled in to the driveway.

"This is it!" my mom said brightly.

The three of us got out of the car, and trudged toward the house in silence, except for the crunching sound our feet made in the gravel. My mom was fiddling with a key that wasn't attached to her main key ring yet. We entered the house through a sliding glass door that led into a bedroom freshly painted swimming pool– blue.

"This room will be for you girls," my mother said, cheerily. We turned through a tiny hall where we passed a very small lilac bedroom, and then into the mint green living room. I could smell a distinct musty odor like a trunk left in a damp garage too long. The wooden floors creaked and echoed as we walked through. Old French doors, black and ornate, thick with being painted so many times, opened off the living room onto a cracked cement patio. Beyond the patio I could see a thriving, overgrown and wild garden, obviously planted and tended to at some time, but now unwieldy and infused with weeds. The last room was a narrow kitchen with cabinets made of white enameled metal. I tentatively opened one, and it squeaked loudly.

I looked around with a critical eye. Despite the gray atmosphere, and the desolation of the house, I was still optimistic. *It could be fixed up*, I thought. At least it would be ours, just my mom and me and Cathy, with no Gogo to make everything crazy. I started thinking that the blue gingham curtains might look cute with the white cabinets, and once our carpet was down, the living room wouldn't echo so badly, and the blue plaid bedspreads my mom had bought Cathy and me from Sears might look fresh in the bright blue bedroom.

Just then, I heard another car crunching into the gravel driveway.

"Who could that be?" I asked my mom, thinking that no one could ever find us way out here in the boonies. My mom was already trotting to the door.

"Oh! That must be Ray!" she said beaming. Ray? I wondered what he was doing at our house already—I mean we hadn't even been there ten minutes yet or brought any boxes in. I knew Ray lived close by, and that he was part of the reason we were moving to the coast, but I didn't expect him to be quite this intrusive. Maybe if we had invited him, it would be okay, but we weren't ready to have company yet, I'd thought.

"Hello, hello!" Ray said heartily. He was carrying a very large canvas over his shoulder. "I brought you a housewarming present!" he said. Ray put his painting against the wall, and stood back a few feet, looking at his work, rubbing his dark beard thoughtfully.

I wandered over to take a look at the painting Ray had done. I generally liked his artwork; I had seen the paintings that hung in his house. I was shocked at this picture though. It was a portrait of a nude woman sitting in a wooden chair. Her legs were spread wide, and her head was cropped out of the painting entirely. My eyes were glued to the huge pubic patch in the middle of the picture. When I tore my eyes away from the image of the headless woman, I saw that Ray had a nail and hammer in his hand. He walked over and pounded it into the biggest expanse of green wall in the living room. Moments later, the painting was hung, the only piece of decor in our new home.

Oh, no, I thought. *No.* We just left a house that I was embarrassed to show my school friends because of the lack of taste and mess and noise, but this, I decided, was worse. How could I ask new friends into my house with this gigantic crotch staring into the room? Who said he could put it up anyway? This was our house, there wasn't going to be anyone to boss us around anymore.

"Great. That looks great there, what do you think, Dorothy?" Ray took a few steps back, crossing his arms over his black turtleneck.

"Oh yes, Ray. Thank you, that's wonderful, darling," my mother said, smiling broadly at Ray.

I stared at my mother. Was she serious? Why would she want a picture of a headless naked lady in our new house? I thought that some paintings I had seen in books of nude women would have been okay, the kind from the old days where the ladies had round tummies and big thighs and white smooth skin. Maybe the kind of painting where the mysterious women were half-smiling, some of their long hair partially covering a plump melon-like breast. But this? The woman had her legs spread open as wide as they would go. She was slumped down in the chair, and her bosom hung down around each armpit. I tried to imagine what expression the woman would have if I could see her face. Would she be sneering? No —her eyes would be closed, —not out of embarrassment, but out of defeat.

"Okay, then. Let's get to work. Girls, don't just stand there, give your mother a hand. Get out to the car and start bringing in those boxes." Ray nudged me toward the door with his hand on the back of my neck.

I wondered who invited him to our moving-in party? I shuffled outside, walking more slowly than normal.

When I got out to the driveway, I saw that three teenage boys had started a fire in an old oil drum in the field next to our house, and were standing around it warming their hands. In the San Mateo suburbs, there had been no fires, no oilcans, and no empty fields, for that matter. I watched the boys laughing, talking, and occasionally spitting over one shoulder.

"Hello Derrick, Bucky," I heard Ray say behind me. "What are you guys doing? Chris, how long does it take you to grab a box? Move it."

"Hey, Ray. Not much. Just burning' some shit," one of the boys was yelling. I was surprised they would swear in front of a grown-up.

"Well, I saw your mother in the bar a few minutes ago and she was wondering where you were, Buck. You better run on home," Ray called back.

"Yep. Okay, thanks Ray."

I watched the boys throw fistfuls of dirt onto the fire until it died down, and a black plume of smoke was all that was left. The three of them, hunched against the cold fog in their hooded sweatshirts, took off down the dirt road. Cathy had wandered out and watched with me.

"Girls! What did I tell you? Let's move it!" Ray said, picking up a box.

I snatched a big one out of the car, and threw it inside the sliding glass door, half of the clothes spilling out onto the carpet. Who was he to tell me how fast or slow I should be moving my stuff?

I had lugged a few boxes out of the car and into what was to be my new room, when I heard the wailing of a siren piercing the quiet, where a moment before all that could be heard was the distant crashing of the waves and the braying of the fog horn. The sirens got closer, and they seemed to be coming right to our isolated spot in the artichoke field. I went out to the road, and could see the ambulances and fire trucks down at the highway, the lights spinning crazily.

Ray came out of the house and took off at a trot toward the highway. I slowly went back to the car to get another box.

About twenty minutes later, Ray came back, winded and pale looking.

"He's dead. Bucky. The kid who was just here. Ran across the highway without looking, it was a damn stupid thing to do. Kids around here think that no one travels that highway, and maybe it used to be like that, but not now, this area is getting populated, and the goddamn cops don't enforce the speed limit."

The three of us stood looking at Ray wide-eyed. Cathy sat down cross-legged in the gravel, and started sucking her thumb. My mother just stared at Ray as if she was looking to him as to how to react. I felt sick inside, but I had felt that way before the news that the car had hit the kid. I took a few steps toward the road, so that I could get a better look at what was going on.

"The girls will not be allowed to cross the highway, of course," Ray said to my mother, and she nodded mutely in agreement.

"No, of course not, Ray, " she finally demurred.

Now my stomach did a flip-flop. I had felt mildly nauseated since the curvy car ride, and the feeling didn't go away, especially when I saw the painting. The death of the kid hardly registered, I realized. I knew in my head that I should feel bad for the dead kid, the kid who only minutes ago had been outside of our new house, but I didn't. What caused my stomach to tighten, and my breathing to quicken was the realization that Ray was in charge. It was suddenly obvious. Ray was going to be telling me what I could and couldn't do. Even though we had left Gogo, my mother now had someone else to answer to. I felt mute, silenced; my tongue was gone again though no one had told me not to speak.

We turned and wordlessly went back to our boxes, moving them in one by one, with only the crashing of the waves and the foghorn in the background again. The light from the lighthouse swept a broad brush of blue-green over our sad little moving scene every half-minute or so, keeping a slow rhythm to my movements, while the flickering red lights down the street kept time to my heart. I felt damp inside, not just because of the fog, not even because of the unexpected death. It was the sense of everything changing, yet nothing changing. The house, the town, the weather was different, but the embarrassment and restrictions were already falling into the familiar pattern, only now it wasn't Gogo, it was Ray.

* * *

That very first night, my mom told me that Ray was going to spend the night. I was shocked.

"What are you going to sleep in?" I asked her accusingly, knowing full well that my mother slept stark naked every night of her life, since I often snuck into bed with her, just to have a little time.

"Oh, I'll just wear my slip to bed," she said vaguely. I tried to picture my mom in her half-white slip and bra getting into bed with Ray. I didn't buy it.

* * *

Ray was pretty much around all the time that first week. He started bringing some of his paints and easels into the garage. He brought an old-fashioned kerosene heater and some old rugs out there too. He hung a dartboard on the wall.

"Is Ray moving into the garage or something?" I asked my mom.

"Oh, no, darling, he just thought he might paint out there once in a while since he doesn't have that much space at his place. He's going to Mexico for a painting trip soon, and thought some of his things would be safer in our garage where we could keep an eye on them. "

"Well, he's moving a lot of stuff in there."

* * *

One night Ray didn't show up at our house when my mother came home from work, and my mother took us out for hamburgers at a place called The Shelter that was right on the beach in Miramar. The restaurant had a loud, boisterous crowd of men surrounding the island bar in the middle, so there was a lot to look at. She ordered a glass of wine along with her hamburger, something I had never seen her do. She was very preoccupied, and kept looking around the restaurant towards the bar. I was happy to be out to dinner with my mom, especially since this was only about the third time I had ever eaten in a restaurant, but the absentmindedness I felt radiating from her was ruining my good time. We had been eating our huge drippy burgers that came in a plastic basket in silence.

"Mom? Mom!" I had to say twice to get her attention. Her gray eyes focused on me for a second, and she put down the glass of wine and lit up a cigarette.

"Yes, darling. What?"

"Are you looking for Ray or something? What, are you worried because he didn't come over tonight?"

"No, no, darling, nothing like that. Ray can come when he likes, he doesn't have to come over every night." She took in a large drag of smoke.

I took a few more mouthfuls of my gushy cheeseburger. My mother sat staring off into space, her hamburger only half-eaten, and she was already on her second cigarette. I stuffed in the last chunk of the cheeseburger, and, wiping my mouth with the back of my hand, asked, "Why don't you just call him?"

I felt a pang when I talked about using a phone so casually, since I missed having a telephone very much. It intensified my feeling of isolation out there in the gray artichoke patch. For the first few days after we moved in, I kept asking when the phone was going to be installed, and only got indefinite murmurs from my mom. Finally Ray told us that we weren't going to be having a phone, there was really no need for one. This killed the pre-teenage me, and I took to hanging out at the pay phone booth at the Union 76 station down the street, sitting on the ground with my orange transistor radio, waiting for KYA to give the signal to be the twelfth caller so that I could win tickets to a concert. Of course, by the time I dropped my dime in and waited for the dial tone, it was too late to get through. But my mom could use a pay phone too, and I wished she would.

"I'll never call him!" her vehemence surprised me. "I made a vow when I started dating Ray, that this time, I would never, *ever* call a man. If he wanted to, *he* could call *me*."

"How can he when we don't have a phone?"

"He could have called me at work, or else stopped by, or—I don't know, stop asking so many questions."

At this, even Cathy stopped sucking her thumb, pulling it out with a pop.

"Okay, okay. But tell me. Is that why we came here to this restaurant? In case he was here?"

"No, darling. Don't be silly. I just felt like going out, that's all."

"Well, you never have before." I didn't believe her. That was starting to happen a lot.

* * *

When Ray got back from his month in Mexico, he picked Cathy and me up in the afternoon while my mom was at work and asked us if we wanted to go for a ride. He drove us to the market across the highway, which everyone called Andy's, not Coastside Market like the sign said. When we went inside, Ray told us to pick out anything we wanted. This was very uncharacteristic of him, since he had never bought us anything before. I felt a weird vibe, but wandered around the skinny isles, contemplating what I wanted to have. Cathy chose a jar of Ovaltine, and I took a jar of Tang, two treats that we loved, but weren't in the house anymore since we had moved. Gogo used to let us eat them both straight out of the jar with a spoon. Ray took out his wallet and paid Andy, asking us, "Did you want anything else?" I shook my head no. I wanted to hurry up and find out what he wanted; I felt there was something he was holding in.

On the way back home from the store Ray tapped his fingers on the steering wheel of the Datsun pickup, and made small talk with us. I watched him carefully. Driving down the dirt road of California Ave toward the ocean and our house, he finally said, "So what would you girls think of your mother and me getting married?" He said this looking straight ahead through the windshield. Neither of us said anything. "We're getting married next Saturday." He glanced to his right to gauge our reaction.

"You are? Okay, good," Cathy said, using her nail to poke into the protective paper on the top of the Ovaltine jar. I quickly looked out the passenger window so that Ray wouldn't see the tears that had unexpectedly sprung to my eyes. Didn't my mother say it was finally just going to be us?

I'd been waiting to have my mother to myself and now this guy was going to be in the picture. It wasn't Papa, it wasn't even Beba. Ray was almost a complete stranger to me. Now he was going to be my dad?

I stared out the window at the cypress trees, blinking hard, wishing away my tears. Cathy and my mom and I had only just left Gogo's house, and we hadn't even lived alone much more than a month. *Maybe this was my mother's plan all along*, I thought. Why was *he* telling us, anyway? If she told us the news of their marriage, then at least I could cry freely, and ask questions and see what the story was. I was pretty much intimidated by Ray and his manner. He scared me. I swallowed hard a couple of times, and turned to face him with the best smile I could muster, though he must have detected that I'd been crying.

"Chris?" he was saying. "What do you think of that?" I didn't answer, just twisted the top of the brown paper bag that held my Tang very hard.

* * *

My mom and Ray invited people to their wedding by tacking leaflets up on telephone poles around Montara and Moss Beach and liberally passing a bunch out at the local bar, the Montara Inn. The flyer simply stated, "Ray and Dorothy are getting married on Saturday. Please Come."

It only took them about four days to put the whole thing together. Ray dug a pit in the back yard, and covered it with the box springs of an old mattress, which was to serve as a huge barbecue pit for the dozens of chicken quarters that were piled up in the fridge. Their friend Jessica made the cake, a three-tiered psychedelic wonder. The frosting was bright primary colors, the bottom layer blue; the smaller second layer yellow, with a red top layer. On top of the cake was a cutout from a magazine of a young bride and groom, and on the back was another picture of an old couple. The cake had a cascade of nasturtiums flowing down the layers and spilling onto the tray. Some local boys, whose parents they'd met at the bar, came over to talk about playing music.

Gogo and Beba drove me over the hill the day of the wedding, along with George. Cathy and I had spent the night there with them. I didn't like the idea of *arriving* at my mother's wedding. I felt I should host, but for some reason we needed to be babysat the night before. The Saturday of the wedding turned out to be a rare, blue, breezy coastal day, and when I arrived, our newly trimmed yard was filled with friends, relatives, and all sorts of local characters I had seen around town, but I didn't know three quarters of the people, I realized, looking around. The air smelled of the chicken that was roasting on the mattress springs, while a friend of Ray's basted the pieces with a long branch of rosemary, squinting from the smoke of the barbecue and the cigarette he held in the side of his mouth. A giant seesaw was set up in the side yard for the kids. The smell of those funny kinds of cigarettes wafted through the air, and there were lots of bottles of red jug wine.

I went out to the huge seesaw, and when a kid got off one side I straddled the rough board despite the thin pink plaid cotton dress I was wearing. I felt pretty, but the smocked baby-doll dress seemed too young for the way I was feeling. I was the oldest one on the seesaw, but the boy on the other side was big enough to make it work. I was startled at how high the plank took me, how my stomach dropped on the way down. I figured if the kid on the other side jumped off, as kids tend to do on seesaws, I would die I was so high up. With each lift I was surveying the colorful scene of the wedding in staccato freeze frames. The familiar, and oddly comforting, feeling of being an observer rather than a participant washed over me with each slow lift of the seesaw. I stayed on the plank a long time, even though the other kids said I was hogging my turn, and didn't get off until I saw people starting to gather around the patio.

After much tuning and fiddling around with equipment, the band started playing a rough, raucous rendition of "Satisfaction" on their electric guitars, and my mom, in a modest knee-length blue dress trimmed in white lace, stepped up to the concrete patio and stood under the French doors. Cathy strode up in her five-year-old sureness and took my mother's hand. She remained there throughout the ceremony. I stood way back, behind most of the people, still feeling strangely detached and not part of the scene. At that moment, our family dynamic was defined: my mom and Ray, so very married, Cathy holding my mother's hand, and me, in the background, looking on.

When the band bashed out the last, "Hey, hey, hey, that's what I say," the crowd quieted to a low murmur. A minister friend of theirs, dressed in a white collar, black shirt, and jeans, asked my mother if she would take Ray as her lawfully wedded husband.

"I do," said my mother, looking adoringly at Ray, who looked handsome with his black curly hair, beard, and customary black beatnik-style turtleneck.

"And do you, Ray, take Dorothy to be your lawfully wedded wife, to have and to hold, in sickness and in health, until death do you part?"

"I do," Ray said.

"Right on, Ray! OooWEE!" yelled someone in the crowd.

"I now pronounce you man and wife," the collared man said, as Ray gave my mother a big kiss on the lips and the crowd started hooting and yelling and throwing hats up into the air.

I watched in silence. I felt invisible. It was done; I was resigned. There was nothing I could do.

The party went into full afternoon swing. In one corner I saw Gogo gnawing on a huge piece of chicken, the juice running down her chin. Mario from the Inn, the ninety-five-year-old legend of the town, sat peacefully in his chair, looking handsome in his dark suit and nodding off every once in a while, despite the fact that he was sitting next to the cacophony the band was making. Groups of women swirled on the lawn, barefoot, with flowers in their hair. The cake was cut, with surprising secondary colors of orange, purple, and green inside. Evidence of blue and yellow frosting could be seen all around the kids' mouths. Jugs of red wine were passed around among the men. I spent most of the sunny afternoon with Cathy and George and the other kids, in the field next to the house, playing on the seesaw.

Hours later, when things started winding down, Gogo came out to get me and to tell me I was going back to their house that evening, to stay a few days until the honeymoon was over. I caught my mom before she left.

"I feel like I'm invited to this wedding like everyone else, instead of being *in* it," I said.

"What do you mean, darling?" My mom asked, hurriedly. She looked very happy and pretty, her eyes glassy and her cheeks flushed with the wine she had been drinking.

"I mean, I drove to this wedding from over the hill, now I'm driving back. I don't feel like I'm a part of this at all."

"Oh, of course you are, sweetheart, don't be silly."

"Yeah, I guess, but where are you going, and when are you coming home?"

"Oh, we're just going up the coast, and I'll be home soon sweetheart, very soon..." she said, and kissed me.

"Dorothy, there's someone I want you to meet," Ray was calling to her from behind the fence.

"I have to go darling, be a good girl and find Gogo and Beba."

"But Mom, wait, how many days are...."

"Dorothy! Did you hear me?" There was some impatience in Ray's voice now. My mother looked over at the fence where Ray was standing, looked back momentarily at me, and without saying another word to me, called back.

"Yes, Ray, I hear you. I'm coming."

And she half-skipped, half-trotted toward the fence.

I was left standing alone in the yard, with the same, familiar, empty feeling I always had when she left.

CHAPTER 9

Power Struggles (Loopholes)

"I was thinking of starting you girls on an allowance," Ray said to Cathy and me. "That way you could have some money to spend as you like. What do you think?"

I studied Ray's face carefully looking for clues. I didn't know what to think, and I certainly didn't know what to say. At almost the halfway point through that interminable grizzly, gray summer, I didn't know this man who was suddenly taking care of us, suddenly married to my mother, and suddenly… my stepfather.

Stepfather. I didn't use the word much, because it wasn't that familiar to me, but it sounded mean, as mean as the stepmothers in the fairy tales. I didn't know too many people who had a stepfather back then. I knew this: he wasn't Papa, with the love and passion and anger oozing out of his pores, or Beba with his patience and soft spots everywhere, or Gogo, who I at least knew how to read, and could avoid her at the first sign of a meltdown. He was a stranger, the next in line to take care of me, and it felt as if my very survival was in his hands. I didn't trust him. I had to be careful.

* * *

The three of us were sitting in the musty smelling kitchen, around the Formica table covered with the hopeful blue-gingham tablecloth my mom sewed when I was so optimistic about the move. I looked out the window to the rows of gray-green artichokes and thought about Ray's question.

Money was the last thing I would wish for at this point. My mother home and taking care of Cathy and me would probably top the list. Moving back to San Mateo was secretly second, secret even to myself, since I couldn't admit after all that wishing to move that I was more miserable than before. An image of kids running through the sprinklers in the sunny suburbs with the manicured lawns flashed through my head, but I quickly chased it away with the consideration of money.

My mom had always given me a quarter on Monday for Bank Day at school, and I enjoyed putting it in the envelope with the string fastener and adding up the twenty-five cents week after week in the little blue bankbook. Sometimes I'd hand my mother a pile of change I had collected and found, hoping it was enough for "paper money" so I could buy a ring with a fake stone, or a Beatles 45. Until this point, I didn't really want or need money; there were other areas of lacking that were so gaping that trinkets could never fill it. That was about to change.

"Yeah, sure, that would be great," I finally said. I tried to put more enthusiasm in my voice than I actually felt, thinking that maybe he was trying to please us and that I should be grateful.

"I was thinking of starting you at a dollar and a quarter a week," Ray said casually, looking at our faces for a reaction.

"A dollar *and* a quarter!? Wow!" I stopped to gain my composure. I didn't want to let him know what a shockingly large amount that was to me. "I mean, uh, great, good, I mean... that would be okay." The jolting zapper of such a huge sum of money had made me sit up and blurt out—now I was carefully slouching back down in my chair and arranging my face into a look of semi-boredom, but my mind was swirling with possibilities. This amount of money could be entertaining. Even though there was nowhere to shop in this Land of Sprouts and Fog located exactly in the middle of nowhere, there was always the Sears catalog. Hell, with that kind of money I could catch the Greyhound over the hill and shop at the mall with my old friends. I glanced over at Cathy, but her face remained expressionless. Obviously, at six, she had no concept of what a fortune was being handed to her, but for me, the Desire was planted. Little did I know that this was a calculated sowing on Ray's part, for without desire, the Scarcity that he was about to introduce could never work to control us.

"And, " Ray went on, "you can get the chance to earn even more money if you help out with a few chores. I've made a list here." Ray showed us a large piece of yellow ruled paper he had drawn up to look like a chart. "Cleaning the bathroom would earn you an extra seventy-five cents, and ironing will earn you a dollar. Washing the car— you have to do a good job mind you, including waxing it of course—will earn you another dollar and a quarter, so you can double your allowance by helping your mother and me out."

I could hardly believe my good fortune. Maybe having Ray live with us wasn't going to be as bad as I thought. He wasn't Papa, but maybe he was going to be fun in other ways. I imagined myself walking into my new fifth grade classroom wearing the short white go-go boots I would buy with all the money I'd be earning. Everyone would want to be friends with the new girl. My fantasies of being the most popular girl in the class were cut into by Ray's next remarks.

"Now besides the awards for doing extra chores, there of course will be a fine if you fail to do any of your regular chores—the nightly dishes for instance. The standard fine will be fifteen cents."

I nodded at Ray absently. He was interrupting my calculations to see if I would have enough money for the boots *and* a new Beatles album by the end of the summer, securing my Most Liked New Girl status. Then I digested what he was implying. Why would he think I wouldn't do my chores? I pretty much always did what grown-ups told me to do. I thought that being good was the ticket with grown-ups; at least it worked at school. It was true that I had never really had any chores before—Gogo had done everything for us—but I didn't really mind doing these new tasks that Ray had Cathy and me do. Work took my mind off things, and I had nothing else to do since we had moved anyway, I had no friends yet, and no phone. I thought I would never be "fined," another word and concept I was not really familiar with, but was about to know intimately.

The next day when I trudged out of my bed in my nightie and went to stand at my usual spot by the heater in the wall, I saw that Ray had hung a cork message board, and on it was the charts he had shown us, one for Cathy and one for me. At the top of my chart was a large "$1.25," the amount of my allowance. Underneath that amount was the notation, "Left light on in kitchen: -$.15. A new subtotal was written in red: $1.10.

I stared at my already dwindled allowance with annoyance. Ray had said we'd be fined if we didn't do our chores, and I had certainly done the dishes the night before, and didn't even try to say that the pots and pans needed soaking overnight. He hadn't said anything about being fined for leaving the lights on. I swallowed my irritation, and made a mental note to myself to turn out the lights.

On day two, when I got up and checked the corkboard by the heater, I was shocked that lines of subtractions on both Cathy and my chart greeted me. "Water not wiped off kitchen counter: -$.15. Left books in living room: -$.15. Talking back to your mother: -$.15." After the subtractions were made, my allowance was already down to a measly sixty-five cents for the week, and it was only day two. I felt the anger churning in the pit of my stomach. I'd been duped.

After that, every false move I made was fined. Of course I never knew what would earn me the fine until after the fact. After a while, some of the fines were more than the original fifteen cents. Opening the freezer without permission I found out cost a quarter. Changing the channel on the TV was the same. Leaving a door ajar so that the heat could escape could cost up to fifty cents to "defray the PG& E bills." Ray started timing our showers with the kitchen timer, and we were fined fifteen cents for every minute over ten.

I was jittery. I was being Watched. My self-worth was starting to be defined by a lousy fifteen cents. After a while, just the words *fifteen cents* sent a Pavlovian wave of nausea and self-hatred through me.

* * *

I didn't see my mother a lot that summer, but when she was home in the evenings or on the weekends, I looked to her to gauge her reaction to all these rules; all this rigidity. She acted as if it was the most normal thing in the world to have our every move monitored and calculated for its monetary value. She herself wasn't fined, but she was set up on a Budget, despite the fact that she was the only one working and bringing home a steady paycheck. The Budget consisted of a steno pad that was prominently left out on the desk in the living room. Each page of the pad had a different heading: food, entertainment, clothing, gas, and the amount allowed for each category for the month. My mother was responsible for paying for these items from her check, while Ray took care of rent and utilities and booze from the money he had saved from when he was a businessman, instead of a full-time artist. Whenever my mother spent any money, she was required to go to the steno pad and subtract the amount she spent from the amount allocated for that area. If she bought herself a pack of cigarettes, for example, she would have to make an entry on the "Entertainment" page, and subtract the $.37 from the ten dollars allowed. If Ray bought her a pack of cigarettes, or anything else in her part of the budget, then she had to pay him back the cash.

"I picked up some bananas at the market; they were on sale," Ray might say. "You owe me twenty-eight cents." And my mom would trot dutifully to her purse and count out the amount to the penny, asking for change if she needed to.

I watched these little vignettes, these exchanges between my mother and her new husband, with a combination of fascination and horror. On the one hand, I was amazed at how adoringly sweet and obedient she was to this man, but on the other hand, to see my mother once again controlled, to see that *she wasn't in charge*, filled me with fear, since she was what I thought was my only lifeline.

* * *

Money wasn't the only thing carefully supervised under Ray's Regime. Food was also a controlled and regulated commodity. At Gogo's house I had longed for, and fantasized about, eating dinner as a family around a dining room table, but I didn't imagine a one-way conversation that consisted of listening to Ray mandate how much food we should take. "Put that back, that's too much butter, Chris. No more, you don't need that much on your potato," and comments to the like, were pretty much the extent of the mealtime communication.

Between meals, there was no more of the Open Pantry policy we enjoyed at Gogo's house. We were told that we needed to ask if we wanted a snack, and the first time I did, I stared in disbelief at the three wheat checks Ray put on the blue-gingham tablecloth. Ray's face remained expressionless, so I didn't know whether to laugh, or wait for the punch line. Finally I asked him if he was joking.

"Are you serious? Three pieces of cereal for my snack?"

"What, that's not enough? It will be dinner in a couple of hours."

When I didn't say anything, he went to the squeaky kitchen cabinet and brought out the vat of econo-sized peanut butter, and with the tip of a knife, dabbed each square.

"There! That should hold you!"

Later that afternoon, when I was feeding the cat, I tried one of the dry pieces of cat food that was covered in powdered milk to make whitish gravy when a little water was added to the bowl. It tasted kind of good. I felt a little bit guilty about eating cat food, but I figured if the cats could eat it, it couldn't be *that* bad. After that, I took to sneaking a few pieces of it whenever I fed the cats, or even sometimes when I wasn't.

One morning, at breakfast, my jelly glass contained a translucent gray-blue liquid with little lumps floating on top. It looked suspiciously like the gravy the cat food made when I mixed it with water. I brought the glass up to my nose, and it smelled funny, like yeast.

"Mom, what is this stuff?" I said with exaggerated disgust, wrinkling up my nose.

"It's milk."

"This is *not* milk." There was that familiar "She's Lying To Me" neon sign flashing brightly in front of my face.

"It's pure milk, I swear to God," she said, *way* too defensively to ring true.

"Well then, what's wrong with it? Is it goat's milk or something? It's gross!"

"It's just powdered, that's all. They take the water out, and I put it back in. It's exactly the same, only it's a lot cheaper."

This was too much for me. It was bad enough I was sneaking the cat food covered with powdered milk, but now I was expected to drink it for breakfast. At Gogo's house I was used to guzzling milk straight out of the carton all day long. I made a stand, probably because Ray happened not to be at the table.

"I'm not drinking it."

"What about if I mix it with half regular milk?" I noticed my mother was pleading, so I felt I had the upper hand.

"No. Just give me the half a glass of regular milk without the mix."

And for a while, that's just what I had for breakfast: a Flintstones jelly glass with about an inch of milk in the bottom of it. That is, until I told Gogo about it one weekend when Cathy and I were visiting.

Gogo immediately called Andy's Market, the little store near our house in Moss Beach, and set up a tab. She told us that from now on, we could go to the store and take as much milk as we wanted, and that she would pay for it.

That first Monday after coming home from visiting Gogo's house, I walked to the store and grabbed a half a gallon of milk, and Andy wrote it down on a little pad. I made a big deal about guzzling it straight from the carton in front of Ray, rolling my eyeballs around the carton to gauge his reaction. His look of defeat didn't make me feel good; I almost felt sorry for him. I could see that winning this control game was a lot more important to him than it was to me. I decided after that not to flaunt the milk in his face.

But my victory in that small battle didn't go unpunished. Soon there was a new rule: no walking around the house in your socks.

"Put your shoes on or go barefoot," was the way Ray announced the new rule.

"Why?" I asked.

"Because I said so, and I'm tired of your insolence."

"What's insolence?"

"Being a smart-ass, that's what." That he would call me a name like that made me cringe inside. This new attitude came on so fast; I still felt as if I hardly knew him.

"I just want to know why I can't walk around in my socks. I like to."

"Because it gets them dirty and your mother has to do more laundry."

"She has to wash them anyway."

"It wears them out, that's why. Now take them off, or put on your shoes."

I didn't want to be drawn into this battle of wills again, but I couldn't help myself. I felt the anger in me rising, because I thought he was doing this sock thing to pay me back for the milk. He had me engaged. I fought back. The next time I went to Andy's to get my milk, I also picked up a pair of black socks, unlike all my white ones.

When Ray saw me walking around outside in the socks, he started in, "What did I tell you about not wearing shoes? Don't you listen? I'm going to need to fine you at least..."

I cut him off. "These are *my* socks that I bought with my own money. I got black ones so you would be able to tell."

I faced him, and could see that he was fuming. His face was a mixture of fury and defeat. He looked so mad I was almost tempted to let him think he had control over me, because I knew with such a deep conviction that he would never own me; my spirit was far too strong. I might have been my mother's daughter, but my will ran so much deeper.

Maybe Ray sensed this strength and took it as a challenge to tear it down, just like Gogo did when we fought. What he didn't know, what I never let him see, was that gaping hole in my heart that absorbed everything Ray said as evidence of my unworthiness. Every "smart-ass," every "you're not *that* pretty," every "insolent," every "wash your hands, who knows what you touched in the night," every fucking "fifteen cents," was not affecting my strength—quite the opposite: I was getting stronger and tougher every day. But it was eroding what little was left of my self worth.

I didn't understand why Scarcity had entered our lives, living in every wall, creeping its way into every conversation, and sitting in the middle of our dinner table every night. It wasn't only the money, there was suddenly not *enough.* Not enough time, not enough heat, not enough clothes to wear, not enough opportunities to talk, not enough food to eat. I felt as though *I* wasn't enough.

* * *

I was surprised when I felt the urge to go to church.

I thought back to my second grade confessions, when I would have to make up my transgressions just to have something to say. Back then, I knew that I was Good, no matter what I did or said, but now I wasn't so sure. Maybe Ray was right. Maybe I should do as I was told and not fight back. Maybe I *was* bad.

There was a little Catholic church in Moss Beach. Ray had pointed it out when we had driven by one day, because he had been commissioned to paint a mural of a crucifixion for the church. The church looked nothing like the big old St. Gregory's I was used to going to in San Mateo. It looked more like a wood plank cabin you might find in the woods.

One Sunday morning I woke up early before anyone else in the house. I had that Sunday morning feeling of longing. I missed the purpose I had on

Sunday, I missed getting up early and getting dressed up to go to church with Beba and George. I missed the sacrifice of skipping breakfast. I decided to make a daring move and go to the little church I had seen by myself.

I got dressed quietly, not in fancy church clothes, but in my nice pants. I was careful not to wake up Cathy, who was sleeping in the bed next to mine with her thumb in her mouth. I tiptoed to the closed door of my mom and Ray's room, putting my ear close to the door to see if I could detect any sounds. I couldn't. Then I walked outside, silently closing the door behind me.

I ran. I ran as hard as I could the whole four or five blocks along the side of the highway, my heart pounding in my chest, partly due to the exertion, and partly due to the fact that I had snuck out of the house and was doing something on my own for the first time ever. The town was still, and few cars passed me as I ran down the highway. The sun was still low on the horizon and reddish gold, slanting into my watering eyes, and it was cold; my breath came out in visible puffs.

When I got to the little church, I stopped outside the door, catching my breath. I could hear singing going on inside. It felt funny to be going to church without a grown-up, without Beba to ask the priest if it was okay to take communion since I had not gone to confession. I knew I would just have to do the best I could. I was on my own.

I opened the heavy door, and knelt in the back pew of the cool, dim building. Immediately, the feeling of calm washed over me. The priest was standing behind a simple alter covered with a white cloth and fresh flowers.

"Peace be with you," he said, and I answered, "And also with you," automatically with the rest of the congregation, although it seemed like a long time since I had been in church.

I wanted communion, so I decided to do my own confession. I convinced myself that God wouldn't mind if I communicated with him directly instead of using the priest liaison. Kneeling, and holding my hands in prayer, I told God that I was sorry for all the things that I was obviously doing wrong, and asked for help in being a better person so that I wouldn't get in trouble so much. Then I got in line with the rest of the people for the host, carefully swallowing it without letting it touch my tongue, as I had been instructed to do. Nobody looked at me like I was out of place or doing anything wrong.

I ran all the way home again, afraid that the house would be up and wondering where I was, but I when I got there, they were all still asleep.

I kept up this secret ritual every week, willing myself to wake up early every Sunday. I felt myself feeling a little bit better, and the weight of all the new rules seemed lighter. I could let things go a lot easier, without fighting back.

One morning I got up for breakfast and my mom and Ray were sitting at the table reading the local newspaper.

"They think it may have been arson," Ray was saying.

"Oh, I'm so sorry Sweetheart," my mom said, putting her hand on top of Ray's. "And you had just finished that painting for them."

"Yeah, it would have been great exposure for my work," Ray said, shaking his head.

"What are you guys talking about?" I asked.

"Oh, that little Catholic church here in Moss Beach burned down, that's all. They think someone did it on purpose. Your father had a painting in there—it's a shame," my mom said.

"I went to that church!" I burst out, surprised at my audacity and grief. I braced myself for the punishment that was sure to follow for sneaking out of the house without permission. They both just stared at me.

"How pious of you," my mother finally said. Ray said nothing but went back to the paper he was reading.

I didn't know what pious meant exactly, but I did know this: she didn't approve.

* * *

I had lost the little anchor I had found in my solo church excursions, but as the long gray summer — the summer in the middle of the artichoke field, the summer of gaining a stepfather, the summer of hearing "Wipe Out" playing weakly on the old Grundig radio — came to an end, life became so distracting I couldn't hear that voice inside of me, let alone know that it was ailing. I was too busy to feel anything as school started and all my attention went into being a perfect student and the most-liked girl in the class. On top of that, we were moving again.

Ray built us a house a few blocks away from our sixty-dollars-a-month rental, the shabby little house I had held such high hopes for only a few months before. As weird and run-down as that house was, it was going to be *our* house, just my mom and Cathy and me—or so I had thought. This new house was definitely *Ray's* house, and it was infused with qualities of Ray's personality: minimalist, monastic, thrifty, unorthodox, no frills. It was small and boxy, with rough wood exterior walls, unfinished pine interior walls, and brick-red linoleum tiled floors. It was heated with a Franklin stove, and the kitchen had rough plank shelves with no cabinet doors. There was no dishwasher, washer, dryer, bathtub, or telephone. The house was furnished with things Ray found at the dump and refurbished. Cathy and I shared a partially divided room.

The new house was Ray's in more than the physical sense. New rules and stipulations began to emerge. Now we were instructed to break toothpicks and tear paper towels in half, and to reuse the tea bags and the towels by hanging them on a special nail for this purpose.

Ray's house was also hip and artistic. The house hung. Ray's art was hung on all the walls, wicker chairs were hung by chains, and plants were hung with macramé. A large canopy embroidered by my mother at Ray's request hung over their bed.

As if Ray's house was a mirror of his soul, there were doors that couldn't be opened. The front door to the house, the one that faced the street, was not to be touched by anyone, including Ray. "We don't use that door" was the reason why. The garage door was a false front, and couldn't be opened. The bedroom that Cathy and I shared had two doors leading to it, one for each of us, but the door on my side after a while was blocked by furniture, and eventually turned into a closet. We couldn't go through the door to my mother and Ray's room without express permission, and the door was always closed.

Gogo, Beba, and George moved too. The house at sixtyeastfortieth was too big for the three of them, and they found a small apartment in Millbrae. Cathy and I stayed with them every other weekend so that my mother and Ray could have their Alone Time. The craziness, the friction, the drama of Gogo was not evident during the four days a month I saw her now. Starting with the milk incident, she had mysteriously turned into my champion, spoiling me like crazy when I visited. Her kitchen was always full of Pop Tarts and pizza and anything else I wanted. She ran hot baths for me and brought me magazines to read while I soaked in bubbles. When she saw the state of my dingy and worn underwear my mother packed for one of my weekend stays, she said, "You would only wear new, snowy-white knickers if you lived with me!" and I knew that it was true.

I watched as the life I was living started juxtaposing sharply with George's, where they used to be identically intertwined. My uncle, George — who used to be so much like me that everyone thought we were twins — and I were living very different lives, and it was becoming apparent in our appearance, our proclivities, and our levels of confidence.

Taped to the door of George's room was a sign made by Gogo saying "George Golda, You are the Pro, oh yes you are, you are!" George obviously believed this affirmation, because he exuded an easy, nerd-like confidence. The twin beds in George's room were covered with pale blue eiderdown comforters from England. Gogo and Beba took turns sleeping in the extra twin bed when they weren't getting along. Half of his bedroom was taken up by a ham radio, and on the wall was a map of the world with dozens of colored pins to show where George had made contact. He played the trombone in the marching band, and Beba took him to swimming and tennis lessons. He traveled around the world for free, since Beba worked for United. At only ten years of age, he was a national Judo champion. He dressed like a geek, wearing white socks and sandals, and didn't care when Cathy and I made fun of him. The background sound in George's apartment was the ever-present television, or occasional Lawrence Welk or Polish Polka albums, and the place smelled like the lard in Gogo's chip pot, and Beba's kielbasa sausage.

Our friends already dubbed the house that Cathy and I lived in "the hippie house." Ray had let me paint a psychedelic mural on the back of the closet that semi-divided the room I shared with Cathy. My bedspread and curtains were made out of dark brown felt trimmed in orange dingle-balls, chosen by me and sewn by my mother. The background sound in our house was the plaintive Judy Collins singing "The White Freighter," or else Iron Butterfly's "In-a-Gada-da-Vida," or George Harrison on the moog synthesizer. I dressed in jeans and go-go boots, fishnets and pink plastic belts. Cathy and I had no extra-curricular activities besides completing the chores we were required to do, and had to earn the money if we wanted anything. We both were hesitant to speak around grown-ups. Our house smelled like Ray's pipe tobacco, and one time like the banana peel he had tried to roast and smoke.

* * *

During my fifth grade school year, I tried very hard to shine and be good, and then had to try just as hard to lose the status of Mrs. Johnson's Teacher's Pet. I discovered that I cared more about being popular with the kids than being top of the class, so after a while I dimmed my own light. I manipulated and cajoled my way into hanging around the popular rich girls instead of the shy girl who tried to befriend me the first day. Except for in February, when I was sick in bed for a month with pneumonia, the rest of the school year was busy, and I was too distracted with the urge to please, to be liked and popular, to get straight As with no one knowing, and moving to the new house to feel much of anything. Only when my body broke around Valentine's Day did I find myself crying to my mother that "I wanted to go home." I was devastated when she said I *was* home.

When the next summer rolled around, though, life slowed down, and I felt as if I was moving in slow motion through the drippy gray fog that had once again swirled onto the coast, as if on cue. It rolled in at the beginning of June, and remained unmoving, day after day, a thick, heavy blanket shrouding the days. Without school and the bustle of moving to divert my attention, the damp drizzle landed in the Hole in my heart, filling me with loneliness, though I wasn't sure what I longed for. It wasn't George, Gogo, and Beba, exactly, although a year later, I missed them more than I thought I would. It wasn't Papa; that sharp pain was fading from the front of my consciousness, and had turned into a vague dull ache. No, what I was feeling now was more like a longing for connection and familiarity and wholesomeness. I had my mom and Cathy, I reasoned, and I had lots of friends now, so I didn't know why I felt so lonely. I wished I could go to church again, for relief, but the little church was gone, so the feelings in me had no outlet, but rather bounced around inside of me, springing to the surface when I least expected them.

I woke up early to the smell of oniony, garlicky Guest Food that third of July. I remember it was the third, because the fourth was the day my mind spiraled and skipped. When I shuffled into the kitchen in my pajamas, the avocado-green electric frying pan was plugged in, and when I lifted the lid, a meaty gravy dish was bubbling away, the telltale Company Pearl Onions dancing on the surface, announcing that my parents were going to have one of Those Parties.

"Put the lid back on—that's for the Company!" my mom said, as she rushed around the corner, a bottle of Windex in one hand and a rag in the other. I liked the bustle of the house on the day when people were coming over, though the parties themselves made me uneasy.

"What is it?" I asked. "That boof borg in yo you made last time?"

"No, silly. That's with beef. And you pronounce it *boeuf bourguignon.* This is *coq au vin.*"

"Coca what?" I said, just wanting to carry on the conversation with my mother, as it was Saturday, and she was home—but she was in her usual Rush-Busy mode, and shooed me off.

"Go clean up your room and make your bed! We're having people over tonight!"

I know, I know, I thought, as I drug my feet back to my room. They had a lot of parties since we had moved to the new house, and they were all sort of the same. Eight or ten hiply dressed people would arrive, younger than my parents, some of them familiar by now, others friends of Ray from the Art Institute. Big jugs of red wine were passed around, and there was a lot of smoking and talking and drinking, with loud Rolling Stones songs playing on the stereo. On those nights, the little black-and-white TV would be put in our room, which was a treat, even though we weren't allowed to change the channel. We were expected to stay in our room for the duration of the party, coming out only to get a plate of dinner.

That evening proved to be no exception. After the guests arrived with a lot of loud, hardy greetings, and my mother brought out the eclectic mix of jelly jars and Mexican green glasses for the wine, I wandered off to my room to watch TV with Cathy as I was expected to do. For some reason though, the novelty of having the TV in my room was not working to hold my attention, and I soon became bored and antsy. The loud music and laughing in the next room made me curious. I kept wandering out to go to the bathroom, and then meandering into the living room and kitchen, to observe what was going on without being noticed.

I saw that although most of the adults were smoking, they were very interested in passing around one particular misshapen cigarette. Everyone was laughing, even though I didn't see anything particularly funny, and there was also a lot of kissing going on among the guests, not always with his or her respective partners. I stood behind the counter and listened to snatches of conversation damning the war, expressing naked fear over Ronald Regan being the governor, swearing that there would be no choice but to move to Europe if he ever became president. The lyrics to Beatles songs were discussed, and then Ray started going on about something called acid.

"Man, you have to try eating a tangerine on acid. It was wild!" Ray said to the crowd. Then to my mom: "Dorothy, I'm going to have to get you some LSD. You have to try it. It will change how you see things forever."

I drifted back in the bedroom and tried to watch the TV, but my stomach was jittery, and then I noticed that Fear had taken over my being. That same icky Fear of the flies, the Fear of the Drummer Boy, the Fear of "I'm going to California, *domane,* Christina." I couldn't concentrate on what I was watching, and when it was time to eat the special wine-infused chicken, I could only pick at it.

Finally, my mom poked her head in our room. "You girls better think about turning off the TV and going to sleep pretty soon," she said. Her cheeks were pink and I could see her eyes were sparkling and shiny, even through her glasses.

"Mom! Come here!" I said. When she walked over to the bed, I pulled her down close to me by wrapping my hands around her neck. I said very close to her face, "What is acid? Whatever it is, I don't want you taking it! And why are you guys all passing around that same cigarette?" Although I didn't know that much about drugs, I Knew.

"Oh, it's nothing. It's just a special cigarette that makes you giggle, that's all."

"What about the acid?" I persisted. "Promise me you won't ever take it! Promise me!" I was holding on to her tightly.

"Don't worry, darling, it will probably never come up..." she trailed off.

"Promise!!"

"Oh, okay. I promise. Now go to sleep, it's late," she said, extracting herself from my grip, and stepping lightly out the door, closing it behind her.

Cathy's eyes were already closed, and she had her thumb in her mouth. I roused her enough to get her into her own bed, and then I went back to my bed to watch some more TV, trying hard to let it do its magic and get me numb. I woke late in the night with all my clothes still on, and the lonesome test pattern on the television, and its accompanying static the only noise in the house. I quickly changed and thankfully fell back into the abyss of sleep.

I woke up on the Fourth of July to find my proper English mother on her hands and knees, wearing her weekend black sweats, her blond curly hair bobbing as she scraped some awful-looking gook off the kitchen floor with a spatula and blopping it into a brown plastic bucket. The entire floor was covered with the stuff. At first I thought it was vomit—it looked like it—but no, there was too much of it. Then I thought it could be oatmeal, but there were other lumps in it that didn't belong in porridge.

"Good morning, darling!" she said in her overly cheerful British way. I didn't answer, waiting for her explanation as to what happened. When she offered none, I prompted her.

"Uh, what are you doing?" I winced as she scraped up a big lump of stuff.

"Oh, nothing darling, some of the people last night just got silly, and started making this mess..." she trailed off, smiling at the memory.

"What do you mean? What were you doing?" That Fear thing was waking up.

"Oh, I don't know, I guess Jessica spilled a little of her gravy on the kitchen floor, and she started playing with it with her bare toe. It was a little greasy, so she started sliding her foot in it, sort of dancing in it, keeping time to the music. She made it look like fun, so other people put their toes in as well. Then someone thought of adding an egg to make it easier to slide around. I think it was Joe who said that they needed some texture, so he added some oatmeal, maybe cornmeal..." She pushed her glasses up with her shoulder since her hands were covered in the stuff. "Most of the people at the party were dancing barefoot in it after a while. It was nothing really. Would you like some breakfast?"

I stood in the doorway in silence trying to digest this. At another place, another time, I might have found this scenario hilariously funny. Another me, with the Fear excised, might have thought it was cool to have such Weird, Wild, Whacky parents. The prepubescent me of *that* gray summer, however, the me who only ever wanted beige, who only ever wanted to blend in, had reached the saturation point for being able to absorb craziness, and this little scene may have been the straw that broke the proverbial camel's back, though I didn't know it yet.

"Go on! Don't just stand there staring at me, go get dressed!" my mother said over her shoulder.

That evening, I paced back and forth between the two windows in the living room waiting for the sky to turn to a darker shade of gray so that we could light the fireworks we had bought at the Red Devil stand in Pacifica. I kept glancing over at my mother who was fast asleep on the couch Ray had made from a frame he found at the dump and fitted with a piece of foam rubber covered in Naugahyde. She was always so tired after they had one of Those Parties.

Finally, I could see that the cars had their headlights on up on the highway. It was time.

"Mom, when are we going to light the fireworks? It's pretty dark outside now." I wobbled her cheek a little. "Mom, wake up! Let's light them now!" She opened her eyes again, but I could mostly just see the whites of them.

"Oh, I don't know," she murmured. "You'll have to ask Dad."

* * *

That's when it happened. I looked down at my mother's face, and the Fear and the loneliness that I had tried to keep contained washed over me with such force that I was jolted out of my denial. She wasn't There. She hadn't been There in a very long time. Her eyelids looked waxy and sort of translucent, and I jerked my face back away from hers, suddenly creeped out by my proximity. She didn't look Real to me. She was a Fake. It was as if I could see inside of her, and underneath the calm mask of her sleeping face there was no soul, just wires and gears inside. Then a single word floated to the surface of my mind as if it were spoken to me—a word that, although uninvited, lodged itself at the forefront of my consciousness, and would stay, as annoying as a chipped tooth you have to constantly visit with your tongue, as grating as a skipping record, as painful as a deep splinter that can't be removed even with the sharpest tweezers—and the word was "Robot."

It could have been another word. It could have been "Puppet," but no, that was too playful, too innocent, too friendly for what I was feeling. My soul was speaking very loudly to me, but I didn't understand the language. My concrete knowledge of the world didn't allow for the poetic terms of metaphor outside of my vivid dreams. My conscious twelve-year-old self didn't know about being controlled, about abdicating the steering wheel of life to someone else. I didn't know about vacating, and I didn't want to know or admit that she wasn't there for me, because she was the only one. Unable to process the meaning, I took the word literally, and at that moment the obsessive thought of 'Robot' grew autonomous robotic arms that grabbed hold of my psyche and wouldn't let go.

It followed me through the sparklers and the Piccolo Pete's that night. I didn't want my mother to suspect that I knew she was a robot, so I tried to act nonchalant as I observed her, looking for any robotic-like moves. I noticed she didn't light any of the fireworks herself, always handing the cones to Ray to light while he instructed us to move back. Maybe she wasn't programmed for fireworks. Robot. I mechanically went through the motions of enjoying the Golden Fountains, oohing and aahhing at the appropriate times, but secretly wanting to go to bed so the night could be over, the Knowing could be over, the Robot could go away.

The next day I opened my eyes from the top bunk and stared at the knotholes in the beamed ceiling. There was a moment of confusion, where I knew something was wrong, but didn't know exactly what, and then it came flooding in. The 'it' being a heavy shroud over my being, a darkness, a weight I had to bear. I didn't know that obsessive-compulsive behavior had a name, and I didn't know the word for depression, but I had made up my own name—my own word—Robot.

I climbed slowly down the bunk bed ladder, waking up my body, trying to see if I could shake it off. I stood in the middle of my room. I couldn't let it go. Robot. I walked out to the living room, and sat down at my place at the table that already set for breakfast. I didn't want to look at my mom in the eye. She was whisking around the kitchen, stirring scrambled eggs. She looked the same, except that I knew she was a robot. Not Really, not on the physical plane, but Really.

All that day, my mind registered and re-registered the word robot. I thought it might leave on that fifth of July—the feeling was too intense to possibly last longer—but it didn't. On the sixth of July: robot. And the seventh, and the eighth: robot, robot, robot. I couldn't concentrate on anything for more than a minute or two without 'robot' distracting me, punctuating every conversation.

The thought of Robot followed me to Girl Scout camp that August. When I got the letter from my mother at Camp Sugar Pine, I felt horrible guilt that she was writing me so lovingly and innocently when I secretly knew she was a robot. I was afraid my tent mate, such a nice, normal girl, would see through me, and detect the 'robot' that was repeatedly tumbling through the dryer of my mind.

I started to believe I was crazy. It was now serious enough that I thought I should talk to someone about it, but the only person I could tell was my mother, and she was, well, a robot. I decided to broach the subject anyway, the next time we were alone.

That opportunity came when I was helping her put away the groceries, folding the paper bags while she put the cans on the shelves.

"Mom, I have to talk to you about something," I said, exhaling slowly.

"Yes, sweetheart?" she said, in her usual absent-minded, robotic kind of way, as she got out the stepladder for the high shelves.

"I know this might sound kind of weird, but I can't get it out of my head that you're a robot." I said this in a fast blurt. I wanted to explain more, but I couldn't.

She glanced over at me with one hand still reaching for the high shelf, and said, "Robot?"

"I mean, I know you're not really a robot, not for real, but it's this mood I have, and I can't get rid of the thought."

"Of course I'm not a robot, silly girl." She pushed her glasses up on her nose and looked at me for a moment, a slightly annoyed frown on her face.

"I know; I just can't stop thinking about it."

"Well, try not to think about it, think of something nice. Like our Disneyland trip coming up. That's something good to think about, isn't it?"

But I wouldn't allow myself to enjoy that rare family trip to Disneyland that August. My anger and fear was turned inward, and I would continue to punish myself, even through Disneyland. Sitting in the backseat of the black VW bug, rolling south down Highway 101, staring at the back of my mother's curly head, my only thought was 'robot.' I knew she was just going through the motions. I knew she was lying, but I didn't know exactly what about, so I believed it was her covering up the fact that she wasn't a human. I listened to everything she said with suspicion. Or maybe I did Know, and that buried seed of knowledge was coming to the surface.

At one point on that endless car ride down south, she and Ray started discussing the lyrics to a song on the radio, and what exactly Billy Joe

McAllister threw off the Tallahassee Bridge. They switched to speaking in French, a tactic they always used when they didn't want Cathy and me to overhear their conversation.

"What? What do you guys think he threw off the bridge?" I had my face lodged between the crack in the front seats.

"Oh, nothing darling. We don't know. No one knows for sure."

Yeah right, I thought. Robot.

After that trip, the cloud changed focus and became more encompassing. Instead of only my mom being a robot, the obsession morphed into the perception of the whole world somehow being mechanical, that no one was his or her true self. I hadn't read Shakespeare yet, and didn't know of the concept of the world being a stage, and the men and women merely players. This was my first realization that hardly anyone was authentic, and it filled me with dread and terror. Instead of a word, 'robot,' the repetitive thought changed into an image, that of a drawing of the world.

I was getting desperate. I needed to talk to someone. The next time I stayed at Gogo's, I decided to talk to her about it. Gogo was in the bedroom putting clean sheets on the bed I was going to sleep in. She hadn't bothered putting on the bedroom light, so the room was half lit by the light in the hall, and half by the streetlight outside of the window, giving the room a surreal mood to match the one in my head.

"Gogo? I have this weird feeling." I stared out the window into the night.

"Yes, Duckie? What feeling is that?" She stopped shaking open the sheet and looked straight at me. It felt good, and I was encouraged to go on.

"Well, I can't get it out of my head that all the people in the world are sort of like robots. It started with thinking that mom was a robot." I glanced at Gogo to gauge her reaction, but her face remained expressionless so I went on. "Then it turned into the whole world, and now, I don't know, I can't get it out of me, no matter what I do... It just feels like everything is fake all of a sudden."

Gogo sat on the edge of the unmade bed, and stared out of the same window I was looking out of. I couldn't tell what she was focused on since the streetlight reflected off of her glasses, but I could sense that she was far away.

"Everyone feels like that sometimes, Duckie. The world is a funny place. No one understands it."

I let out the breath I didn't know I was holding. The cloud didn't lift that instant, but I could feel the coolness of relief sort of blowing around my being.

A couple of weeks later, as the mornings got colder and the scent of autumn started to creep into the air, a couple of days before I was to start seventh grade, I woke up and was shocked to find the feeling gone. I stayed very still on my top bunk, waiting to see if the dark would come swirling back. It didn't. I rolled off the bunk without using the ladder and looked out the window. The summer fog had lifted. The day was a crisp and cloudless blue. I closed my eyes and rested my forehead against the cold pane of the window, wet with condensation, and let the relief wash over me. I mouthed a simple one-word prayer: "thank you."

* * *

I wanted to think the Fear was gone, but the Fear, and all its little ugly disguises of depression, obsession, sadness, and anger was only lying flat and dormant, after having its way with me during that seemingly endless summer. I didn't know it, but the Fear was still growing during its hibernation, fueled by a combination of hormones, abuse that I didn't know was abuse, and neglect. I felt it coming to the surface, and held it as long as I could. When I could contain it no longer, instead of attacking myself again, I let it out; or rather it involuntarily exploded out of me, in the form of rage.

* * *

Anger made its debut in me in spring, a couple of weeks after Easter. Cathy had taken to carrying around a small purple foil-covered chocolate chicken she had saved. She personified the candy, turning it into her pet, and named it Chick-Chick. This wasn't the first time that Cathy breathed her imagination into inanimate objects until they took on a life of their own; she had done it with spools of thread and index cards, drawing me into her games every time, though I tried to act disinterested.

Cathy took to carrying the chocolate hen everywhere she went, using it as her alter ego. When my mother made breakfast, she'd ask, "Where's

Chick-Chick's breakfast?" Then in a lower voice, "She obviously doesn't want eggs, Mom." When she couldn't do her homework, it was Chick-Chick's fault for hopping all over the paper, which she would demonstrate by bouncing the chicken across her binder as if the matter was out of her hands.

Chick-Chick was funny. I started liking Chick-Chick. Once I woke up and the thing was on my pillow, an inch from my nose.

"Chick-Chick wanted you to wake up," Cathy said from the lower bunk, which started me laughing right out of sleep. Then when I went to brush my teeth, the thing was already in the sink. Cathy poked her wild curly head into the door. "Chick-Chick wants a bath."

The night my Fear first rose, we were typically sitting around the dinner table, in our assigned seats, with the usual strained, somber dinnertime atmosphere. Meal times were always an ordeal for me, since Cathy and I were only allowed to talk minimally, as Ray had told us that he didn't want his dinner "monopolized with kid talk." Ray also told us that we had no opinions until we were adults, which worked well to keep us quiet, as we weren't allowed to voice our non-existent beliefs. Ray admonishing us for eating too much or correcting us for our bad table manners was the punctuation for any conversation.

This night, it was one of those times he seemed to be in a pretty good mood though, laughing and joking with my mother. I noticed he seemed a lot happier after he spent the afternoon in the Montara Inn. Chick-Chick was sitting next to Cathy, and I noticed that every time Ray laughed, Cathy jiggled the chicken to make it laugh too. My mom served the food, and when the adults had taken their first bite to signal we could start eating, Cathy tipped Chick-Chick over her plate in a pecking motion, saying under her breath: "Chick-Chick, I want you to eat more. You like noodles—no, there isn't any egg in these noodles."

I watched Ray observing Cathy. Instead of being annoyed, he seemed to have a twinkle in his eye.

"Would you like to see something really humorous?" Ray asked. Cathy and I looked at him warily. "I mean, really, truly, absolutely humorous?" He looked back and forth between Cathy and me, and at my mom. We solemnly nodded.

"Hand me that chicken."

Cathy grabbed Chick-Chick and held it protectively under the table.

"What are you going to do?" Cathy asked, eying him up and down.

"I'm going to show you something funny. You'll laugh. I promise."

Cathy slowly brought the purple-foiled chicken, a little worn and misshapen now from all the carrying around she had done, out from under the table, and reached across me to hand it to Ray. He plucked it quickly out of her hand, and before I could register what was happening, he bit the head off, foil and all, and put the decapitated Chick-Chick on the table, it's hollow insides exposed.

There was silence for what seemed an eternity, but was probably only ten seconds, while we stared at the chicken with its head bitten off.

Then Ray broke the spell by spitting the head out of his mouth where he had been holding it, and into his hand. He started laughing hard, forcefully expelling the breath he had been holding, saying, "Don't you think that's funny?"

Cathy burst into tears.

My mother said, "Oh Ray…" in a "you silly boy" tone.

And I felt, for the very first time, an anger rising from the pit of my stomach that was so huge I didn't know what to do with it. I sat there shaking, looking down, and holding on to the sides of my chair. I was paralyzed with a fear that if I let this thing out it would envelop and then consume me.

Then an unwanted and uninvited image came into my mind. I was bludgeoning Ray, blood splattering as I hit him repeatedly over the head with a club, his face becoming pulverized, until he fell down dead. The rage, which had traveled up to my chest, reversed directions, and instead of bursting out of my head, retreated back down with this oddly soothing fantasy, back down to the pit of my stomach where it lay like a hot coal.

I don't remember the rest of the dinner that night, I don't remember if Cathy continued crying, I don't remember the food, I don't remember if there were recriminations, I don't remember remorse. I imagine the rest of the table time was uneventful and that we went on eating as usual, because nothing snapped me out of my head where I relived the anger, and the power, and the fantasy over and over again. Ray was my anger's target, and as far as I let myself Know, also my anger's origin. My mother's paralysis, my sister's blooming persona of a victim, my own inability to speak, none of these hidden stokes to my anger's fire were recognized by me.

The Fear disguised as anger lived in me after that. I would indulge in my murderous fantasy whenever I felt powerless. The daydream gave me instant relief to my anxieties, but also filled me with guilt, especially when Ray was trying to do something nice for me, like making banana splits for dinner, or caring for me when I broke my arm, painting my cast a psychedelic green and red. Even if Ray had been the most nurturing and caring a stepfather could be, I'm convinced that this anger would have still grown, maybe not at the same rate, because Ray's narcissistic behavior was excellent fertilizer for those seeds that were planted way back when I begged my Papa not to leave, way back when I had the fly dream, but the anger would have grown anyway, I'm sure.

This anger took on a life of its own, but I was very careful not to let it out. I was smug in the knowing that I had control over this wild and untamed beast that lived in me. I could let it rise up to the point of release, and with a thought, albeit a nasty, guilt-inducing thought, could tame it, make it lie down, make it do what I said.

That's not to say that there were times I thought the anger might win, might break out of the careful cage I kept it in. Over the next couple of years, there were quite a few close calls. The time my mother and Ray were having one of their arguments, more of a heated discussion really, and Ray, having conceded defeat, deliberately walked around the table and emptied the contents of his wine glass on top of my mom's curly head, the ruby rivulets streaming down her glasses; *that* was a *very* close call. That time I could recognize that it was also directed at my mother. I couldn't believe that she wasn't standing up for herself. The anger and me were playing tug-of-war right in my throat, the struggle almost strangling me, but I clenched my teeth tight, summoned my flight of imagination, this time punching Ray in the nose to make red drips on his face to match my mother's, and the anger backed off. As time went on, the anger was becoming harder and harder to contain, until one day, at the very same wooden table, it blew.

* * *

If you took a freeze-frame of our dinner table that fateful night that Chick-Chick was so unceremoniously beheaded, fast forwarded through three years of film, and stopped the reel again at one of our supper-times, you would hardly be able to tell that any time had passed at all. There we'd be at the appointed time, our not-so-new-anymore family-of-four sitting in the very same seats, eating tuna noodles or spaghetti with mussels. I would be a fifteen-year-old teenager, but you would see I hadn't changed much at all, being a late bloomer, but Cathy at ten, was flowering early, right along side of me.

Ray would still be at the head of the table spewing out a nonstop stream of directives at us, correcting our manners, limiting our food intake, and discounting what opinions we managed to eek out, while my mom would still be at the other end watching, as if matters were out of her hands. But you might notice a slight air of complacency on my part, as I now let the orders and commands drift over my head, or more classically, in one ear and out the other.

I had learned over the three years to take the Opossum Defense to Ray's criticisms and punitive actions, and play dead. Ray still infuriated me all right, but I had learned to control that beast of anger that was growing in me. Fine me fifteen cents? I'll show off my babysitting money. Rip my favorite hurricane lamp off the wall and replace it with an old brass gooseneck as punishment for leaving the light on? No reaction, not a word from me. Sure I raged inside when I saw the desk lamp haphazardly nailed to the wall, but I swallowed it down. Then I proceeded to decorate the ugly light by hanging colored beads from its neck and pasting Ganesha stickers all over it, as if I loved it, and it was the best lamp in the world. Yeah, nothing could affect *me*, or at least I wouldn't give Ray the satisfaction of knowing it.

Maybe you'd notice, because you'd be comparing films three years apart, that Ray had stepped it up a little with Cathy at dinnertime. It was imperceptible to me, partly because the behavior escalated over time, and partly because I was mostly tuning it out, but you would notice his admonishments had become a little harsher, a little more frequent, a little more condescending. Now, if you would compare Cathy's table manners from the time she was seven until the time she was ten, you may think that you had mixed up the films, but what you would be seeing would be correct: 1,245 corrections later, Cathy's dinner etiquette had not improved; in fact, it was worse.

Okay, let's roll the projector again.

On this night, as on many nights, Ray was focused on making sure that Cathy kept her plate close to the edge of the table, a particular pet peeve of his. The "move your plate closer" order was given so often, so repeatedly, every meal, that I didn't even hear it anymore. Every time he said it, Cathy would automatically pull her plate closer, but inevitably it would creep away from her again until the next admonishment. This night was no different. At first.

"CATHY! What did I tell you?" Ray said, in a voice more exasperated and authoritative than the norm, I thought. "Move your plate closer, damn it!"

Cathy hung her head and moved the plate toward her, but as usual, five minutes later it had migrated six or so inches away from her. When Ray noticed this time, he put down his fork forcefully, making a bang on the table, the noise grabbing my attention. I looked up, expecting Ray's face to be contorted in anger, but instead he wore a mask of calm, his eyes thoughtfully narrowed and shifting as he looked over at Cathy. This look of calculation shot a cold, narrow stream of fear down my spine.

"Well, Cathy," Ray said, almost affectionately, although the underlying patronizing tone was evident to me, "it seems as though you *enjoy* eating far away from your plate. You want to eat far away from your plate, I'll let you eat far away from your plate if that's the way you want it." There was a slight pause here as we all glanced at each other in confusion. "STAND UP!" he barked.

Now my heart was pounding a little, but this was nothing I wasn't used to, nothing I couldn't handle. Cathy obediently stood up, and Ray walked behind her and picked up her chair, and moved it as far away from the table as it would go in the living room, about fifteen feet away. He put it down hard, with a thud muffled by the carpet.

"Sit there," Ray said, and Cathy did. Ray went back to his place, and the room was still, as if the air had been sucked out of it and we were sitting in a vacuum. There was complete silence, except for my heart pounding in my ears so loudly that I was sure everyone could hear it. My mother looked down at her plate. Ray started eating. Finally Cathy spoke.

"Uh, how am I supposed to eat?" she asked plaintively from across the room. I didn't turn around to look at her. I couldn't stand to see her back there.

"You may walk up, take a bite, leave your fork, walk back, chew the food, swallow it, and then you may walk up for another bite," Ray said.

I tried to catch my mother's eye, but she was eating and still looking down at her plate as if nothing were going on. Finally I swiveled around in my chair to take a look at Cathy to see what she was going to do. I knew that I would never go along with such a scheme, but Cathy stood up, walked the eight or nine agonizing steps across the room, took a bite, and then, as instructed, walked back to her chair and began to chew.

Then the anger mostly contained these past three years by acting nonchalant no matter what Ray said or did, suddenly whooshed in and consumed my body. I couldn't fake it this time. I was boiling inside, a hard, roiling, and forceful boil so powerful that I thought I might lose my food and throw up right then. I dropped my fork and held on to my seat. I had no time to conjure up any of my violent retaliatory fantasies because I was so mesmerized by the insanity of the scene playing out in front of me: Cathy getting up for the second time, pushing her bedraggled hair out of her face, one stirrup of her stretch-pants unhooked from her sock, getting a bite of food, and walking back to her seat to chew with a look of resignation that weirdly, could almost be confused with contentment on her face. Ray eating his food heartily, with an air of satisfaction and triumph surrounding him. And my mother, *my mother,* not saying anything, sitting there eating as if this degradation her husband was making her daughter endure was the most normal thing in the world.

When Cathy got up for the third time, everything slowed way down for me, and then stopped, along with my pounding heart. Suddenly, I could see everything clearly, as if I had hyper-vision. Not only could I see the vivid staccato images of Cathy's pant leg askew as her socks shuffled across the Persian carpet, or of my mother pushing her glasses up her nose with one finger because they had slipped while she had been hanging her head, but also underneath the images to Cathy's willing compliance, her possible enjoyment of the humiliation, to my mother's submission and inability to protect us, but I didn't want to Know, I didn't want to see all that, so it was Ray's fault, completely Ray's fault for making me see what I didn't want to see, and to my complete surprise, I found myself standing up and facing him. I involuntarily opened my mouth, and what came out was a strong, drawn out, roaring, "FUUUUCK YOOOOOOOOOOU!"

If you saw this scene in a cartoon, everyone's hair would be blown back with the velocity of what had just come whooshing out of me. The words would hang over the table in big block letters while all four of us stared at them in eye-bulging shock. The sturdy three-dimensional words would stay suspended for a good five seconds before shattering and crashing on to the table.

I stared at the little cloud of dust left by those words. I didn't know all I was feeling yet; at first I was just stunned. I couldn't believe that the profanity had come out of me; it never had before.

After I digested that I was capable of this reflex, I began to feel something else, like an emptying, and then the Vacancy sign went on inside of me. The Fear, when exposed, left the premises. Suddenly I knew The Fear had no substance behind it, it hadn't been born of anything tangible, really. I had never been in physical danger, I was only afraid of my withering spirit being crushed out of me by being called insolent, or a smart-ass. I was afraid of being punished or shamed. Now I knew that Ray couldn't do anything to me. That Fear had been living in my body for so long now that I didn't even feel its presence, let alone realize it had been holding me hostage.

As voids tend to do, it immediately filled up again, and suddenly I realized that I felt wonderful, powerful, soaring, free! The transformation of the horrible anger and Fear into euphoria was dizzying.

"How *dare* you talk to your father that way!" my mother piped up, snapping me back into the scene. *Oh,* now *she says something*, I thought. I looked at her for a moment, and thought that she was too pitiful for even the "oh shut up" I was about to give her, and turned and glared directly at Ray.

"LEAVE HER ALONE!" I still said this with the authority of my highest self, but though I hadn't lost it yet, I could feel the adrenaline draining out of me, and did not want my power to be replaced by some sissy tears.

"Dinner time is SICKENING! I can't take it ANYMORE!" I screamed.

Ray was seated way back in his chair as if repelled by my very presence. I could see him trying to regain his composure and power.

"Go to your room. You're grounded," he sputtered out, none too convincingly.

"Yeah, I'll go to my room, and I'll STAY in my room from now on. It's better than being out here with YOU!" I flounced out of the room with my head held high although I was shaking so badly I could barely make it to my bed, where I flung myself on my stomach, heaving.

That Fear that I had tried to keep in, that had turned on me in the form of depression and obsession, finally had come out disguised as anger. I wasn't going along with the program anymore, I didn't have to do anything anyone said. Trying to be nice and good and loving didn't pay off. It didn't make Papa stay; it didn't make Ray nice.

My heart surged with power so much so that it broke, and then shut down tight.

I was free.

Or so I thought.

CHAPTER 10

Keeping the Faith (The Doughnut not the Hole)

The tone of the house changed after that night. The tension was gone and the atmosphere was flat. I had been all geared up to test out my new-found freedom of speech to Ray, but it never really happened because he had backed off. No more fifteen-cent fines, no extra mandates, no punitive actions directed at us. Even the conversation at the dinner table had turned strangely neutral. At first I felt all-powerful, as if I had single-handedly stopped the abuse with my single ugly outcry, but soon enough the reason for the lack of negative attention became apparent. Ray was preoccupied with a New Project.

He was going to build us a new house in the empty lot adjacent to our house, and we were going to be moving — right next door. Day after day Ray sat at the wooden dinner table drawing the plans for the house himself. As the pages of blueprints piled up, and I pieced together fragments of conversations that drifted about, our new house slowly came into focus in my mind's eye, and when that picture was clear enough, it was suddenly ripped down the middle into two. As Ray showed me the technical drawings he was working on, I could see that there was not one floor plan, but two. Ray was going to build two houses: one for him and my mother, and a separate one for Cathy and me. This was a little more freedom than I had bargained for.

Of course I thought it was all my fault. I was so bad, so abhorrent, that it became necessary for Ray to build us a completely separate house. I'm not saying that my outburst caused the blueprints to be drawn up the way they were, but I do think it was one of the many nails that contributed to the building of our new home.

* * *

"Bless me Father, for I have sinned..." I knelt in the dark booth. Even though the routine was still familiar to me after such a long time, at sixteen, the confessional still intimidated me. I was staying at Gogo's for the weekend, and Beba had suggested, as he often did when I came to visit, that we go to confession that Saturday afternoon. Usually, I said no, I didn't feel like going, but lately some of the things I was doing with the freedom from being the Good Girl were weighing me down.

"...It has been over a year since my last confession, and these are my sins..." I tried to launch right into my first sin, but the father stopped me, as I knew he would.

"How long has it been?" The deep voice on the other side of the mustard-colored glass asked.

"A year."

"Have you received holy communion in the past year?"

I told him I hadn't, and sighed, knowing the next inevitable question.

"Have you attended Mass?"

"No," I murmured. I knew that this was supposedly a mortal sin, but I really didn't feel like it was my fault. I had more important things to talk about, like swearing at my step-dad and causing him to build us a separate house.

"Why not?" The Monsignor persisted.

"I don't have anybody to take me to church anymore. I used to walk by myself to a church near my house, but it burned down. I don't have my license yet." I said this quickly, in a forced whisper, hoping we could get past this subject.

"You'll need to find your own way," the father said. He was cutting me no slack. There was not a hint of sympathy for my predicament. The statement was more profound than I realized, but instead of ingesting it, I rolled my eyes and made a sarcastic face, bold and protected by the opaque yellow glass.

"Your penance is one rosary," he said, before I could go on. I was shocked. A whole rosary! My usual penance was three *Hail Marys*, maybe once in a while an *Our Father* but a whole rosary! I really must be bad.

I knelt in the pew, half-heartedly fingering the white pearly beads of my rosary. *Hail Mary, full of grace, the lord is with thee...* This was being recited in the part of my brain that can go on autopilot, while another part of my mind was starting to fume. This church was a joke. All they did was hand out stupid punishments for things that weren't even bad. It was just like Ray. *Blessed art thou among women, and blessed is the fruit of thy womb, Jesus...* How does he think that I'm going to get to church, when I don't know anybody who is Catholic in Moss Beach? This is the last time I'm going to that stupid confession... *Holy Mary, mother of God, pray for us sinners...* I didn't even get a chance to tell him any of my other sins. What would the father have thought about drinking a beer? Was that a mortal sin too? *Now, and at the hour of our death...* Was having sex a sin?

* * *

My main joy, my escape, my addiction, for the year before I turned sixteen, was making out with Kevin. Kevin Buckley, the baddest boy in the tenth grade. Kevin, the one who stopped the eighth grade dance by breaking in through the principal's window, drunk. Kevin with his green eyes, long curly hair, and motorcycle boots. Kevin, his breath a combination of unfiltered Camel cigarettes and Wrigley's Spearmint gum. Nothing else really mattered. Sure, I still did my schoolwork, but mainly that was to pass the time until the next time I could kiss Kevin. Whenever I wasn't kissing Kevin, I was thinking forward to the next time I could, or reliving our last encounter in my mind.

Kevin wasn't like the other boys I had loved so far. Not like Robert Hunt, the guy who gave me my first thrilling slow dance, whose blond hair bounced along with the ball he dribbled to make the winning basket, or Jay Alves with the twinkly eyes that matched the glint of his braces when he smiled at me in Algebra class, or Pete Peterson, every eighth grade girl's crush. Those had been good, smart, straight A-type of guys that I knew from my advanced classes in junior high. I had never even held hands with them, let alone kissed them. Acknowledging me by throwing a candy wrapper in class had been enough to keep me doodling their names on my binder for days.

At first, I couldn't admit that I would like a guy who disrupted our class meetings with his loud, obnoxious remarks, or a guy who was barely literate. But there was something in his complete lack of self-consciousness that drew me to him, since I was so much the opposite. That, and Ray always telling me that I was going to marry a *doctor,* the word dripping with sarcasm, implying that I was so straight-laced. I'd show him doctor. I started writing "KB" everywhere, even on my body with soapsuds when I took a shower. If I saw the combination of letters on a license plate, that was extra lucky, it meant he loved me too in my compulsive mind.

The first time that Kevin put his meaty, grease-infused hand on mine, when I was sitting next to him during the Battle of the Bands at Von's Cinema, a jagged jolt of electricity shot through my body that was so powerful I was sure he felt it too. Later that night, when he kissed me under the street lamp, my hands in his pea coat pockets along with his, the contrast of the hard calluses on his hands with the full softness of his lips almost made me swoon. I didn't sleep all night, reliving the moment over and over in my mind.

After that, that was all we would do. He gave me his big 'K' ring, asking me roughly if I would "go with" him, and I carefully wrapped the ring with red yarn, sealing it with clear nail polish, so that I could wear it proudly on my left hand. It was official: he was my boyfriend, which made it *okay* to constantly make out. For the first time, I felt 'love,' and I was instantly addicted to it. I couldn't get enough. I would wait impatiently for Kevin to snub out his cigarette so we could get down to the business of taking me out of reality.

Now I couldn't wait for my parents to go out so that Kevin and I could roll around on the living room floor for hours, or even if Ray was in his studio painting, we could at least mess around while under the guise of watching TV. Ray got wind of what was going on, and forbade me to have Kevin in the house, as if that would stop us. Every day after school we would go to the beach, or to the middle of a field with tall grass, and if the weather wasn't so good, there were half-built houses we could sneak into.

After a while, our hands started roaming everywhere, and then our mouths. By then the "I love you" declarations had been made, so wasn't it okay? "Make Love Not War" was the sentiment of the day, so I didn't think it was wrong. Except sometimes. Like the time we were at a dance in the bottom of the old Montara School house and Marcia's mother came over to the corner where Kevin and I were tangled and said we were the only ones at the dance not behaving. I was genuinely shocked; I didn't know we were doing anything wrong—we were just kissing.

At least we made it to *that* dance—there was the other time we missed the sophomore dance that had a huge pre-buzz that an up-and-coming group called the Doobie Brothers were going to be playing. We never made it past the parking lot. We started kissing in Kevin's red and white souped up Impala, and then I lost track of time—I was only there, there on the back seat of the red leather upholstery, the windows steamed up, our mouths roaming to places they had never gone before, and when I came to, our clothes were half off, and people were coming out of the dance. I didn't feel so good about that night; I was starting to lose control.

Yet control was what I tried to do for a while. We had been together for almost a year, and Kevin started bugging me every day (but it felt like every hour) to "do it" since he had never "done it" either. I had no intention of "doing it." Even though I had declared freedom, and that I made up my own rules, I still had a nagging inner voice bugging me about what was wrong or right. I wasn't sure why– no one had ever talked to me about it, but I thought I should wait until marriage to have sex. That is, until my mother told me she *expected* me to do it.

* * *

One day, when I was in the kitchen doing dishes with my mother, and chatting away about Kevin, my favorite subject, my mother broke in with a random bombshell.

"Your dad and I think that you should think about going on the pill," she said, without looking at me.

I cringed. Questions fired off in my brain, like sparks when a wire has been short-circuited. What was she suggesting? Did she think I was actually going to do it? Why was she discussing stuff like *that* with *him*, and why couldn't she speak for herself? And he *wasn't* my Dad. Red-faced, I continued drying the dishes, trying to process what she was saying, but hoping she would stop talking about it.

"We noticed he is a very good-looking boy," she went on glancing at me. What was her point? Was that when it was okay to do it, if the guy was good-looking?

"And well, we think that he might, well, *expect* things." So if a guy expects it, I'm supposed to give in?

Even though I had a burning desire for Kevin, deep down I knew that part of the attraction was that I was dabbling in forbidden territory. This was a guy from a large, poor family with an alcoholic stepfather who beat him, a guy with a dark room full of skulls and transmission parts, a guy who was failing most of his classes not because he was lazy, but because he was illiterate. A guy who could sometimes turn mean, the pupils in his pond-green eyes closing down to a pinpoint, a guy whose rough housing "play" left teeth marks on my arm. A guy who smoked cigarettes and marijuana daily. Did my mother know any of these things about Kevin? If she did, would she still be advising me to go on the pill? The one thing that kept me from going there was the fear of pregnancy.

"Mom! Shut up! I'm not planning on doing anything with Kevin! Ew!"

"Darling, we just want you to be safe."

I wished she would stop saying 'we.' *He* had put her up to it; I knew it.

"We want you to think about it."

* * *

After that, I didn't know what was wearing on me more, my mother's constant haranguing to go on the pill, or Kevin's insistence to go all the way, or worse, the pouting and withdrawing from me when I refused.

I was conflicted. What part of me was saying no? Kevin wanted it, my parents expected it, society was touting it, and even though none of my friends were having sex yet, a part of me could hardly resist it. Yet, to my annoyance, the deep part of me knew that I shouldn't. I thought it was God trying to spoil my good time, and I kept telling God that I didn't have to do what He said anymore either; I wasn't going back to that dumb confession.

Finally I decided to go and get the pill, just to get my mother off my back, or so I told myself. I had a girlfriend drive me over the hill to the Planned Parenthood office, where I entered through the curtained door and sat in one of the orange plastic bucket seats in the quiet linoleum lobby full of teenaged girls to wait my turn. There was no 'type' of girl there, I noticed. Quiet, pretty, demure girls sat next to bored-looking, gum-cracking made-up girls, who sat next to hippie chicks in their long granny dresses holding hands with their pony-tailed boyfriends. We may have entered that lobby with nothing in common, but when we left, we each carried a six-month supply of happy little pink pills displayed in a foil circle, like candy, and a plastic purple carrying case, all in a plain brown paper bag that we clutched to our chests as we left to go back to our separate corners of the world.

* * *

The next time my mom started bugging me about getting the pill, probably that very same day, I cut her off mid-sentence with an "I got it." This hardly registered on her face, and she started to go on, and then stopped mid-nag.

"Did you say you got it?"

"Yeah, I got it."

"B-b-but how did you do that?" She stammered. I felt some satisfaction at throwing her.

"I had someone drive me over the hill to Planned Parenthood and I got it." I was dying during this exchange.

"Well. Yes, Chris, I'm very proud of you for taking the initiative like that, and figuring out how to go about it without any help from me. It is very grown-up of you. Good girl."

I wanted to vomit.

* * *

I still had no intention of having sex. I told this to Kevin when I showed him the little purple carrying case, snapping it open to show him the cute little circle of pills. Then, impulsively, I popped one out and swallowed it.

"They said I would have to be on them a full month before they're guaranteed to be effective," I said, looking into Kevin's pale-green eyes.

Nanoseconds later, we were on my narrower-than-a-single, army-cot-sized bed Ray had built, on top of the brown felt bedspread with the orange dingle balls my mother had made, that was now developing a hole down where our feet were, from all the wear and tear it had received during this past year every time my parents left the house. We did what was now so familiar to us, effortlessly moving and kissing and touching and pressing, to an unheard, internal rhythm, the world leaving, the hurt leaving; there was just us, breathing hard in unison, our hands and mouths moving to the perfect places without our having to command them.

I didn't have to do anything; I didn't have to think or try, I just didn't stop what we had started so many times. There was that sharp unexpected pain, but then only pleasure, not only the physical so much, but that blissful tangling of our spirits that rose above us, morphing into One, a One that on a divine level could never be undone, and then floating back down and encircling us like a soft, cotton-candy cocoon. At dusk, my room darkening, sixteen and no longer a virgin, I had never felt so calm, or safe, or loved. Whatever this magic was, I wanted more, it didn't matter anymore if Kevin was right for me; *he was now*.

* * *

I remember the night I stopped believing in God.

Not long after giving into Kevin, lying in my narrow single bed, I gazed out at the clear night sky, and started my ritual of wishing on a star: "Star light, star bright, first star I see tonight..."

Here I paused. For once, I didn't really know what to wish for. When I was little, I would wish for impossible things, like meeting the Beatles, or being able to fly. Later, my wishes to the stars were like a combination of a prayer, an oral diary, and a counseling session. I talked to the stars about getting Pete Peterson to notice me, or I asked them to help my period start in eighth grade, since everyone else's had.

Now, since I had Kevin, I really didn't need anything else. I used to wish for Papa to come back, or for Ray to be nicer, but now I didn't really care.

As I stared out the window, and beyond to the heavens and the sky, instead of filling me we with a feeling expansiveness and infinity, instead of filling me with possibilities and optimism, it withdrew and turned opaque. It looked flat. Suddenly, I saw how pathetic I was, believing in this childish ritual. I was sixteen. I had reluctantly accepted the fact long before that there was no such thing as Santa Claus, and that Gogo had concocted Joey the Fairy. Why was I holding on to this ridiculous star wishing? I decided I wasn't going to bother doing it anymore. "And," I said out loud, before I knew how I would finish the sentence, "there isn't a God either."

I rolled onto my back and stared at the ceiling with trepidation. I thought about the scary declaration that had come out of me, and I knew that I meant it. My fear gave way to relief. Now, not only would I not have Ray's rules to answer to, I wouldn't have God's either. Now I could be like the rest of the family: atheist, amoral, free! They couldn't make fun of my beliefs anymore, or call me pious. I wouldn't have to say a whole rosary for missing church. I didn't need religion. I had Kevin.

I rolled back over and looked out at the stars, now only distant suns instead of points of hope, and let them go. And, like the rebellious teenager I was, I turned my back on God, and turned towards what I thought was even more freedom. That priest who gave me the full rosary for penance wasn't *all* wrong: I *was* going to have to find my own way.

* * *

But how could I find my own way if I didn't even have my driver's license?

Driving was the Key. Driving would set me free. I would never have to ask my mom or Ray for a ride again. I would never have to hear them reply 'no,' as they did ninety percent of the time, again. I would never be grounded for missing the school bus again. No more scrounging for change to catch the Greyhound bus, no more walking miles, no more sneakily hitchhiking, no more knocking on people's windows at stop signs to ask for a ride, *again.* I could get a real job, instead of just babysitting in the neighborhood, my wallet would be full of fives and tens, my closet full of cute clothes, not just from the army navy surplus, from real stores like Macy's, and my spirit would be full of freedom, blessed freedom from *them.*

I pictured myself breezily announcing to my parents that I was "going out" and after pulling out the jangly set of keys from my Indian weave bag, slinging it over my shoulder and heading out the door, ignoring their nosy questions and protests. I imagined lightly stepping into my car, *my car*, I couldn't see what it looked like yet, just that it was definitely adorable, and more importantly mine, and rolling down the highway, window down, hair blowing all over the place, radio tuned to KFRC blasting Elton John, and me singing "Oh, I finally decided my future lies... beyond the yellow brick ro-oh-oh...ah ah ah ah ah..."

My fantasy was cut into though, like a needle scratching over the Elton John LP, when I considered the reality of the catch-22 that was currently confounding me. Although I had gone through the required Driver's Training at school, I still couldn't drive well enough to get my license. This I knew to be true. In fact, the boy who had taken the behind-the-wheel part of the course with me wore a motorcycle helmet on our second day, saying he feared for his life. I needed more practice, but Ray refused to let me even *touch* either of their cars, not his Datsun pickup or my mother's black VW bug, not even if they were in the car with me.

Here was the seemingly impossible-to-solve conundrum that rolled around my head day after day: How could I learn to drive without a car, how could I get a car without a job, and how could I get a job without a car?

The first part of my problem was solved the summer before my junior year, when I got a local job at the candle factory, like a lot of kids on the coast, and got one of my friends to give me a ride. I had been Asking the universe for a job, (I can only call it asking, since I officially didn't pray anymore) *any* job, just to get me money, but I wasn't prepared for my first exposure to the world of work.

We stood in rows in the cavernous building, the atmosphere heavy with the perfume of candle wax, placing wicks in the metal canisters of hot wax that came by on conveyer belts. Sometimes we'd be moved to a table of hardened candles to shake them out of the greased molds. We worked for eight hours standing, on a piece of cardboard if we complained that our feet hurt, with two ten-minute breaks, and a half-hour lunch.

After the first day, I wanted to die.

After four days, I got demoted to the votive section. After eight days, I was fired. My shame of being fired soon turned to jubilation when they handed me a check for two hundred and fifty dollars, way more money than I had ever seen in my whole life.

* * *

I took my newfound fortune, and immediately plunked two hundred of it down on a newly painted red Opal Cadet being sold by a friend of my parents who lived up the street. I thought it was the cutest car I'd ever seen. I didn't care that it had a manual transmission, I was sure I could learn how to use a clutch. Ray reminded me that I still couldn't drive without insurance, so I called the local State Farm office, and gave them my last fifty dollars.

I was finally ready to learn how to drive.

The next problem was who was going to teach me. I begged my mom to take me out every day when she got home from work, but she always said she was too tired. I never even considered that she was perhaps not the best teacher, having received her license when she was thirty-five, and never really feeling comfortable behind the wheel. Ray wasn't interested in teaching me. I stared out of my bedroom window, frustrated, day after day, looking at my new little red car, just sitting there, waiting to be driven. Sometimes I'd sit in my car in the driveway, fiddling with the gearshift, imagining myself driving.

Finally, on a Saturday, after I'd had the car about a month, my mom gave into my constant pleading, and consented to take me out. She drove my car, with me in the passenger seat, to Sunshine Valley, a curvy narrow road that joined Montara and Moss Beach back through the canyons and horse ranches. As soon as we switched seats, my mother's nervousness was palpable. She smoked a cigarette, blowing the smoke out the window while giving me a rudimentary talk about letting out the clutch while applying the gas. She stubbed her cigarette out in the ashtray, and fumbled and shook while she fastened her seat belt. Finally she gave me the nod to start.

I turned the key to the right, taking pleasure in revving up the engine in neutral, pushed the stick to the left and up into first, and jerked and lurched the clutch, bolting the little Opal forward like the horses that surrounded us, only to stall. Back to first. Lurch, squeal, peel out; stall. Start up. Back to first. Pitch forward, hit the throttle to save it, clutch in, and second gear achieved! Thirty thrilling miles per hour, hit the breaks, and stall.

Start up again.

During this ordeal of dozens of false starts, my mother held tightly to the plastic loop-strap that hung down from the roof. I'd glance furtively at that hand, and could see her knuckles white, her nails digging into her palm. With her other hand she clutched at her neck. This posture was not giving me much encouragement or increasing my confidence.

"Mom, what are you doing? You don't have to hold onto that thing like that," I said, with a momentary glance in her direction.

"For Christ's sake, Chris! Keep your eyes on the road! And *slow down*!" She used her other hand now to brace herself against the dashboard. I braked, and the car died.

"Put...the...gear...back...in...first," my mom said slowly with extreme exaggerated measured patience that made me furious.

After about an hour, both of us angry and exhausted, we agreed the lesson should be over.

The next weekend we tried again, but this time she made a point of taking a Valium before we went out. She offered me one too, which almost tempted me after the ordeal the week before, but I politely declined. Properly drugged, my mother was a little calmer during this next session, but it was pretty much a shortened version of the first session.

This ended my driving instruction.

* * *

Kevin had his license, so he took to driving us around in my car. He'd give me impatient, condescending lessons once in a while, that I enjoyed perhaps less than my mother's coaching. Once he got so frustrated with my gear shifting that he reached over to roughly jam it into a new gear, and broke the skinny gearshift out of the socket, which luckily he knew how to fix. I guess neither of us knew enough to put oil in the engine, because after a couple of months it blew up. I had to spend all the money I'd earned at my new art gallery job to get it rebuilt.

Like the priest said, I had to find my own way. I had to teach myself how to drive; the steering wheel of my increasingly rudderless ship was in my hands. I knew I had no choice but to sneak the car out whenever I could, to practice in my neighborhood, going slowly and lurchingly, with starts and stops that mirrored my life's journey. Finally, I thought I could work the clutch well enough to pass the all-important Driving Test, the test that would determine my freedom and independence at last.

My mother drove me, in my little rattler of a car, to Daly City to take the test. Her obvious anxiety flowed out of her, filling the car with heaviness, and swirled into my veins. I almost wished I had accepted her second offer of Valium she had given me right before we left. I flunked the test out of sheer anxiety. That and turning right on a red light that said "no turn on red," having never had any lights or signs to deal with before. A couple of weeks later I tried again, and failed again, this time for taking too many tries to parallel park the car, then ending up a few feet from the curb. I didn't succeed on my third attempt either, and they said I had to wait at least six months, (they may as well have said forever) before I could try again.

* * *

I drove anyway. I felt I had no choice. I snuck the car out behind my parents' backs, and took myself where I needed to go, always afraid of getting home too late and being caught, or worse, being pulled over by a cop. I was driving myself around in my own car, just like I had imagined, but that light, breezy, Yellow Brick Road feeling of freedom was missing, and in its place was the Renegade feeling, with a frosting of fear.

* * *

Ray nailed the finishing touches on the house next door, and we moved, carrying things over piece by piece. The new house looked very much like the other one, the same rectangular box with unfinished wooden siding, only I should say rectangular *boxes,* plural. Two identical houses on the outside, joined by a graveled courtyard in between. My parents' house had the living room, kitchen, bath, and their bedroom. Cathy and I shared half of the other house, the other half being a studio for Ray. Our area included our bedrooms, which were two partially partitioned cubicles, a small living room, and a bathroom.

Now here was freedom. Our own house.

But there was no reveling for me. Instead I felt banished. I soon learned that the main house would be locked when hey weren't home, which meant no access to the kitchen for snacks. I also realized that only their house had the only real heating, with a blow heater and a wood fireplace. Our part of the house only had a coil bathroom heater, which did little to heat the house, and we were only allowed to have it on for ten minutes anyway. I did my best to try to fix up our little space and make it homey, finding a scavenged white shag carpet, and putting a waterbed in the living room to serve as a couch.

Our friends, and friends of friends, took to hanging out at our unsupervised house day and night, using it as a haven for meeting up, watching TV or smoking pot.

* * *

The car. The house. The driving. Small worries. The lack of faith in God, the lack of interest in schoolwork, the lack of direction. Meaningless. I could dull the pain and fill the void with Kevin. Kevin was my drug, Kevin was my religion, and Kevin was my Purpose for Living.

Except that I Knew — in that part of me that Knows but is often ignored, in the part of me with the clear, low, mostly unheard voice, the voice drowned out by the static of the berating worry in my head — that he Wasn't. He wasn't The One. Not even close. He wasn't the one for me in my future, and he shouldn't have been the one hanging around in my present.

Sometimes that whispering voice of reason demanded to be heard, and swirled up into my consciousness like a throbbing, banging headache. Like the time Kevin and I went camping in Yosemite with Mrs. Henson, the eccentric music teacher who befriended all the teens in Kevin's neighborhood. I should have been ecstatic, alone with Kevin, unsupervised, in a Tent of Our Own. On one of the nights Mrs. Henson let us sleep in the camper, handing us a bottle of Slo Gin with a wink and a "have fun."

When my wise-self broke through on that trip, I was sitting on Kevin's lap under the stars, the smoky scent of the campfire wafting through the chilly night air, when that voice, the exact same voice that said "robot" to me on that Fourth of July when I was twelve, penetrated my denial. This was wrong. I had no business at sixteen to be on an unsupervised camping trip, drinking and having sex with this boy, the emphasis on *this boy*.

This Yosemite Moment cast me down into my second bout of depression, my second bout of obsessive thinking. The rest of the trip was ruined; I was trying to hide my anguish as we rode around the valley floor on the tourist bus, looking up at Half Dome for stability and support, but it was useless. I couldn't fight the enemy in my head. This episode of depression had no name like 'robot,' it was just the Knowing that Kevin was no good for me, and the bout wasn't as severe in intensity or duration. After a few weeks, the feeling passed, and I was back to being in love with Kevin.

There was always an element of worry in my love though, because it seemed to take more and more to make him happy, and I was always afraid of making him mad. Nothing was more painful than being ignored by him, so I tried harder and harder to please him. I started noticing that when I was on my period he wouldn't bother hitchhiking over to my house. There was a rumor at school that he kissed another girl at a party when I wasn't there, and when I finally got up the nerve to confront him under the trees during passing time at school, he shrugged unapologetically. Instead of being thrilled to have sex with me, like he was at first, he started saying that he didn't want me to be his *only* experience.

You might think that I had more than enough reason to dump him, but I stayed with him even after I caught him with my best friend Kerry, at my own house, in a compromising sixty-nine position. I felt the moment of power, of temporarily gaining the upper hand when I flicked on the light and saw them both struggling to pull up their jeans that were pushed down around their ankles. I felt my spirit soar at Kerry's remorse and her immediate threat of suicide. I felt calm and superior as I rummaged around the medicine cabinet looking for something she could take to end it all, coming up only with some Bayer aspirin, that she dramatically downed, shaking the bottle into her mouth.

That night, I told Kevin we were through. The next day, as the three of us walked twenty miles to raise money for leukemia, I loved the feeling of Kevin tentatively trying to put his arm around me, of taking my hand and rubbing it as we walked along. I tried hard to ignore his gestures, but I was far too ravenous for any kind of affection to keep up the guise for long. By that evening, I had forgiven him officially, telling him I'd give him another chance as we sat on the stairs of Von's Cinema.

We swam along that next summer, in water that was not too tumultuous, and then we found ourselves under the influence of the heady drug called Senioritus. Kevin was a kicker on our winning football team, and I was his proud girlfriend. The buzz around the school was that we had a potential to win the championship for the first time in Half Moon Bay history, but like a lot of the other girls, the excitement was dulled, because I felt like a football widow. Kevin hardly had time to see me, and when he did, he often refused to sleep with me because the coach told the team to abstain a couple of days before the game to keep their edge on.

DeeDee Fudge, the womanly, mature head cheerleader, decided to remedy things by throwing a big party at her house for the football players and their girlfriends only. At first I didn't get one of the invitations I saw circulating, so I found her at lunch and asked her why.

"Oh, sorry Chris, I'd love for you to come, but it's for the football players and their girlfriends only."

When I reminded her that Kevin was on the team, and that I was his girlfriend, she frowned.

"Oh! Right. He's on the kick squad isn't he? I guess that counts. I just don't think of him as really being on the team, he just isn't... well, he's really not the type." She reached into the pocket of her backpack and pulled out one of the hand written invitations.

I really didn't care how I got invited, I just knew that I wanted to go to the exclusive, rare invitation-only party that everyone was talking about, and I wanted to go with Kevin.

The tentacles of electricity radiated down the unpaved Strawberry Ranch Road as Kevin and I bumped our way toward the beach. The October night was cold and clear; the entire Milky Way glowed sharply in the sky. I could see the multiple bonfires outside, and could hear the stereo blasting before we pulled up to park in the field. The song "There's Gonna be a Heartache Tonight" came out a few years later, but must have been inspired by a night with a mood like this one.

Kevin and I walked up together, but soon friends pulled us in various directions, and after a while I had lost Kevin completely in the throngs of high school kids wandering around inside and outside of the house. I was sitting on the couch in the living room when I got wrapped up in a conversation with Robert Young, a cute, funny, skinny guy on the football team, who was kind of effeminate with his gestures.

"Hey, Chris, did you know I got a new car? It's sweet. I scored a '65 Mustang, and it is completely cherry, man. It's white with a red interior."

Robert said this so close to my face that I could smell his very beery breath. He was slurring his words a little.

"I drove it here, you know. Come out and take a look at it. C'mon, Chris! It is such a beauty, I know you'll appreciate it."

"Well…I dunno." I looked around the room, my eye always in the habit of searching out Kevin. "I don't know where Kevin went, and I was sorta looking for him..."

"Aah, I just saw him go out back to smoke a doob with Chris Wade. He'll probably be out there a while. Come see my car, it'll only take a minute."

I hesitated, but I stood up and followed Robert out into the chilly air. It was a moment I would regret for a long time to come. We went past the driveway to where all the cars were parked in the field. He stopped at his car, and opened the door proudly, the light showing off the perfect interior.

"This is it!" He was glowing, but also wobbling a little.

"Wow, Robert. Nice. Really nice." I felt obligated to act like I was more impressed than I actually was. I couldn't really get that excited over a car. I was leaning against the back door, when suddenly Robert stepped out in front of me, positioning his hands on the roof of the car on either side of me.

"Uh, this probably wouldn't look too good, Robert, if Kevin came out here," I said, trying to duck under one of his arms, but he lowered his elbow, catching me, and holding me in.

"Oh, come on, Chris. Mellow out. We're friends, we're not doing anything." He was swaying from side to side, actually needing the car to hold him up.

I could have made my break. I could have probably knocked him over. But, no, I was too 'polite' for that. I was a nice girl.

"Yeah, I know, Robert," I tried to reason with him even though he was obviously drunk, "but Kevin and I have sort of been fighting a lot, and, you know, I don't want to do anything to get him mad."

The visible breath from my words had not even evaporated into the cold night air, when suddenly Kevin materialized only inches away from us. He pulled Robert away from me by the back of his Block H jacket, swung him around to face him, and pulled his fist back and slugged him in the face. Robert dropped down to his knees, but miraculously regained some composure, shot up, and started swinging his arms wildly. What seemed like the entire party had abruptly surrounded us, and people were yelling and cheering. Kevin and Robert were rolling around on the ground, grunting, fists flying.

I watched this scene with an odd detachment, as if I were observing from outside of my body. Part of me was thinking, "Oh he cares!" and part of me was thinking, "Uh-oh."

Someone pulled Kevin off of Robert, and DeeDee pushed through the crowd saying, "I knew I didn't want him at my party."

Robert stood up, brushed himself off, and wiped the blood that was trickling out of his nose with the back of his hand. He jumped into the still open door of his car and sped off. The crowd started meandering back toward the house. Only Kevin and I were left. He stood looking at me, breathing hard. I didn't know what he was going to do or say.

"That's it. I'm done. We're through. Gimme back my ring" is what he said.

Panic flowed through me, turning me cold inside, making me feel lightheaded.

"No! Wait, Kevin! It wasn't what it looked like!"

"Maybe you didn't hear me. I said, *I'm done.*" His voice was flat, devoid of emotion.

"We weren't dong anything…" I started sobbing. I was scared, and a little bit drunk, and the steely look in Kevin's eyes reflected by the moon looked mean and serious, his pupils small pinpricks. I started feeling panicky.

"Kevin, please, *don't*. Haven't I been trying lately? It's been good, hasn't it? Please! I told Robert I didn't want to go, he was just…" I was crying hard—I didn't want to be, but I was starting to lose control.

"What part of 'we're through' don't you understand?" He spat this out, and turned and walked away.

"No, please." I dropped on my knees, crying from a deep, raw part of my chest. I was terrified of what I was feeling, it was too big, and it was old, and wild. I had kept this Fear down for a long time, and now it bubbled up uncontrollably. The same blackness that swirled around me when my bedroom swarmed with flies, the Fear that was born when I was standing on the toilet begging Papa not to go, the feeling that I was alone, and that my mother, and maybe the world, was somehow pretending, robotically going through the motions, now all converged and enveloped me, and none of my tricks would work now to keep this monster at bay.

Suddenly I felt the sensation of literally wanting to jump out of my skin. I couldn't take the pain of being in my body; the effort to suppress this thing was too much. To my complete shame and sadness, the thought of suicide landed in my psyche for the first, but far from the last, time, giving me a slight relief. I could end this. I could escape. I didn't want drama and attention, like Kerry when she tried to swallow all the aspirin; I just wanted to Leave without anyone knowing, without saying goodbye.

I stood in the field alone, and could hear the ocean crashing not far away. I would walk down to the beach, and then just keep walking in; it would feel cold at first but I would just force myself to put one foot in front of the other no matter how cold it got, then I would be floating and churning, letting the waves do what they wanted; the cold would feel good when it froze my head and all this fucked up shit that was floating around in it, and then it wouldn't be long, just a gulp or two of salt going down my throat.

I actually walked down to the beach, carrying this fantasy. I remember standing in the sand, and that's it. The moon must've gone behind the clouds, because the rest of the night is too dark to remember.

* * *

I was cast down into the shadows, into the darkest part of my soul, a place I had never gone, and would not revisit for another twenty years. Every step I took felt like I was walking in thick cement. Every bite of food was like a mouthful of dust. My breath was shallow, all the colors dimmed, and that old feeling of being an observer rather than a participant was dominating me; all I could do was watch everyone talking from afar; I was invisible.

At first I tried to get Kevin back, groveling, pleading, begging him to give me another chance; I called him from the phone at my art gallery job, hiding under the big front desk so that the customers wouldn't see me crying. For a while there was no limit as to how I would humiliate myself. I gave up when I saw his arm around Cathy Prescott, an impossibly adorable freshman cheerleader with a popping bubble butt that flashed in orange dance-pants whenever she walked across the quad in her short uniform skirt.

I stopped eating.

I had been dieting since I was fourteen, but now weight was dropping off of me effortlessly. The thought of food made me nauseous, and if I did take a bite, the task of chewing and swallowing seemed impossible, and I'd often spit it out. I quickly lost twenty-five pounds, and was down to a very skinny-for-me 105. I would weigh myself for amusement, and look down at the scale with detachment.

I stopped caring.

I used to feel guilty for trying so little in school, yet still receiving As and Bs. Now I got my first F, in my senior government class. I stared at the 'F' the same way I looked at the 105 on the scale. It was unreal. I was just watching. This wasn't me. My friends started doing my assignments and turning them in with my name so that I would be able to graduate.

I started smoking.

One day in the car, as I was crying my usual lament, Kerry offered me one of her cigarettes. I took it without thinking, smoking my first cigarette as if I had been doing it all of my life. That day, I went out and bought myself a pack, and became a half-a-pack-a-day girl instantaneously.

I wanted to die.

After that first time, it was easier and easier to fantasize about suicide. It gave me relief from the Fear, the same way the violent fantasies about Ray did. I always imagined a cold bullet entering my brain, flash freezing it, and I would be free of my head's obsessive clutches. Sometimes I'd pretend I was actually going to do it, and would go into my parents' bathroom, lock the door, and line up all their pills on the counter, unscrewing each bottle one by one.

Part of me, maybe it was the part that was observing this other, suffering girl, knew all of this wasn't normal. I'd seen lots of other girls have their boyfriends dump them and they never went off the deep end. A little crying, a little whining, and they'd be on to the next guy. When I considered this, I thought I should ask for help. I didn't have God anymore; I could only turn to my mother, who somehow had not noticed that anything was wrong.

When I told her I didn't think I was functioning properly, she had a combination of surprise and worry on her face. She set me up for my first (but far from last) shrink, at the free clinic at the county hospital. I only lasted for three sessions, despite the sincere young psychologist, because sitting in the ugly, linoleum-floored waiting room full of old crazy-looking street people, made me feel worse instead of better.

I continued spiraling down, for almost three months, (though it seemed like a lifetime) and then I drove my car off the cliff at Skyline.

* * *

All my days were slow now, but this gray day a couple of days after Christmas seemed particularly sluggish. At noon, I had not bothered getting dressed, lying on the couch in my pajamas and reading a book when the phone rang. I considered not answering it, then shuffled over to the hallway in my slippers.

"Hello." My voice was flat; I barely slurred the word out.

It was my friend Cheryl, voice hopped up, on fire, agitated, excited. I held the phone away from my ear at this unwanted intrusion of drama, and I started zoning out.

"Are you listening to me? You gotta drive us over the hill right now!"

"What? Why?" I said sleepily.

"I told you. Jordan is fucking pregnant, goddamn it!"

"Really?" This was mildly interesting to me. I wondered how anyone could get pregnant when all the girls were taking free birth control pills.

"Get your ass over here and pick us up now. We have to get to the clinic!"

* * *

I went through the motions of getting dressed, putting on jeans and a sweatshirt, but didn't bother brushing my hair. Just as I was walking out into the drizzle, my neighborhood friend Kim walked up my driveway. I asked her if she wanted to go for a ride, and she shrugged yes, and got into the passenger side of my car, since she didn't have a license yet either.

I was so used to sneaking my car out now, it didn't even seem like I was sneaking. *They know*, I thought, as I turned the key in the ignition, *that I take this car out without having a license.* I tried to remember how many times I had ventured off the coast and over the hill by myself. Not too many, I decided, if any.

We headed south to Miramar, skinny wipers cutting a low pie shape on the wet, drippy windshield, the slight squeak, squeak punctuating the staccato conversation I was having with Kim as to why we were going over the hill. I pulled into the driveway, and a frantic looking Cheryl and a subdued looking Jordan, the hood on her sweatshirt pulled tightly over her head, got into the back seat of my car.

* * *

I felt a little wobbly driving on the curvy road out of town. I tried to act more confident than I was, doing my best to join in with the talk of the abortion, while trying to concentrate on the winding road. We made it to Planned Parenthood, and Cheryl got out with a protective arm around Jordan, the wind whipping Cheryl's hair, and they disappeared behind the curtained door while Kim and I waited in the car. Less than half an hour later, they were back out, Jordan visibly shaken and crying as they got into the back seat. The subdued talk of the now-impending abortion, and whether or not the boyfriend should be told, bounced back and forth like a Ping-Pong ball from the back to the front of the little rattly car, the squeak and slap of the wipers keeping the somber beat.

As we headed up Sharp Park road, I saw a lone hitchhiker, a cute boy around our age, standing forlornly with his thumb out, his brown mop of curls dripping with the rain.

"Should I pick him up, you guys?" I asked into the rear view mirror.

Jordan sniffled a 'yes' by nodding her head, which gave Kim and Cheryl the okay to say, "Yeah, yeah, pick the guy up." I clumsily pulled off to the dirt on the side of the road, and I could see him in the mirror running toward the car. Kim dove into the back seat, butt first, and the hitchhiker took the front.

"Hey, hi, like thanks a lot for picking me up you guys; really appreciate it. Hey, I'll take the back … well okay, thanks. Wow, it's really starting to rain, looks like a storm," the guy rambled amiably as he got in.

We headed up the winding mountain, the conversation, and the music on the radio, muffled by the sound of the rain hitting the tin roof of the small car. At the peak of the mountain, we came out of a ring of the very thick fog, but still in the rain, and started heading down the hill.

We glided down the first curve, the second curve, and the third big curve. Without warning, I got that feeling I had had before, that of being in a gray dream. I felt calm, except that the part of me Observing saw my hands clutching the steering wheel tight. We were two-thirds of the way down the mountain, Pacifica sprawled in front of us, when I felt the car start to hydroplane, the rear wheels floating, not any sound, and when I spun the wheel the other way to try and compensate, the car started fishtailing, and all the chatting in the car was over, and it was silent and slow motion, then the inside of the car matched the outside by turning black and white, and we were moving in jerky freeze frames, and then there was that split second eternity (it was then that I knew that we manufacture time and all its constraints) of realization when I knew I wasn't going to be able to stop what I knew was happening, and maybe there was a gleaming but fleeting pinpoint of admitting to myself that I didn't really *want* to stop it, I didn't try to steer any more, I was just going to let whatever was going to happen, happen, and I was fully aware and watching as the car sailed quietly off the side of the cliff into the gray abyss.

If I could stop the movie right here, when my little red Opal Cadet was airborne against the gray sky, with its five teenaged inhabitants in wide-eyed anticipation, I could probably label that freeze frame the lowest, yet the highest moment of my eighteen years. I had been wishing away my one precious life for the previous three months, with the selfish, shortsightedness of a frightened child, playing with it by starving myself and smoking, and now, this death wish was about to reach fruition. But during that flex time of seconds that seemed like hours, I was already sorry. I knew I didn't want to die, and I think God heard me and bashed my car up against the only skinny tree on the cliff, instead of letting us tumble to the bottom and our deaths.

We landed with a dull thud against our saving tree. It was very quiet, until suddenly Cheryl started screaming, "It's gonna blow! Get the fuck out!" while she kicked wildly on the back door that opened without argument.

I carefully and tentatively put my left pinky in my door handle, (I was too afraid to move any other part of my body) and with the slightest movement unlatched it. I leaned on the door and rolled onto the ground. I sat cross-legged in the wet and musty-smelling leaves and pine needles, the rain pattering on my hair. The main thing I was concentrating on was getting a breath—my stomach felt inside out—and all I wanted was one good breath. Then my body kicked into a self-medicating mode, and everything slowed way down, things were hazy with no sharp edges, and there were no colors, no pain, no noise, only a kind of *waa-waa* in the background when someone was trying to talk to me. I intently watched the pattern the blood dripping from my face was making on the knee of my jeans, moving my head slightly, to fill in new spots in the design on the faded denim. I was thinking, devising a plan. I could see the windshield was cracked, and I knew my chin was bleeding. All I would have to do is take my car to the shop and get the glass fixed before my parents got home. I could put a bandage on my chin, say it was for a zit, and my parents would never know that I had taken my car over the hill. I felt calm with my planned course of action, and sat in my cross-legged serenity.

"Honey? Can you hear me?" I turned my head slightly, and a motherly figure came into view. I wondered how she got down there with her heels and nylons.

"Can you get up, honey? The ambulance is here for you."

"Hmmm. No, thank you. I gotta go home." I had stuff to do. Auto body shop. Band-Aid.

"She's in shock, could someone cover her up?" The lady was saying. The background came into focus, and I could see lots of people were down there with me. Someone draped a coat over my hunched shoulders. I didn't know what they were talking about; I felt fine.

Next thing I knew, I was at the top of the hill, two grown-ups holding on to me. Everything turned into color and noise, like when your ears pop. Red and blue lights were flashing, lots of cars, lots of people talking. I wondered how all these people had known that I had crashed.

I saw Cheryl, Jordan, and Kim in a circle. Then I thought of something. I shrugged off the people who were holding me up, and walked towards my friends.

"Hey, you guys? If anyone asks, Cheryl was driving, okay? You have your license, so you won't get in trouble," I said, holding onto Kim for support. They all stared at me, and I could see revulsion in their eyes.

"God, Chris. Your face!" Cheryl blurted out.

"Yeah, I know, but I'm fine, really. But you were driving, not me. Okay?" I wanted to make sure she understood.

"Sure, okay, but you better get in the ambulance."

"Where's the hitchhiker?"

"He's already in there."

I was being led to the back of the flashing ambulance. I turned and saw my friends get into a cop car. An attendant in white put me on one of the beds, and I could see the hitchhiker next to me, already lying down with a big bloody bandage wrapped around his head.

"Hey," he said weakly, but managed to give me a thumbs up.

"Hey," I said uncertainly, as I lay down. Then the thought of those guys in the cop car sent a jolt of fear through me. This is how afraid I was. I was more afraid of being punished by Ray than I was of mutilating my face.

"I gotta go tell my friends something!"

"You can talk to them later—right now you better rest," a black guy in a white coat was saying to me.

"No, I have to go," I said, and I sat up and bolted out of the ambulance, impervious to any pain, ignoring the protest coming from the van, and pushed past the milling people towards the cop car. I knocked on the window of the black-and-white car, and the policeman, an alarmed look on his face, rolled it down I stuck my head in.

"So don't forget what we talked about, right?" I was saying none too discretely to my three friends behind the wire barricade. "About who was driving?"

The three of them simultaneously hung their heads down, but I didn't get why.

"Yeah, Chris, you better go," Kim said.

I hobbled back to the ambulance, and allowed them to strap me down. As we took off, I took the outstretched hand of the hitchhiker next to me, and squeezed it. He squeezed my hand in return.

The black guy with the kind face stared down at me. He kept talking to me, saying different variations of, "Don't you worry, you're gong to be just as pretty as you ever were, they can fix you right up."

Jeesh, I thought, it must be bad for him to keep going on like that.

* * *

While checking into Seton Hospital, there were two things I was adamant about: I wasn't driving, and I wasn't going to call my parents. I was eighteen, and had been for a few days. I was a legal adult, so there was no need to call them.

I was on a gurney, and various people talked to me as I stared up at the ceiling.

A nurse: "Honey, I think it would be better if your mom knew you were here." One doctor to another as he fiddled at my chin with some tweezers: "Should we cut the flap of skin off? Damn, hard call. Could be too large. Call a plastic surgeon." A cop: "Why don't you tell us who was driving?" I stared at him upside down. "Everyone else, well, except for the boy you picked up, admits it was you."

As the people bustled around asking me questions, I realized that I felt a sense of relief. The physical pain was overshadowing that dark emotion that had been plaguing me for almost three months. I was embarrassed to have everyone fussing over me like they were. This was nothing. Why didn't people fuss over me when I was really hurting? I was saying, "I'm sorry, I'm sorry" over and over again in my head, like a prayer-mantra; I really didn't want to die.

"Listen, sweetheart." The cop was leaning over, his face close to mine. "We know it was you driving. I'm not going to cite you for not having a license; you're going to be suffering enough. I just want to close out this report and get out of here."

"How do you know I was driving?" I finally said.

"You have pieces of the steering wheel in your chin," the cop said squinting his eyes a little and lowering his voice.

"Oh." I digested this. "Okay, yeah, it was me."

A man in a suit, rather than a white doctor's coat, rushed in. "Try to save the flap, she'll have nothing left."

"Okay, let's operate," the doctor said. "Are you sure you don't want to call your parents? You're going to be here for at least three or four days."

Up until that point I was still thinking I was going to take care of everything before they came home to dinner. Everyone was bustling around so fast I felt like I didn't have time to make a good decision. I needed to think.

"Where's my car?" I said into the room.

"It's totaled. It got towed to a junk yard," the cop said.

"Totaled? I thought the windshield was just cracked."

"The engine was half way into the front seat. It's a wonder you kids weren't killed."

I thought of my car being pulled to its grave. I would never see it again.

"Okay, call my parents," I said, giving up all hope of getting away with this.

* * *

They gave me some drugs before they operated, so the next images are cloudy and disjointed. There was the hitchhiker, standing in the doorway, a big gauzy bandage around his forehead, his arm in a sling. He smiled and gave me a 'thumbs up' with his good hand. I thought how he was the only one who didn't tell on me. Then my mom and Ray were both there, their eyebrows tied in knots of concern. I thought they were going to start yelling at me for taking the car and wrecking it, but they didn't say anything.

I was wheeled into a room with a bright spotlight, and they worked on my face for a long time, sewing it up. I was in and out of consciousness, and couldn't feel a thing. Once in a while I could catch a glimpse of what was going on in the reflection of the surgeon's glasses, and I could hear scissors cutting, but my eyes were so heavy and tired that I didn't care.

I woke up in a bed, weak sun slanting through the blinds of the window. I could hear the Lord's Prayer being recited by a low, droning voice, and could see nuns in white habits wandering around. Where was I? I thought I must be dying, with all the praying and nuns, I couldn't remembered what happened. Then the events of the previous day started seeping into my mind, and I figured out that I was in a religious hospital.

I had a lot of time to think over the next days, while they were waiting to see how bad my internal injuries were. Few people visited me, as it was Christmas vacation, so most of the people at school didn't even know I was there. I did have an ongoing phone relationship with a guy from the boys' teenaged ward who called the girls' ward randomly, and I happened to answer. We talked on the phone dozens of times a day, and he sent me up Marlboro's that I smoked in my hospital bed. He kept me distracted. We flirted and romanced on the phone.

Talking to him dulled the pain of Kevin. I couldn't help but hope he would find out what happened, and maybe I would get some sympathy. Maybe he would even come back. But something had changed; I didn't feel like thinking about him too much, or for too long. The wreck jolted something out of me. I needed to concentrate on getting better and getting back into the game of life. The doctors and nurses told me not to get out of bed without calling for assistance, because they hadn't fully diagnosed my internal injuries, but every chance I got I would gingerly slide over the side of my bed until my bare feet touched the cold floor, and would carefully stretch and bend and move, wincing a lot, to see what parts of me were broken, and what part still worked okay. I coughed and laughed over and over until I could stand the pain in my belly.

I was scared to see my face though. I knew it was bad because of how my parents' and Cathy's eyes widened with what I perceived as repulsion when they saw me.

I also noticed how everyone said I was going to be pretty again. Every time I went to the bathroom, I carefully avoided the mirror. Then one time, I accidentally caught a glimpse of myself in the aluminum paper towel dispenser. I could see three dark patches where my eyes and mouth were. Curiosity won over my denial, so I went to the mirror and looked at my eyes, carefully using my hand to cover my mouth. Not that bad. Black, swollen, but I could see that it was going to go away, some of the black was already fading to a yellowish green. Only around ten stitches around one eye, and my nose was all fat. Then I slowly lowered my hand, and had to take a sharp intake of breath when I saw what looked like a full black goatee, there were so many stitches. I gingerly put one finger up to my chin, and two little black stitches, loops carefully tied with knots, fell onto the ledge of the white porcelain sink.

I stared into the mirror, looking deeply into my own eyes. There was no Papa. There was no God. There was no Kevin. At least I had my mom and Cathy to love, and I knew they loved me, but they couldn't take care of me. I looked at my skinny beat up body and bruised and smashed face, and knew it was up to me.

CHAPTER 11

Phone Call (Half Truth, Whole Lie)

"I'm going to call our real father," Cathy said from the middle of the white shag carpet. She sat with her blue-jeaned legs crossed, a tattered piece of paper by her side. The heavy black phone was pulled as far as the cord would allow, and was nestled in Cathy's lap.

My heart, which had been in a healing dormancy for the past four years, stirred and fluttered to life. The hole, the one that I had been born with, the one I vowed to close in this lifetime, had been diminishing, protected by the bubble wrap I had personally (and I thought, artfully) created using a combination of busyness, sedation, and denial, now became exposed. A light shone from this hole, directly onto an array of carefully dimmed memories, bringing the pixelated images into focus.

I had promised myself, when I stared at my battered face in the hospital mirror, that I was through with feeling sorry for myself. Self-pity had almost gotten me killed. I was faithful to that promise, though there were a few times when I almost faltered, especially right after the wreck, back when I was still vulnerable.

* * *

When my parents sent me to San Francisco on the Greyhound to get my nose re-broken and set, I admit I felt a little sympathy for myself, but that was during the first tender weeks of wearing my shiny-new impenetrable armor of independence. I didn't expect the pain to be so bad. When the doctor put the two-pronged fork up my nostrils and pulled up with a sharp crack, I didn't expect to see the stars, not stars like the Road Runner has floating above his head after some collision, but the sensation of moving backwards through a tunnel with pinpoints of light whizzing by; it hurt so bad. I didn't expect to have to wear a full-face brace. I still would have been okay though, if it wasn't for a lady who stopped me on California Street as I was heading back to the Greyhound station, high on doctor-administered cocaine, my face covered in bandages, and chain-smoking cigarettes. She was so motherly. She took me by my shoulders saying, "You poor dear, where on earth are your parents?" Then my eyes welled up a little.

I was so mad at myself for Asking. I found a dime and a phone booth at the bus station, and lighting up another cigarette called my mother at work and asked her if she'd pick me up in San Francisco. I was starting to feel dizzy.

"I'm sorry darling, I'm working. Can you make it here to Pacifica? Then I can take you the rest of the way home." I closed my eyes and leaned against the phone booth, vowing to never ask anything from them ever again.

I had to though, one more time. After the crash, my little Opal Cadet was towed to a junkyard for scrap metal, and I was back to square one as far as needing a good job to pay for a good car to get me there. I wanted to do it on my own, I really did. I took the bus to the dealership in Pacifica where I had seen the powder blue VW bug in front, a big '$900' painted in yellow on the windshield. I went inside and asked the man if they gave out loans.

"You banged your face up pretty good. Hope that's not why you need a car." He was chuckling, but I told him that it was exactly why I needed a car, without smiling. "How old are you honey? You don't look old enough to drive, let alone borrow money." When I told him that I was eighteen, a legal adult, he smiled and said, "Sure honey, you can get a loan, but your parents will have to sign on it. Let them help you out this time," and he winked.

I had no choice but to ask. I got the expected answer from Ray. "What makes you think that we should be responsible for your loan? If you stopped paying, we'd be stuck with it. Take the bus." I had to swallow my pride and grovel. I begged and pleaded, and cajoled, and asked and asked and asked until the *No*s didn't bother me, day after day, until I wore Ray down, and he agreed to co-sign the loan papers. *That* was the last time I Asked, but it was a big one.

What helped me keep going during those first months was my mental checklist of 'To Do' items. I think maybe it was like funeral planning that gives a grieving person a purpose, a focus that helps them put one foot in front of the other. Get a new job: check. Get a new car: check. Make enough money to pay for my senior ring, prom, yearbook, ski trip, trip to Disneyland, as well as my car payment and gas: check. Get a new boyfriend: no check.

At first, I admit I held a tiny sliver of hope that I would get back with Kevin. I am even less proud to admit that I thought that holding the Sympathy Card might give me an advantageous hand. My first day back at school after the fateful Christmas vacation, I ran into him during break in the gym. He had on my favorite green sweater, and the familiar smell of Wrigley's Spearmint and unfiltered Camels floated toward me, instantly activating my arousal sensor, which I tried to ignore.

"I heard what happened" is what he said. His green eyes, made even greener by the sweater, were flat and opaque. I tried to stare deeply into those eyes, looking for a hint of recognition, of acknowledgment of our shared intimacies, but I found none; I was shut out.

"Yeah," was my witty reply, as I watched him now staring at me, not into my eyes, but roaming around the rest of my face, to my bandaged chin, to the stitches in my brow, to the nose brace.

"Well, see ya around," he said, turning and lumbering out of the gym and across the quad, his awkward gait made even more awkward because of his big motorcycle boots. He headed over to a tree where the Frosh-Soph cheerleaders hung out, their bright orange outfits glowing in the sun. He put one arm heavily and territorially around Cathy Prescott, the freshman that everyone called Bubble Butt because of the way her orange dance pants flashed and winked from beneath her short-short pleated cheerleading skirt.

She was adorable, and I hated her for it, but my heart had started to form the protective scab over itself, and didn't feel much of anything, even as I watched the two of them; I was detached, observing. I went to my trusty mental 'To Do' list, and moved 'Get a New Boyfriend' to the top, underlining it twice in red.

It didn't take long to find Geno. I spotted him because he was one of the few faces in our class that I hadn't known for all of high school, if not most of my life. He stood out from the crowd with his mop of curly black hair, and tall and husky body. I asked around and found out that he was on the wrestling team, had just moved here from Oceanside, and already had a girlfriend. I started going to the wrestling matches.

At the Valentine's Ball I maneuvered myself to be standing in a spot in the gym where he would ask me to dance, not the least self-conscious about my battered chin. He came by and pulled me towards him during a slow song. I laid my head against his hard chest, and thought I liked his smell. He smelled like sweat, but it was a clean, sweet scent. I ran my hands down the back of his damp light-blue collared work shirt, enjoying the way he seemed almost preppy in his appearance compared to Kevin. I brought my face up to look into his eyes, but the glare from his wire rimmed glasses made it impossible to see his eyes.

He came over to my house the next week with a bunch of guys that already hung out in our detached house that had become the official Party House. "So I hear you're a real Half Moon Bay girl. Why don't you show me around this town? It reminds me of Andy of Mayberry."

Get a boyfriend: check.

I drifted in with him. It wasn't like I had fallen madly in love like I had with Kevin, though love was declared on both sides. I waited a couple of months before I slept with him, and when I did give in to his constant wheedling it was more out of habit than anything else. Afterward, he told me I should have held out longer; it was classier. He didn't respect 'easy' girls. It also confused me when he said he usually wasn't attracted to "skinny girls." I had to ask him who he was talking about, and when he said me, I was jolted a little bit back into the reality of just how sick I had been, how little time had passed since I was at my bottom, and how I may not be that far from the bottom still.

I liked that Geno was sort of a nerd, but I teased him endlessly about it. He played the trumpet and wanted to be an accountant. I showed him how to separate the seeds from the leaves in a ten-dollar lid of marijuana, the Baggies that were constantly floating around our detached house. I wanted to believe he was straight and clean, so I played up my bad girl living situation more for contrast and juxtaposition than enthusiasm for my role.

Geno fit right into my story. I didn't trust him right off. The mistrust of my Papa, that fed into the mistrust of Ray, that fed into the mistrust of Kevin, fed nicely into Geno, and I wasn't surprised, in fact I might have been comforted, that first time we drove my bug down to Oceanside to visit his old friends, and he left me at a party of strangers, returning at three in the morning with his ex-girlfriend Diane Runkel in tow, who was sporting a freshly sucked purple hickey on her neck.

"Babe. It's not like that. C'mon babe, it was nothing, don't be that way." It was the first, but far from the last time I heard this patter, this banter, this bullshit. I protested, I got mad and pouted, but I couldn't feel anything enough to really care. I figured if I wanted a boyfriend, (and there was no way I could be without one at this point) that this kind of behavior went along with the territory; this was the nature of the beast.

* * *

With my heart still beating heavily at the thought of talking to my bio father, I turned to look at my sister Cathy, with her wild mop of curly hair, sitting in the middle of the carpet from my anti-vantage point of The Pit. I wanted to tell her *No, don't call*, but I knew if I did, she might do the opposite. I hadn't admitted it to myself yet, but I didn't trust her.

The Pit was the frame of the waterbed I had bought to serve as a couch in the living room of the house I had shared with Cathy for the past four years. After the Flash Flood and Fire, the name we gave the infamous party Cathy had, I covered as many old pillows as I could with the one Indian bedspread I bought from Cost Plus, and used them to fill the void that used to be occupied by the sloshy plastic water-filled mattress.

I wasn't supposed to let Cathy have the key to the house that weekend, since I was going to drive to LA with Geno, and our parents were out of town. Cathy was to stay at her friend Lindy's house — at sixteen my parents wouldn't leave her alone — but she asked me if she could have the key because she might need to get some clothes. I didn't think anything about it when I pulled the key off my ring and handed it to her.

When Geno's car broke down in Saugus, and we had to fly home unexpectedly, I walked into our house to find a raging party full of stoned high school kids oblivious to the four or five inches of water they were dancing in. Album covers were actually floating on the surface. Kids were still laying on the wet half-deflated waterbed.

Before I could get all the kids kicked out, the house caught on fire. More than once. It turned out one of Cathy's friends was a little bit of an arsonist. That Saturday night was surreal, with the house full of smoke and water, and later cops and firemen.

Instead of letting Cathy take the consequences for her lying to me, I helped her clean and repair the wrecked house all day that Sunday, before my Mom and Ray came home, using my own money for supplies. Cathy didn't thank me, but was mad that I left her alone to face my parents Sunday night.

The key may have been a little thing, a typical thing for a sister to lie about, but it was a key I should have paid attention to, a key I should have put in the lock of denial in the door marked Cathy and Geno.

Granted, I had been busy. Too busy to notice anything, too busy to feel anything. Too busy to look behind the door of denial. If you looked at the reel of film starting at my high school graduation (that's me in the powder blue cap and gown ...yes I am clutching a half-pint of vodka... my mother bought it for me) and fast forwarded it through the next two or three years until the moment I was sitting in the Pit with Cathy's finger poised above the dial of the heavy black phone, you could stop it any random place and see me doing one of three things: working, going to school, and partying in our detached house. I did all three full-time. Let's try it. Okay, stop. That's me working at the Bank of America. Me at the bank again. Me going to night school at the junior college. Me working. Random kids in our bathroom smoking pot in the middle of the night, me yelling at them to get out. Okay, work. School. Work, school, partying with Geno and gang, school.

If you look at the shots of the partying in my house, I am absent in many of the photos. Sometimes I was gone from the house up to sixteen hours a day. Geno and his friends are there. So is Cathy.

I sort of liked that Geno was at my house waiting for me, and I even liked that he took a big-brotherly attitude toward my kid sister. But it really bugged me when my mother started insisting that Cathy come along with us on the few dates that I had with Geno. She didn't like me taking away her full-time babysitter.

"It wouldn't hurt, would it, if you took your sister along to the movies with you two?" My mother asked one weekend afternoon, intercepting Geno and me at the beaded door, as we were about to leave.

"Mom! I never get any time alone with Geno. Cathy doesn't have to hang around with us every minute… no offense, Cath," I said as an aside to Cathy, who was hanging her head dejectedly.

"*You* don't mind, do you sweetheart?" She touched Geno lightly on the arm.

On the way to the movies that night, as Cathy babbled to Geno from the back seat about TV shows they had watched during the week, and the ice cream he had bought her the night before, I started getting a weird feeling. It wasn't anything I could articulate, all feelings were still pretty dead, but I made a mental note to myself to have a talk with Cathy about hanging out with Geno so much.

"It's not that I don't trust you, or anything," I said later that night. "I just think you should be doing something else, like your homework, or practicing your flute, or hanging around your own friends, instead." Then I set down the mandate I had wanted for a long time, although I didn't really know it until that moment. "I want you to promise me you won't go anywhere with Geno if I'm not there."

She did. She promised, but I felt the promise came topped with a heavy dollop of reluctance, and this reluctance landed in my heart, fertilizing all my seeds of mistrust that were planted so long ago.

The next night, during my Poli-Sci class, I was restless and agitated. I couldn't concentrate on what the professor was saying. Impulsively, I threw my books in my Indian weave bag during the break and drove home, smoking and nervous, but the feelings were down below the surface, so I wasn't sure why I felt so disturbed. When I burst through the door of our usually raucous party house, the only sound was the reverberation of the beads on the glass.

"Cath?"

Nothing. Silence.

I ran back out to my car, and lighting up another cigarette, started driving without knowing exactly where I was going. (But I did Know.) It came into my consciousness that Cathy Baker was having a rare weekday party that night, since her Mom was out of town. I drove the two minutes across the highway to her house, parked my car haphazardly in the street, and ran toward the Steve Miller music that was blasting from inside. The front porch was packed with kids that I pushed past to get into the living room, the living room that was famous around town for being completely covered in burlap. Two stoned guys I didn't recognize were half-asleep on beanbags, unaware of how loud the music was.

"You guys know Geno? Is he here?" I yelled breathlessly.

One guy tipped his baseball cap up, and I could see he was trying to focus on me.

"Geno? Oh yeah, he's here. He's out back with his girlfriend, last I seen him." He pulled his cap back down over his eyes. I bolted past them.

When I got into the back bedroom, I could see their shadowy silhouettes through the screen door. I pushed on the latch and stepped out. There they were, bathed in the yellow porch light, sitting on the brick-colored cement steps. Geno had one arm over Cathy's shoulder, and as I watched, they turned toward each other, and their lips met, very naturally I thought, as if they had kissed a thousand times. Geno's hand migrated up to the back of Cathy's head, and they mooshed their open mouths together for a good thirty seconds.

At first I was too shocked to even have this picture be able to register in my mind, but when it did, I involuntarily gasped. I didn't react beyond that sudden intake of breath though, because immediately afterward that ice-cold calm came over me, as I wondered if I looked like that when he was kissing me. They must have heard the gasp though, because they simultaneously turned and looked straight at me over their shoulders.

I could hear a weak "Babe! Wait!" from Geno as I turned and fled through the bedroom, back through the burlap living room, out into the cold night, and drove by instinct, I was so blind with grief. My head was thrumming, but I was too distraught to listen to what it was saying. Something like, *I told you, Mom, I told you I didn't want her hanging around with Geno and me, why'd you let them hang out when I wasn't home?* I felt sickened, but hardly surprised by Geno, and the thought of Cathy, the one closest to me in life betraying me was too much to bear or consider, so somehow the brunt of my anguish was directed at my mother. It was all her fault.

Of course none of this was being articulated in my brain, it was just firing and snapping as I drove to my driveway, jumped out of the car, and straight to my parents' side of the house, which was miraculously unlocked since Ray was out of town, and jumped into bed with my mother with everything on including my shoes. I let out a wail like I'd been shot.

My mother sat bolt upright exposing her nude torso.

"What? Chris? Whatever is the matter?"

I didn't answer. I let out another dramatic howl, and then broke into sobbing. My mother slowly eased down under the covers, and I buried my head in her shoulder, wiping my runny nose on her skin.

"Chris. You must tell me what's wrong. Darling, I can't help you unless you talk to me."

Between intakes of breath and sobs I blurted out, "Cathy... was... kissing... GENO!!" and I howled even louder. "She was wearing my clothes! I told you I didn't want her hanging around him, *I told you!*"

As I was crying, I was slightly anticipating my moment of victory, of vindication. Finally, my mother was going to be on my side for once, instead of Cathy's. Finally, she was going to see her error for making me take Cathy with me everywhere I went with Geno. Finally, I would get my due, instead of always being told to compensate for my little sister. And finally, my mother would have to lay down some moral guidelines, to give some me some wisdom; something she had never done, but that I yearned for.

I cried longer than I needed to, waiting for the sympathy, the indignation, the promise of putting things right; that never came. She said nothing. I cried louder, and finally she said, "That's enough now."

At that moment, the bedroom door opened, and to my surprise, in came Cathy. Just as I had, she got into the other side of the bed with all her clothes on, including her shoes.

She nuzzled her face in my mother's other bare shoulder and started crying too.

My mother stared straight up at the embroidered canopy over her bed, a sobbing daughter under each arm. I waited for some sort of apology or recognition from Cathy, outraged that *she* was acting as if she were the one wronged somehow.

Decisively, my mother spoke, but not what I wanted to hear.

"That's enough now girls. I want you to be nice to each other. Now make up and go to bed."

A big red exclamation mark popped out of my head, and hovered above me as I left my mother's side of the house, and numbly crunched across the courtyard to our house, saying nothing to Cathy. There were no rules. I mean, there were plenty of rules, and punishments: no leaving lights on, no taking food or turning the heater on without permission; sure, there were plenty of rules like that.

But no Real Rules. My parents let us drink and smoke pot, and when they had dinner parties they all kissed each other's spouses. They didn't care if our boyfriends spent the night. Part of me thought this must all be all right, since my parents let it go on, but part of me, maybe the part that got trained in Sin and Guilt as a little girl, or maybe it was just the moral compass I was born with, knew that it wasn't

(I didn't know Cathy was sleeping with Geno, but she was. I wouldn't know that until years later when she blurted out something about rape. It was years later still that I learned that there were hundreds of "rapes" that lasted over a three-year period.)

* * *

Now I looked at my sister and plotted my move, trying to outmaneuver the sister I thought I knew, but didn't know at all. There was nothing I wanted less at that moment than to talk to my biological father. I no longer thought of, or referred to him as Papa; just hearing or thinking the double beat of those syllables was enough to shroud me in shame for ever loving and trusting the man, and despair because of the aching hole in my heart since he left.

No, the man I remembered, the vague wavy figure in my mind, the handsome one I gazed at while he was shaving in the steamy bathroom mirror, was now only his first name, Toni, in my mind, and Toni when I had to mention him out loud, which was as little as possible. The double syllabic beat of *Papa*, the emphasis on the second pa, like the pa-rum-*pa-pa*-pum of the little drummer boy, terrorized me.

I knew I had to act nonchalant. If I protested too much, it would only spur Cathy on. I considered grabbing at the tattered piece of paper. I had seen her going through some phone books when we were at one of the many of my parents' friends' parties, the parties where we were told to go watch TV in the back bedroom while the adults carried on with their drinking and eating. I didn't pay much attention to her as she thumbed through the books, scribbling and drawing on some scrap paper. Now I knew what she had been up to.

"Cathy, forget it, you're crazy," I said with as much boredom in my voice as I could muster. She shot me a smirk that said, *Oh yeah, watch me.*

I tried not to look at her as she dialed the number, instead staring at the hanging candle above me, displacing my anger at Cathy at the moment to Geno, and the time he got my pet rat stoned by blowing smoke in his face, then terrorized him by putting him up on the candle and twisting it around until the rat was dizzy and clinging on for life.

"Yes, I'm looking for Toni Sottile. Is this is house? Toni Sottile. S-O-T-T-I-L-E."

I was surprised that Cathy even remembered how to spell our old last name. Hearing it said out loud washed a wave of nostalgia over me. My mind went back to second grade, when I was learning how to write the capital cursive "S" for my last name.

"Who is this? Mike? Oh, you must be Toni's brother. This is Toni's daughter, Cathy. Could you give me his number please?" She took the cap off the pen with her teeth. "Yes, three-eight-eight..."

When Cathy hung up the phone, I felt the inevitability of what was about to happen, and I lost my feigned cool.

"Cathy, DON'T!! I'm not going to talk to him, please! Don't' you dare say I'm here, I'll leave, I swear to God."

Her look said, *oh please, you'll have to do better than that*. She smiled, and in a sing-song kind of voice said,

"I'm cal-ling!"

As I listened to the slow click-click-clicking of the dial, I felt the anxiety spread down my limbs. The room was cold, but not cold enough to make my hands feel all tingly. I wondered if I still had the two quarters in the bottom of my backpack so I could buy enough gas to get over to Geno's house.

"Yes, hello, is this the residence of Toni Sottile? It is? May I speak to him please? This is his daughter calling. No, I'm not mistaken."

At this pause, I shot straight up onto my knees staring at Cathy, and her identical brown eyes met mine and stared right back.

"Yeah?" Cathy went on. "Well, I'm his daughter too." Both our eyes simultaneously grew wider, communicating the revelation that he had other kids.

"Hello? Is this Toni Sottile? This is your daughter. No, Cathy! Yes, that's right!"

Cathy had stood up, taking the phone by two fingers and placing it back on the stand by the door. She was swaying back and forth, a look of devilish delight on her round baby face. Her mop of blond curls bobbed during her animated conversation.

But I wasn't listening to a word she said. I didn't run out of the house, but I had vacated, as I tended to do, when a situation was too painful to be present. I was lying back down on my back in The Pit, blocking out the room, and Cathy's voice, and trying to stuff down the welling jitters that started deep in the pit of my stomach, that were hurting my chest, that would turn into tears if I let them reach my throat. I came back into the room when she got to the inevitable part, the part I was dreading: the part where she mentioned me.

"Christina? You mean Chris?" I sat up again, and she looked over at me. I shook my head back and forth with such force that my earrings slapped me in the face. My palm was up like a traffic cop stopping traffic, also waving a frenetic 'no'. She watched my frantic protestations for a second and then turned her attention back to the phone.

"Yeah, she's here. Hold on a second, I'll get her for you."

My eyes narrowed to I'll-never-forgive-you-for-this slits, but the resignation had set in. I slowly climbed out of The Pit, and heavily shuffled across the carpet in my socks, Cathy jerking her head in a *hurry up* motion. I snatched the receiver roughly out of Cathy's outstretched hand.

Cathy put her hand up to her mouth to stifle a giggle.

I blew my bangs out of my face, put the phone up to my ear, and gave my father, the father I hadn't spoken to in at least a decade and a half, a composed, cold, single word.

"Hello?"

"Hello, Christina?" I heard the same nasally voice. The still-thick Italian accent startling me. "*Come stai?*"

Cathy was watching me intently, so I turned my back to her and faced the wall for privacy. I didn't want to give her the satisfaction of my discomfort.

Toni started throwing me a rapid-fire of superficial questions, half in English, half in Italian; how is your mother, are you doing well in school, how tall are you? I answered in mumbled monosyllables. Everything was going too fast, I wasn't really there, my mind was split, half of it racing forward to "Are you going to be my Dad now?" and the other half on a parallel track racing backwards to "You left me and I hate you," and I was so confused by the simultaneous love and repulsion that I felt that I couldn't really get my head synchronized with my mouth, until he got to that one question, the question that shimmered brightly with meaning, the question that jerked me roughly back into my body, whether I liked it or not.

"And how is your brother, George?"

That's when all the mental gymnastics stopped. I snapped sharply into the moment, acutely aware of every knothole in the rough pine paneling, of the different shades of green in the bamboo beads that hung silently against the glass door. Everything slowed way down, and a deep, dark, swelling wave of Knowing was right underneath my ribs; a wave that I knew could envelope me, so I tried desperately to ride on top.

"My *brother* George? You mean my *uncle*."

This came out thickly, like my mouth was full of molasses.

"No, your brother! Christina! You mean to say they never told you? My God!"

"What?"

I was buying time, trying to surf that wave, knowing that if I let my mind run free for only a second, then droplets from that roiling surge would leak into my brain and I would have to face the Truth, that I already Knew. If I let myself see it, I would also have to admit that up to this point in my life, everyone important to me had betrayed me. I gripped tight to the moment, turning so that the phone cord wrapped around my body, only allowing myself to wonder what made the cord keep its curl no matter how hard I pulled on it.

"He's fine. George is fine, but you mean my uncle. George is my *uncle*."

I already Knew of course. I knew the second Toni uttered the words "your brother." Right then the computer in my brain went rifling through its database at lightning speed, pulling out files of archival doubts about my uncle being younger than me, pausing at the file when Mrs. Graham marveled at the likeness in our appearance, seeking out the file where George and I calculated that Gogo was almost as old as The Oldest Woman to Ever Give Birth in *Ripley's Believe It or Not*, and even going way back to my old and tattered baby files, the ones that are usually closed, but still faithfully stored, and plucking out one where I was less than two and rubbing my mother's pregnant tummy. My brain gathered these files and had them stacked neatly, ready for me to review, but my heart turned away, trying to protect itself. If I just kept repeating the word 'uncle' to my father, I wouldn't have to look at the tidy stack of brain-folders my mind had produced, each file labeled "Brother."

There was a silence, and I couldn't stand the vacuum of that silence between my father and me; the void that had been there for sixteen years was already too huge to comprehend. So I filled it with the very question I didn't want to ask.

"Never told me what?"

I felt my face burning, and I had stopped twirling around and stared fixedly at the base of the phone. I didn't want to move again until the talk was over.

"Christina, perhaps soon we can meet and talk in person." I suddenly wanted very badly to end this conversation, to get off the phone and talk to Cathy. I was glad he didn't answer my question. I didn't trust him, and wouldn't have believed him anyway.

"Yeah, maybe we can. Okay, it was nice talking to you again." I hated myself for being so polite, after all the times I had fantasized about screaming at him.

"I would like that very much Christina. My God, if you only knew how many times I have thought of you."

Right.

* * *

I quickly spun around to unwrap the cord from my body, slammed the phone down, and turned to face Cathy. The thought of yelling at her for orchestrating this latest uncomfortable drama was overshadowed by three of the words that Toni had said: *your brother, George.*

Before I even spoke, I was digesting very small pieces of what I knew to be the Truth, revealed to me by my long lost father.

"Cathy, did he say anything to you about George being our brother?"

"Yeah, he did say that, but I thought he was just getting mixed up."

"How could he get mixed up with that? Hello, he's our *father.*"

Cathy and I looked each other in the eye for a good half a minute, communicating silently. Then we started bouncing off each other in a verbal volley at lighting speed.

"He does..."

"...look exactly like us. I always thought how it's weird that..."

"...his age is right in between us. And Gogo..."

"...always seemed too old to be a mother... My teacher said..."

"...so did my friends. It's too weird to have an uncle younger than you."

I ran into the bedroom and plucked a photograph of George off of my corkboard. I came out and held it next to my face.

"George is our brother." The proclamation had been made, and that moment we both accepted the fact, before confirming this story with our mother.

I had to move, I had to leave that room. I couldn't think in there, it was too heavy and saturated with sentiments I couldn't name but could feel echoing off the walls.

"Let's go for a drive." I rummaged for my keys in the bottom of my backpack.

I drove Cathy around and around the block in my bug, both of us smoking cigarettes, one after the other, the windows rolled down and the cold, coastal night fog coming into the car. We still only took in little bits of what had happened. We had spoken to our father. George was our brother. Any ramifications beyond those facts were left unspoken, but we decided we had to tell our mother what had transpired, and we had to tell her that very night, even though by now it was well past midnight.

I slapped my open palm on the glass of their locked door. This was unheard of; I had probably never knocked on their door in the night since we had moved to the double house.

"Mom, open up!" Now we were both yelling.

Finally the shadowy figure of my mother came to the door, pulling on her sweats, her cigarette case in hand.

"What on earth?" I could see by the dim light shining from our house that face was drawn with worry. She didn't have her glasses on.

"We have to talk to you," I said, tugging on her sleeve.

"Just a minute. What is it? Is something wrong?" She disappeared for a minute, than came back with her glasses on and followed us across the gravel courtyard to our house. She came in and sat on the edge of The Pit. Cathy sat cross-legged on the rug, but I remained standing.

"What's the matter?" she asked again, snapping open her vinyl cigarette case and putting a cigarette in her mouth. When she held the Bic to light the end, I could see she was trembling slightly; I didn't know if it was because of the cold room, or because of waking her in the night. She inhaled deeply, and blew the smoke out in a thin plume.

"Is George our brother?" I said it directly to her, no prelude, staring at her mouth. I thought of how she had lied to me all that time about having false teeth. She was hunched up in almost a fetal position, and I saw her body relax slightly after I had asked the question that now hung frozen in the cold air of the room along with the puffs of fog our breathing made, and my mother's Camel. She took another long, sucking drag off her cigarette, and exhaled the smoke and the answer all at once.

"Yessss." It came out like a hiss. Like an old beach ball finally being deflated after a summer of fun. She glanced at both Cathy and me, and took another drag.

"WHAT?!!" Cathy and I fairly shrieked in unison, though we had been discussing the revelation for hours now. The velocity was partly about the confirmation, but mostly to impart to our mother our sense of outrage.

The room stood silent now, slightly reverberating from our scream. My mother continued smoking, and Cathy and I stared at her, waiting for some sort of explanation. I looked at this woman sitting in black sweats on the edge of my broken-down waterbed, her blonde curly hair flattened a little from sleeping, the expression in her eyes covered by the glare the table lamp made on her glasses, sucking on a cigarette like a baby on a pacifier, and wondered *who is this woman*? The Robot feeling I had had a decade before resurfaced from the depths of my soul, only now I didn't feel like I was crazy, now I understood.

I suddenly felt very tired, and very cold. I was shaking, and put my hands under my armpits to keep them warm. I didn't really care what she said. I wanted to go to bed.

After one of the slowest minutes in my life, she finally spoke.

"You mustn't tell George under any circumstances." This was said with my mother's Stern Look, her British accent a little more clipped than usual, indicating that she meant business. She looked back and forth between Cathy's face and mine.

"Never. Is that understood?"

Cathy and I both shook our heads up and down solemnly, but at that moment I didn't understand the ramifications of what I was agreeing to. I didn't realize yet that I had any choice but to agree. With that nod of the head, the huge burden of the lie that my mother had been carrying on her back in a pack so gigantic that it hunched her over was now partially transferred to me. I could almost see my mother sitting up a little straighter, the curve of her spine relaxing with the weight released, her head held a little higher, as I agreed to carry some of the load. As soon as I hunched it up on my back I was shocked at how heavy it was, like an anvil had been placed on my shoulders. I thought I could handle it though; I was strong. Little did I know that every step I carried this weight weakened my heart, the heart that still had the hole in it that I had been trying to fix since before I was born.

"I'm going to go tell Dad." As my mother said this last shocking statement, she stood up, and I thought I detected a little spring in her step. Cathy and I stared at her speechless. She hadn't even told her husband? She left the house, the wooden beads on the door rattling noisily in the quiet night.

Part IV

Aftermath

CHAPTER 12

Truth Surfaces (Don't Say Uncle)

"Chris, Shannon and I are going to Mill Valley tomorrow to see if we can spy on Toni. I've got his address, *and* the address of a sewing shop that might be his wife's. Come with us, it's going to be fun!"

I took my eyes off the TV and shifted them over to Cathy across the breakfast table, without moving my head. It was the same table we had always had; only now it was in a new house. Since that fateful phone call to Toni, we had moved one last time as a family, to a beautiful house with large decks and sweeping ocean views, in the next little coastal town of Montara. Now we had all the amenities, like a dishwasher, washer and dryer, carpeting, heating, white stucco walls, kitchen cabinets, and a real room for each of us downstairs, instead of the Spartan existence we were used to, the reason being that we were never supposed to live in this house. Ray had built it for spec, but we ended up living in it for a couple of years while he built another house for my mother and himself, three hours north in Hopland. As soon as Cathy graduated from high school, my mother and Ray were leaving.

The little black-and-white TV sitting on top of the table was on, showing President Ford buttering his own English muffin in the kitchen of the White House, while Cathy and I simultaneously ate our own breakfast of sardines on toast. Things had changed. There was no longer the oppressive atmosphere of the meal table, because Ray was gone most of the time now, building the new house. We ate when we liked. We could change the channel on the TV. The only time a current of tenseness vibrated through the house was a couple of days before Ray was coming home for a weekend, when my mother started nervously scurrying about, telling us to pick up this, and clean that. *"Your father's coming home,"* she would constantly repeat, as if this meant something to us.

"I'm not going to Mill Valley to spy on Toni. I couldn't care less what he's doing. Fuck him." I said this with my mouth full of sardines, my eyes back on the television.

"Oh, Chris, why are you always so mad?" Cathy asked over her tea mug.

I narrowed my eyes at her. Hearing that question made me more mad than I already was. My mother and Cathy sensed this, and so they asked me constantly.

In the last year or so, since I had found out for certain that Toni had been living only an hour away from us, all the resentments I thought I had carefully buried jutted out through the surface. Of course I had already known that he had never bothered to contact me all those years, but now the dreamy memory I had of him when I was four changed to a concrete reality. He was here, right here in the Bay Area. He had been here all this time. He was remarried and had two kids. Two kids not much younger than Cathy and me, two kids that called him Papa instead of me, two kids that hadn't even known that Cathy and I existed, let alone George.

George. *My brother George.* I only let this phrase tumble around in my head, I rarely spoke the words out loud, although I had let The Secret leak to a couple of my friends, and so had Cathy. I had been lying to George about the monumental secret I held regarding his heritage for over a year now, and so had the friends we had told. I didn't even realize how much I resented my mother's mandate to lie to George. It never occurred to me that my mother was making me furious.

No, now all my anger, a roiling, raging, out-of-control thing that intensified when I drank, was directed at Toni. Ray no longer bothered me, except during the occasional times he was home. The thought of Cathy betraying me was too painful to even acknowledge, so I didn't know that she helped fuel my rage either. My outrage at my mother and Cathy stayed simmering on a burner so far back that I couldn't even see the steam; the pot at the front of my Anger Stove was definitely Toni.

I still distracted myself from the monster inside with school and work, and I had saved enough money to go to Europe for a couple of months with my friend T. During the first week in Paris, and over eggs and fries in Madrid, I cried uncontrollably, my usually hardened anger dissolving into tears on foreign soil. I didn't know why. I didn't know that Geno was at home sleeping with Cathy. I didn't know that I was homesick for my mother, the mother I thought I had before I realized that she had been lying to me all of my life and had given her son away, or homesick for the father I never had.

Now, again, Cathy was asking why I was so mad, mimicking my mother's constant query to me. "*Darling—*" it was always prefaced with *Darling—* "why are you so angry all the time? What is wrong with you? What happened to my Sweet Chris?"

As it was designed to do, this line of questioning splashed a wash of guilt and shame over me. I wasn't pleasing her. Anger was bad. Make mental note to stuff anger at all costs. Cathy could read me like a book, and used the same tactics my mother used to her advantage.

"Why am I mad? Who are you, Mom? I'm sick of you guys asking me that all the time. How about this: Why aren't *you* mad? This guy abandoned you before you were even born, never bothering to see or talk to you even once. Now you're going to drive off to Mill Valley and try to catch a glimpse of this Exalted Human just because he got mom pregnant? Go ahead and go if you want to, but I am *out.*"

Cathy considered this while chewing her toast.

"Okay. Fine. But I'm going."

"Go ahead."

I knew she wanted me to go partially because she had just started driving and this was a little bit of a complicated jaunt for her. She didn't care if I saw Toni or not—she needed my help, as she always did. I kept my eyes on the TV.

"How do you get there?" she finally asked.

* * *

Shannon was from our old Moss Beach neighborhood and had become like part of the family, hanging out at our house all the time. But now Shannon was even more like part of the family—she was George's girlfriend. Just like a good family member, she held The Secret, and lied to her boyfriend, her first lover.

I watched them leave in Cathy's copper-colored junky little car from the deck of the house. Cathy sounded the ooga horn she had installed and honked constantly, *ah-OOO-ga*, as they rattled down the steep driveway, waving their hands out of the rolled-down windows, music blasting from the eight-track inside. Halfway down the hill she stopped the car and yelled out the window.

"Are you sure you don't want to come?"

I waved her on, shaking my head *No*. I watched them until I couldn't see them anymore. I waved again when I thought I saw them down on the highway, but they didn't see me, and sped away, heading north.

I shuffled back into the house in my slippers, with nothing in particular to do that day. I had the house to myself since my mom was visiting Ray in Hopland. I went down to my room and flopped down on my bed that was covered the new red bandana bedspread that I had sewed, with all the pillows from The Pit that I had covered to match. I stared up at the ceiling where I had tacked up a huge *Romeo and Juliet* poster.

I tried to imagine the meeting that might take place that day between Cathy and the father she had never met. Would he kiss her and say *Te amo* like he used to do to me? I wondered if he looked old now, since he was getting close to fifty.

I rolled off the bed, and put a Cat Stevens album on the turntable in my room, then flopped back down on the bed, trying to concentrate on the music, waiting for it to transport me somewhere else. I did this most of the day, only leaving my room to get a spoonful of peanut butter out of the jar every once in a while, or to smoke a cigarette on the deck while I looked down at the turbulent gray ocean below.

There were a couple of times during that long day that I went below the surface, and panicked when I could feel myself unable to breathe, drowning in my own emotions. The vastness of these dark waters caused my head to swim and my throat to constrict, and the endless flood of tears that I could feel pushing behind my eyeballs so alarmed me that quickly swam toward the solid rock of anger, where I could stand sure, on solid and high footing, looking down from my place of superiority to the tumultuous waters of emotion that swirled and churned below me like the ocean below our house.

By the time the light started to fade at the end of the day, I was drained and tired. I had smoked too much and eaten too little. I was sluggish from lack of activity. I had never bothered to get fully dressed or wash my face. Every time I heard the sound of a distant car engine, I would look out of the sliding glass door to see if it was Cathy's little car rumbling up the road, a habit I had acquired a long time ago in Chicago, when I used to spend my days looking out of the window to hasten my father's return.

I had gone through many albums that day, and I was listening to Neil Young's plaintive wail of "*old man, look at my life, I'm a lot like you were*" when Cathy burst into my room, fresh faced, red-cheeked and giggling, the adrenaline of her adventure obviously still coursing through her.

With some effort, I propped myself up on one elbow, trying to appear nonchalant though my heart was pounding. Cathy could read me, and sensing my anxiousness, gave me nothing.

"Hey. What are you doing? Did you eat yet?" Cathy said by way of greeting, making no move to take off her tan cord jacket.

"So?" I said, raising my eyebrows.

"So what?" she shrugged.

I rolled over on my side, turning my back to her, mad that she was making me ask, mad that I had to admit to her that I cared enough to ask.

"I'm going to the kitchen to see if there's anything to eat," she called from the hallway.

My curiosity got the better of me, and I shot straight up on my bed cross-legged, and yelled to her.

"Cath-eeee! Come on! Quit it! What happened?"

She called down the stairs, "Well, you said you didn't want to come, that you couldn't care less—why do you care so much now?"

I flung myself back down, fuming over her teasing. A few minutes later she relented, and came back downstairs, flopping herself down on her stomach on my bed, and her story started tumbling out, fast and furious, the way she always talked when words weren't immediate enough.

"Well he's cute and his accent is really strong, and when me and Shannon went up to the door he hugged me right away, I mean he knew for sure which one was his daughter, and I met his wife Regina; I met her *first* actually, and as soon as she saw me she knew it was me and she started crying, and she's nice, and at first we thought he was a perv, you know, because he was staring right at Shannon's crotch, but then we figured out it was..."

"Wait! Slow down! A perv? Start the story at the beginning!"

"Okay. Well, at first we met his wife, Regina, at the sewing shop. We were sitting outside in the car and she saw us. She came out and knew right away who I was, and started crying and hugging me, saying that she remembered the day I was born, which is kind of weird, isn't it? Anyway, she took me up to their house to introduce me to him. As soon as I saw his eyes, oh Chris, you can so totally tell he's our father; he looks just like us. He said 'Caht-tee' in his Italian accent, and hugged and kissed me on both my cheeks. We went in and sat in their living room. It's a really nice house, Chris; you should see it! It's up in the mountains in the redwoods, with huge windows looking over the valley, with fancy-ish furniture. He must be rich or something."

Oh, so he had money, too? I knew he had never paid child support. The camera lens in my mind suddenly snapped on an Envy Green filter as I imagined his *other* kids, the kids he obviously liked better than us, drinking cappuccinos with whipped cream while we had to gag down powdered milk. Jade and lime images floated through my mind, of the *favored* children being showered with designer clothes while I saved up my babysitting money to buy a skirt from the Sears catalog; of *those* kids lounging on expensive Italian furniture while we got yelled at for leaning on the arm of the couch Ray had scrounged at the dump, of *those* kids living in a castle in Emerald City while we suffered in the sixty-dollars-a-month rental in the middle of the olive-green artichoke field. I was so caught up in my green fantasies that I had stopped listening to Cathy—vacating, as I tended to do. Cathy paused, waiting for me to come back.

"Yeah, go on." I forced myself back to the present, embarrassed at being caught.

"So, yeah, we just had a really good chat, and we ate biscotti and drank cappuccinos, and Toni was asking all kinds of questions about you and George. He said he could still remember you as a little girl, and how he had watched this home movie of you a bunch of times. I think he said you were swimming or something ..."

An image of Toni sitting alone in a darkened room floated into my head view, his handsome but sad face half lit from below by the flickering projector, the only sound in the room the *tic tic tic* of the film threading through the spools. I knew exactly what movie Cathy was talking about—I remembered Toni filming the three-year-old me in my pink polka-dot bikini when we were on that trip to California, in San Diego. I was showing off for the camera by framing my face with my little doughnut floatie, splashing water and laughing. Could I imagine Toni crying while he was watching this? No, I could not.

"Yeah, whatever. What did he say about George?"

"Well, he went on and on about how he couldn't believe that we never knew he was our brother until he told us. He said he thought for *sure* the secret would have come out by now. He's sort of pissed off that George still doesn't know the truth about who his real parents are, and he said he wanted to tell him..."

A wave of panic washed over me at the thought of George finding out. Not only who his parents were, but that they lied to him all this time, and now I was lying too.

"No! He can't! George would die! Mom told us not to!"

"I know! I mean it's weird enough for us to find out that George is our brother, but think of him! Oh my God, he's not even Polish; he's Italian! That alone would freak him out enough. I tried to explain all this to Toni, and I told him how Mom made us promise not to tell, but he doesn't seem to be buying it. He says he wants to tell 'his son' the truth."

"Oh my God."

We looked each other in the eyes in silence, our think-alike sibling minds simultaneously running ahead into the unknown future, skipping and bumping over assumptions that filled us with dread and unfounded, but inherited, Fear of the Truth. Both of us made a mental note to try and Control the Situation, and moved this burden to the top of our To Do list. The problem safely taken on as my own to fix, I returned to the present.

"So what about the other kids? Did you meet them?"

Asking this question turned the rotating Christmas tree color wheel of my mind back to green. Only morbid curiosity drove me to ask any details about the kids that Toni obviously preferred to us.

"No, they weren't there. I think they got them out of the house when they knew we were coming. I saw their pictures on the wall though. Marco is the boy, he's the oldest, and Laura is the girl, only a year or two younger. It's spelled like 'Laura,' but they pronounce it *Lao-ooh-rra*. They don't look exactly like us, but they're cute, and you can tell we're related. I can't believe we have another brother and sister we didn't know about!"

"Yeah, it's great," I said, trying to quell my billowing envy.

"You know, Marco's only like a year younger than me, and I was figuring it out, and Toni must've gotten married again while Mom was still pregnant with me!"

All my porcupine quills stood on end. Contrary to popular belief, a porcupine cannot throw its quills at attackers, they can only be released on contact, and since Toni wasn't in the room with me, I could only sit there like the big, bristled rodent.

"Oh, nice. Mom is stuck in Chicago in that gross, dinky apartment with Gogo and Beba, two kids and one on the way, and Toni is off having a wedding and new babies in sunny California."

"Oh, Chris. So what?" Cathy rolled over on her back and stared at my grainy, black-and-white *Romeo and Juliet* poster. I had to memorize a couple of lines from the prologue to that play in eighth grade, and they floated through my head like a cloud. *"Two households both alike in dignity...from ancient grudge break to new mutiny."* For that second, it was like Shakespeare was talking to me, and the relief of forgiving him, and being grudge-free like Cathy, was tangible and delicious, but the misty feeling passed through quickly.

"Okay, whatever." I was quickly getting tired from this conversation. "Oh yeah, what about the perv part?"

"Oh yeah, oh my God." Cathy sat up and was laughing, her head thrown back making silent little gasps, her wild blond curls shaking.

"Yeah, so Shannon and I were sitting on the couch across from him, right? Shannon had her shoes off, and was sitting cross-legged, and I noticed a couple of times that Toni was staring right at her crotch, I mean *right at it*, while he was talking to us! At first I thought I was imagining it, but then he would just stare, like for a minute at a time."

"Oh my God, do you think he was really checking her out?" A little cold feeling twinkled through me, but I couldn't recognize if it was disgust or excitement, or maybe a little of both.

"I sort of did. She had these tight, white pants on..."

My mind wandered to the time when Shannon "accidentally" French-kissed Ray on New Years. That was her first kiss; George was technically her second. She said she did it because that's how she thought people kissed.

"...So when we got out to the car, I asked Shannon what she thought of him, and she said she could barely concentrate on what he was saying because he was staring so pointedly between her legs. I said, yeah, I had noticed it too, and then we both looked down at her crotch, and there was a huge red splotch of period blood! We both gasped, and then I was laughing hysterically while she was going, 'Oh my God, oh my God, the couch was white too, oh my God what does he think?' Can you imagine the embarrassment?"

At first I tried to hold it in, but then a little chuckle started in the pit of my stomach, worked its way up to my mouth, and burst out. I started laughing so hard that all the tension of that long, dreary day, all my anger at Toni, all my resentment towards his rich house and new family, dissolved into streams of giggles that emanated out of my body, and, bouncing off Cathy, gained momentum, and then ricocheted back through me again. I was laughing way harder than the story warranted. The laughter felt like a wonderful healing balm, but I didn't want to heal. I fought for control, trying to swim back to my solid rock of anger. Finally I regained composure.

"Well, I'm glad you had a good time and all, but I'm never going to go over there. Never."

* * *

A year later, I was sitting in Toni's living room.

I can't remember the moment my heart softened, or what magic word Toni or Cathy had said that turned the key to the somewhat flexible chain armor that encased it, but somehow, some form of Grace had worked its way through. I hadn't absolved Toni from his crimes, the actions I self-centeredly took personally, but there was a very small, feathery seed of forgiveness that perched on this opening to my heart, waiting for me to plant in the hole that was dug for it so long ago.

I also don't remember the first moment I saw my father after so many years. I suppose I got out of the car, and maybe when we got to the front door, he swung it wide-open wide with a big grin on his face, but I don't know. I let the instant pass unrecorded in my memory, more than likely drowned out by the turbulent, gyrating thoughts bouncing around in my monkey mind at the time.

I do remember waiting for him in his living room that day though. The tall, beamed ceiling made room for huge picture windows looking out over a sweeping view of Mill Valley. Majestic redwood trees surrounded the house, and the scent wafting in from the open sliding glass door that led to the deck reminded me of Girl Scout camp— cool and woodsy.

I was looking at a photograph, blown up to a big 8x10, preserved in an ornate white and gold frame. It stood propped up on the shiny mahogany end table, where I guessed it had resided for a couple of decades. The formal wedding picture was in black and white, with slight coloring added so that the skin was a gray-pink, the cheeks a little overly rosy. The groom, my father, was wearing a light-colored suit, and had his arms protectively, almost territorially it seemed to me, around his bride's small waist. His expression was neutral. I picked the portrait up and stared into my father's face, trying to detect a hint of emotion, but Toni's eyes stared at the camera unwaveringly, giving away nothing. The bride looked radiant, as brides tend to look, the obligatory white gown fanning out in front of her into a full three-sixty-degree circle. Her eyes were cast down demurely. She didn't look anything like my mother.

I wondered idly about the photo being snapped while my mother was still pregnant with Cathy, maybe even still married. Was that polygamy? I had never seen a photograph to preserve my mother and father's wedding day because none existed. Maybe the day was never meant to be preserved. When Papa first left me back in blue Chicago, I had asked my mother if she had a picture of herself in a wedding dress. She told me that she got married "at the Town Hall, or some such thing," that she had worn a suit, and had taken no pictures. After that, I started obsessively drawing pictures of brides with veils and bouquets, and grooms in suits, as best as I could draw at four. My mother embroidered one of these pictures on the pocket of my pink smock. The smock is long gone, but I still have the pocket.

* * *

Cathy was in the kitchen talking to Regina while she made dinner. She had come to the house several times over the past year and was comfortable and familiar. Marco and Laura, my new half-brother and sister, were busy setting the beautifully shiny dining room table with fancy china. I had met them before this day, when they came to Half Moon Bay to visit Cathy. My green jealousy faded as soon as I had met them, and was replaced by a feeling of kinship, Cathy and I immediately teasing them over their taste in music, calling them Disco Ducks, while they retaliated by calling us 'Organoes' meaning we were organic hippie types.

Toni walked back into the stylish Italian-furnished room, and I carefully replaced the portrait I had been studying. He came over to where I was sitting in the cream-colored upholstered chair, and knelt on the ground at my feet.

I glanced down near my elbow into Toni's eyes, and he looked up at me imploringly. I tried to pull the chain armor around my heart, but the opening was there, and it was getting more difficult to close. When I looked into his brown eyes, I felt a sudden Knowing that our essences had always been, and forever would be, intertwined. It was like the feeling I got when I stared into my own eyes in a mirror for a long time, when suddenly I could see behind my brown iris to whatever that Depth is behind it. I quickly looked away from him; the impact was too much. Then slowly, shyly, my eyes met his again, and held the gaze. His returning stare said, "What, didn't you know this? Why would you be surprised?" Looking back at me were the same sad, brown, hooded, hiding, sensuous eyes that I saw in the mirror everyday.

"Christina, *ti amo*," is how he started. The memory of him saying that to me back when I was three or four, the memory I had tumbled around my head so many times, came to life as the sound of the words washed over me in real-time. I used to echo the words over and over to myself in bed, I loved how the syllables rolled off my tongue, *ti amo*, *ti amo*, so simple yet so full of meaning. Now it made me cringe a little, because I didn't believe him. If he loved me, he wouldn't have left me. I looked out the window and noticed how one of the redwoods had grown right through the deck, and wondered if there could be anything he said that would break through to my heart.

He took one of my hands in both of his, and kissed it. He held it up like it was a stray kitten, cupping it gently under both of his hands.

"Look, Christine! How little your hand is. How cute!" He kissed it again.

I looked carefully at his hands for the first time in seventeen years. I saw that they looked exactly the same as mine, only a little bigger, a little rougher. They were very small for a man's, with thick, stocky, muscular fingers that matched the rest of his body. I wasn't really surprised that my hands were clones of his. It made sense after seeing his eyes. The hands that held mine were very warm. I eyed the plain gold wedding band he wore on his left hand.

"Christina, I remember the day you were born. I was on my bus route in Chicago, and I got the message over the radio that I had a daughter. I immediately turned the—*Como dite*? Crank? — above my head to show the bus was out of service, and drove as fast as I could through the streets to get to the hospital."

I looked at him with some interest, but didn't give a response. I felt compelled to be polite, to smile and nod, and it pissed me off. What I wanted to say was, *"Who gives a shit that you drove to the hospital when your first baby was born? Was this supposed to be some sort of heroic action on your part? Why weren't you already in the waiting room, pacing with the other fathers? And what does it have to do with me, anyway? You didn't even know me yet."*

"So Christina, I had the film of you, the film when you were three years old, with the cute little curls, and you were dancing at the beach, and over the years I have watched it over and over again, and cry every time."

Now those brown eyes were actually tearing up, but I had an odd feeling that he was mugging for me, lowering his eyes for effect, and then looking up at me with watery sincerity. *"Why didn't you bother calling me then?"* I was thinking, but all I said was "Really?" lamely, even with a hint of sympathy, but I thought; *"Now he's the one who's suffering?"*

My mind started wandering again, flipping through the old photo albums in my head. The image of the three-year-old me sitting in my little red mock-leather rocking chair, and how pleased I had been when he called my name from the other room just to see if I was all right. I smiled at this picture in my head, of the little curly-headed me feeling contented and cared for.

Then my mind unexpectedly flipped to the back of the album, the part I usually tried to keep taped shut. Back there, the pictures were dark and underexposed. There was the one with me standing on the front seat of his car, crying and hiccupping, while he was telling me to stop, hitting me each time, over and over again while I tried explain to him that if he just stopped hitting me I would stop crying. Then another picture of him spanking me in front of his friend, over his knee, after I showed them how well I could Hula-hoop. He hadn't liked the way I wiggled my hips, and I hadn't understand. I closed that page of the album with some effort, and quickly turned back to the happier, full-colored image of Papa giving me a big bowl of hot chocolate with pieces of stale French bread to float in it, and me scooping the soggy chunks up with a spoon. I couldn't ignore the most prominent picture in the album, the one I had blown up to a giant 8x10 like the wedding picture of Toni and Regina, of me standing on the toilet, watching him shave in the mirror, begging him to wait one more day until he moved to California. The picture still made my stomach flop in abject fear all these years later.

"So why didn't you get a hold of me all that time?" I finally blurted. It was hard for me to say this to his face, but I said it. He had some sort of grip on me that demanded politeness. I didn't want to hurt his feelings. The little girl, who wanted to please him, was still alive and well, still afraid he would leave. There was a flicker of the disapproving face that I remembered, his eyebrows knitting together.

"Your mother, and Go-*goh*!" He put the emphasis on the second 'go'.

"My God, I wanted to see you so very badly, but your mother thought that it was best that I did not. Did she tell you that I went to see her at the bank where she worked in San Francisco when you first moved here?"

"Yeah, she told me." She hadn't mentioned it at the time; in fact, she had just told me the story when I informed her I had decided to meet with Toni again.

"I wouldn't advise seeing him. He didn't care about you. He came to see me once you know, came right to the French American Branch. God knows how he found out where I worked. He took me out to lunch, and I accepted, thinking maybe he was going to give me some money for you kids, you know he never paid me a dime towards your care. Well, no, that's not true, he made one payment of what, fifty dollars? Only after Gogo had tracked him down. Big deal, he owes thousands. Well, not only did he not offer any money, but at the end of the lunch he had the nerve to say he was 'a little short' and did I have twenty dollars he could borrow to cover the bill. Imagine the cheek! He drove me back to work, and when he stopped the car to drop me off, he put his hand on my knee, and before I knew it, had slid it all the way up my leg under my skirt. I reminded him that he was a married man, and got out of the car. That's the last I heard from him, and that was when you were, what, eight or nine? I didn't bother saying anything to you at the time, because I didn't want to hurt you with the fact that he didn't want to see you, darling."

"I asked your mother if I could see you, but she told me that she did not think it was a good idea," Toni went on. "What could I do? I tried, I really did."

I eyed him suspiciously. His watery brown eyes looked sincere—or maybe it was just that I wanted to believe him.

* * *

In spite of that wobbly first meeting, I saw him again, and then again. Slowly, slowly, over the next few visits, over the next few months, my heart continued to soften and open. I gave him an inch, and then another one, and then maybe half a yard. Toni was persistent. Toni was charming. Toni continually called me to tell me how much he loved me, how I was his favorite, how he had always held a place in his heart for me, just me, his first-born.

I was attracted to his intellectual mind. Toni talked to me about things nobody had ever talked to me about before. He told me about the Latin roots of words and what they meant, he got passionate over Greek philosophy and language, could name the parts of the human anatomy in minute detail, and had gory books to illustrate how all our parts worked. He showed me how the spiral pattern of a sea-snail shell is based on a mathematical equation, and explained how to pitch a tent in the snow on the side of a steep mountain. He told jokes in a high funny voice that made me laugh, and he sang opera at the dinner table.

I was attracted to his physical self. Toni challenged me to a foot race, and then easily beat me. He rode his bicycle everywhere, taught rock climbing on Mt. Tamalpais, and scrambled up the redwoods in his backyard with a rope and harness just for fun, sawing off branches that he thought might obstruct the view of the mountain from his deck. He took me snow skiing for the first time, even buying me skis and boots, and patiently spent the day with me, showing me how to turn, calming my fears and hesitations.

He was winning me over, and I felt like I had come home. I was no longer the outsider like with Cathy and my mother and Ray; rather, I could feel the newness of connection. What I secretly hoped for more than anything was someone in my life who would be there for me, who I could count on and trust. I didn't trust him yet, but was tentatively inching towards it.

"Christina, when you were small, you called me Papa. Do you remember?"

"Yeah, of course I remember."

"Do you think you could call me that again?"

"I don't think so." Squirming. Hurt and anger rising from below the surface.

"Why not?"

"I don't know if there's enough time in this lifetime for me to trust you enough again to call you that."

I wanted to though. More than anything.

* * *

During that year I was getting to know Toni, Cathy and I were relaying our stories about him to George, who now lived in an apartment with Gogo while he was going to college. After many tentative partings, Beba and Gogo had finally broken up for good. The age difference between them had started showing more now that Gogo was close to seventy, and Beba was in his prime in his mid-fifties. Beba went back to Poland for a visit with his family, and came back with a new wife, Eva, a third cousin of his, and eighteen years his junior. Gogo accepted this fairly well, saying that he could marry whom he pleased, but that he would always love her.

"I'm glad you get to see your Puh-pah, " George would say with a mixture of sincerity and disdain, not knowing that it was actually his Papa too, the one that had been absent for so many years. Every time I talked to George, I felt a numbed guilt about lying to him; numbed only because I had absolved myself from any blame, thinking I had no choice.

For the past dozen or so years, since we had moved out of the house at sixtyeastfortieth, where we had last all lived together, George's life contrasted sharply from that of Cathy's and mine. While Cathy and I had trudged up an austere and rocky path littered with alcohol and marijuana, with detours for peace marches through the Haight, George rolled down a smooth, flat road, stopping to play with his ham radio, or to easily flip a boy over his shoulder to win yet another Judo championship. While Cathy and I went to psychedelic parties decorated with pulsating amoeba shapes projected on the wall and wearing neon colored bell-bottoms, George played tennis in his white shorts and polo shirt, and trombone in his marching band uniform. We ate pasta and mussels, avocados and fondue, while George ate frozen fish sticks and chips, and fried ham sandwiches. Cathy and I sported black armbands in protest of the War, while George was festooned with first place ribbons. The background score to Cathy's and my life was the Rolling Stones and Judi Collins, while George's backdrop was the ever-present television, and the occasional thin strain of Lawrence Welk or Polish Polka accordion hits. Cathy and I had beds covered with Indian prints from Cost Plus, and George's bed was covered in pale blue eiderdown comforters from England. Our rooms were filled with incense burners and Beatles statues, and George's was filled with model cars and airplanes that he meticulously put together. George wanted nothing and got everything. We wanted everything and got nothing.

Cathy and I called George a nerd, and he called us hippies. We begged him to lose the sandals and socks and buy a pair of jeans, and he begged us to quit smoking. We thought he was smart and talented. He thought we were cool.

But now there was this Thing, this Secret I had to keep from him. The elephant that I thought I could feel when we all lived together was now three dimensional and scary and lifelike, and there was no more denying its presence. It stood in the middle of every room I occupied with George. I was sure that George could see it, and I felt a physical pain in my chest when I spread my arms wide to try and block it from him. I was not only guilty for lying, but guilty for even Knowing. I was now a perpetrator instead of a victim. I felt the horrible burden of carrying this gigantic elephant-secret, but I had no idea I could simply put it down.

* * *

"Why? Why shouldn't I tell my son that I am his father? Doesn't he have the right to know? Wouldn't you want to know if you were Gorgio?" Toni said to Cathy and me one afternoon when we were visiting him.

"Toe-neeeee!" Cathy and I said in unison.

"What? I do not understand. I cannot believe that Go-GOH and Fresh Egg never told him the truth all this time."

"Toni, I really think it would kill him if he found out. Especially now that Cathy and I know. Shannon knows. Everyone knows. It's gotten out of hand. He'll know we've all been lying to his face and talking behind his back. It would be horrible. Promise you won't say anything. Promise!"

My loyalty to the Lie was unshakable, and the thought of divulging it sent tremors of terror through me.

"Oh, I don't know. I cannot promise."

Deep down, I knew he was right. It would be a huge relief if George knew. My mother was apparently able to lie for years without any guilt, but it was eating me alive. I didn't realize that if he got hurt it wouldn't be my fault.

"Well, at least can I see my son?" Toni asked us. Cathy and I didn't answer. We didn't trust him to keep his mouth shut.

* * *

When I asked George if he wanted to go to Toni's for dinner, he was open to the idea. He was mildly interested in seeing him, though he hardly remembered him.

"Sure, I'll go. I'd like to see what your Puh-pa looks like again. I can remember him a little you know, Chris," he said in his teasing way.

My heart sank a little. I was hoping he'd say he was busy, like he always did.

George picked Cathy and me up that warm, sunny afternoon, and we drove to Mill Valley together. Cathy and I chatted nervously the whole way there about everything and anything except for the subject at hand, Toni.

The Elephant, the one that moved in with us way back when we moved to sixtyeastfortieth, was not going to be ignored that day. There he was, sitting right in between us in George's red Mazda, taking up so much room that he was squishing the life out of me, making it difficult to breath. I could feel his rough, cracked hide against my skin, and his wiry hairs were scratching me. He smelled particularly elephant-like in the car that day, even with all the windows down, a combination of earthy mud and dung. When I turned my head away from the window, his one black, beady elephant eye was staring right into mine, and the eye was sad and tired. I didn't acknowledge the elephant, even to myself, but I knew someone was going to on that day.

After that suffocating ride, I was glad to get out of the car and stretch my legs when we got to Toni's house. When we knocked on the door, Toni answered it like he had been standing there waiting with his hand on the doorknob. He kissed Cathy, and then me, on both cheeks, quickly and with little interest, looking over my head instead of into my eyes, to George who stood behind us in the doorway. He walked past us slowly, and took George's hand as if to shake it. He gazed up at George, who was a good head taller than Toni, with a look of awe on his face. He didn't shake his hand, but he didn't let go of it either.

"Gorgio! Gorgio," was all he said, his voice cracking. Then he suddenly grabbed George, and hugged him tightly, burying his head in George's chest.

"Uh, hi Toni." George said this easily and casually, with a bemused look on his face as he looked at the top of Toni's head, obviously taken aback by Toni's not-so-discreet outpouring of emotion. "How're ya doing?"

I was cringing at this scene, my heart thumping, willing Toni to cool it. We hadn't even gotten into the house yet; the front door was still wide open. When I looked out through the door onto the front deck, there was the elephant watching, flicking his trunk inside the door like he was going to come in too.

Toni finally pried himself off of George, and stood back a few feet to look up at him. Tears were in his eyes. We all stood uncomfortably in the hallway, until Regina came in, wiping her hands on her apron.

"Come in, come in!" she said, breaking the tension. "Gorgio, so nice to meet you, I am Regina." We soon all followed the delicious aroma coming out of the kitchen. If it had been a cartoon, we would have all had our noses up in the air, following the visible swirly fragrance into the kitchen, our feet off the ground floating behind us, with the elephant taking up the rear, his trunk extended high.

As usual, Regina had put out a beautiful spread, this time consisting of tomato and basil bruschetta, veal stuffed with prosciutto and provolone, and perfectly al dente pasta with pesto and new potatoes. We all sat around the shiny oval dining room table, all five of Toni's offspring in the same room at the same table for the very first time. Cathy and I were chatting, having become comfortable with the dinner routine at the Sottile's during the past year. George was observing, looking around the house for the first time, and Marco and Laura were up and down, helping Regina and cracking jokes. We ate while it was still early in the afternoon, talking, laughing a little uncomfortably to fill in the gaps, and singing Italian ditties. Even though the dinner was delicious, and the conversation flowed like the wine, I had trouble eating with that elephant staring at me the whole time.

"So Gorgio, I understand that you work part-time in a biological technical company, is that correct?" Toni had hardly kept his attention off of George the entire meal.

"Well, yeah, it's called Bio-tech. We're working on developing a machine that sequences DNA."

"Ah, so you study genetics?"

"Yeah, that's right."

"So what do you think is more important, Gorgio, in shaping a person's character and talents—his genetics, or his environment?" Toni had found the perfect opening.

"Well, it's probably some of both, but..."

"Do you not see, with your study of the human genome, that a person is only the composite of his biological parents' genes? You must be familiar with the studies of twins that were raised in completely separate and different environments, yet turn out to be very similar, marrying the same type of woman, even buying the same type of automobile."

I didn't like where this conversation was going. I tried to shoot a meaningful look at Toni, hoping I could get him to change the subject, but he didn't look my way. I looked back and forth between George and Toni, and thought surely George must see that he looked identical to his father, far more so than Marco did. Their mannerisms were exactly the same in the way they would simultaneously twist their eyebrows into an S shape whenever they were perplexed or inquisitive, how their voices raised an octave whenever they were telling a joke, or how they both crossed their arms over their chest when they didn't agree with what was being said.

As we tended to do at the Sottile's, we all overate, and were all groaning and holding our stomachs, saying we couldn't possibly eat another bite of the delicious cream cakes that Regina had put out for dessert.

"Do you know what I like to do when I am very full? I like to walk; there is nothing that can compare. You breathe in the air, you digest the food; it's beautiful," Toni said, still staring directly at George.

We all looked at him half-heartedly. We really didn't like to go walking in those days; Cathy and I would've rather smoked.

"Especially during a beautiful sunset like we will have tonight," Toni went on. "Do you know that right at the top of the ridge, not far up the road, you can see the sun setting behind Mt. Talalpais, Gorgio? Why don't you come with me, I'd love to show you where I hike." I glanced at George, and his arms were not across his chest, indicating to me that he may have been somewhat open to the idea.

"I'll go too, then." Cold fear at being unable to control the situation shot through me. I knew that Toni wanted to get George alone, but it was still almost unfathomable to me that he would actually have the guts to tell George the truth.

"No, Christina, we have walked a lot together, and I have never walked with Gorgio. You just got through saying you were too full to move."

* * *

The two of them slipped out, the front door softly clicking closed behind them, and with that click, a heavy silence hung over the room, silence except for the slow heavy breathing of the elephant. We who were left behind, we who knew the Truth, avoided each other's eyes. Finally Laura stood up and started clearing the table, breaking the spell. The level of conversation elevated, and kept rhythm to the percussion of the clattering plates and clinking silverware; the melody of our small talk carried by the running tap water and dishwasher hum. We moved and paced needlessly. Occasionally, in passing, Cathy's eyes met mine in alarm. We all effortlessly walked around the elephant—we were so used to it by now. The elephant lay on his side, taking up more space than usual, and it was breathing hard, panting, as if in distress.

Though it seemed like an eternity, George and Toni were only gone about half an hour. I heard their voices outside before they walked in, and when they did, it was with little fanfare. They continued talking, and at first I thought that maybe Toni didn't tell him after all; George's face looked ashen to me, but I hoped fervently it was my imagination. He was quiet, subdued, and eerily tranquil.

"So how was your walk?" I ventured.

"Yeah, Chrissy, he told me about Gogo." George said this so calmly, that I thought maybe I had imagined it. He usually responded to everything in full throttle, his nickname being 'A Thousand Volts.'

"He did?" Cathy and I said in a perfectly synchronized delayed reaction.

"I kind of knew, you guys. You know, I found my birth certificate once, and it said something about adoption—I tried to ignore it, but I guess that it was always in the back of my mind, that doubt—but I tried not to think too much about it." This all seemed so anticlimactic; so surreal. All that time I had wasted worrying and stressing that he was going to find out and fall to pieces, for nothing.

I felt my body start to relax. I felt myself tentatively let go of the tension I had been holding in my tightened stomach and neck. My breathing became less shallow, and I stopped jiggling my right knee. Just as I was taking a cleansing sigh of relief, fear shot through my body when the jarring, terrified, screeching trumpet of the elephant pierced the room. I glanced over, and the elephant was no longer lying on its side, but had stood up with his last strength, and was on his hind legs only, the front two heavy stumps clawing at the air. Its long trunk whipped straight up, grazing the high-beamed ceiling of Toni's living room, and let out another dying, melancholic, moan.

I watched the elephant wide-eyed, my body shot through with adrenaline again. Everyone saw it, though nobody said anything. Then, just as the elephant was giving us his last, tortured, off-key saxophone blast, his body suddenly pixelated before our eyes. The little rectangles of gray hide broke apart, and floated weightlessly around the room, swirling and fluttering, the pieces that landed on our bodies instantly absorbed.

I knew that was the last time I would ever see the elephant. Even though it was smelly and invasive and annoying, I knew there was a part of me that would miss it. Having it around was all I knew, and I felt the void immediately, though the remnants that were left inside of me, inside of all of us, would live forever.

"If you already knew, why didn't you say anything?" I said, when I had recovered a little.

"Well, I didn't really know for sure. I just never thought about it. But you know, I know Mama's…uh…Gogo's age. She would have been close to forty-nine when she had me, and would have been one of the few people in the world who had a baby at that age."

The rest of the evening must have been short, since I don't remember any of the conversation. I only remember it being a lot more subdued than the first half. After we had coffee, George said that he had a calculus final in the morning, and he had to go.

Cathy climbed in the back seat of the car, and I sat up front with George. We were very quiet as we headed toward the Golden Gate Bridge, and Cathy fell asleep. I kept glancing sideways at George, looking for signs of distress. Finally I tentatively broke the silence.

"I'm so sorry, George. Are you going to be all right? Talk to me."

"That's okay, Chrissy, don't worry about it." He said this in a calm, small voice.

This seeming serenity surrounding George didn't feel natural. It felt weird that he was showing no reaction to such a monumental revelation. The silence continued after the sun set, and I was about to break it again by apologizing for participating in The Secret, but before I could say it, I saw George's hands clench the steering wheel and his demeanor suddenly changed. The mask of calm on his face was gone. I could see his jaw muscles working, his eyes narrowing.

"Fuck Toni—I never want to see him again," George spat out like he was ridding himself of venom.

It was as if a ball came out of left field and smacked me upside the head.

"What? Why?" The abruptness of the change in his demeanor scared me,

"That idiot had no business telling me that. If Mama and *Tat* wanted me to know, they would have told me themselves. What right does that fucking asshole have to open his goddamn mouth?" George was driving faster, passing cars on the right and left crazily.

"George!" I put my open right palm on his heart, trying to calm him. "Listen! Think about it. Why are you mad at Toni? All he did was tell you the truth, while everyone else, including me, was lying to you. You should be mad at us! Slow down! You're shooting the messenger."

"Why do you think, Chris, that Mama and Tat never told me? Don't you think they had a good reason?"

"They probably didn't want to hurt you."

"That's right. And if that fucking asshole would have kept his mouth shut, I wouldn't be hurt now, would I? I'm done with Toni, and I'm not saying anything to Mama and Tat."

When he mentioned Gogo and Beba, he caught a sob in his throat. My heart was breaking for George; I wished I could take his pain. I wanted to suction all the little square pieces of elephant that landed in him out, and put them in me, and I'd take double my share, I was used to it, I didn't care,

I'd do anything to prevent him from feeling the way I felt. I needed George to keep all thousand of his Thousand Volts, because a lot of the time, he was the only charge I had for my ever-depleting battery.

He was never a thousand volts again, though he still wore the t-shirt Shannon made for him saying that he was. He'd eventually glow brightly again, his energy palpable, but after that, my guess was that 900, maybe 910, was the highest he would ever go.

CHAPTER 13

Concentric Circles (Bullet Holes)

I didn't expect my breathing to quicken and become shallow the way it did, as I watched the plain, gray, particleboard coffin being lowered into the hole in the ground by the two muscular funeral home workers. I tried to slowly inhale the pine scent of the trees and the musty smell of the damp leafy earth in the old overgrown graveyard, to get my bearings back.

I didn't cry when she died, and I didn't feel like crying now, but I felt dizzy as if I might faint. When George had called from the hospital saying that she was gone, waking me from an afternoon nap with my new boyfriend Breen, I calmly thanked him for calling, and immediately got up and did the only thing I could think to do: cook a gigantic pot of pasta. Everyone who walked in the door that long evening got a heaping bowlful of the fettuccini shoved in their face before they had a chance to speak, before they would pile on the condolences I didn't know what to do with.

The last time I had spoken to Gogo had been a week or two beforehand, when I had asked her what she wanted for Christmas.

"Oh, I don't think you should bother buying me a Christmas present this year, Christine." When I tried to protest, she cut in with a haunting, "Goodbye, Christine, Goodbye!" She faded out with that last goodbye, and hung up.

I had bought her a gift anyway, a purple velveteen robe with turquoise trim that zipped up the front. I thought it would be nice for her to have a decent housecoat since that was pretty much all she wore in those last days. I had no idea that Gogo was going to be buried in that robe when I plunked down my credit card to buy it, but she was. A few days before Christmas,

I rummaged around the presents I had wrapped and placed under the tree, found the tag that said, "Merry Christmas Gogo!" and unwrapped it, giving the unadorned Macy's box to the undertaker.

George had kept his promise of not letting on to Gogo and Beba that he knew The Secret — for a while. When he graduated from college a little more than a year after that revealing afternoon at Toni's, unbeknownst to us, Gogo had tentatively broached the subject with George, but before she could get into any details, George stopped her by telling her he Knew, it was okay, she didn't need to explain, he Knew, and he loved her, and *don't say anything more, please.*

During the last couple of years of Gogo's life, it was as if she were hanging on in order to fulfill the promise she had made to raise the boy she asked my mother to carry for her. After all that fuss, it wouldn't really have been right if she died before she finished the job, but toward the end she seemed as if she was tiring of the task. She spent her days in an induced doze in the armchair with the television on, swallowing handfuls of prescription drugs every day, the array of little brown bottles displayed haphazardly on a wicker shelf I had bought for her from Cost Plus the previous Christmas, because I was tired of seeing the bottles scattered all over the stool and floor by her armchair. She was waiting, waiting, wading into the murky waters of the next life, barely treading the water in this one, certainly not swimming, waiting until George got his degree, and was ready to be on his own. Less than half a year after George graduated from college, Gogo exited.

George was convinced it was suicide, an intentional drug overdose, but since Gogo had insisted years before her death that no autopsy would be done, we would never know exactly how she died. She hadn't been well, she had been in and out of the hospital with pneumonia, and was sometimes talking crazy-talk, forgetting who I was when I went to visit her after work. The last time I had seen her, she was back home again, and was washing her face, which was puffed up with the steroids they had given her, but she seemed in good spirits, and I had noticed that she still applied her face cream carefully, appearing to be concerned with her looks.

It was up to George and me to look at coffins and arrange a burial place. My mother had moved to the house Ray had built in Hopland as soon as Cathy had graduated from high school, and she had said she was too distraught to make the three-hour car drive to help us.

George and I stared wide-eyed as the funeral director showed us cutaway models of the different caskets we could buy; did we want eighteen- or twenty-gauge, mahogany or stainless steel, and how much padding did we want for our loved one? The syrupy Muzak floating around the pale blue reception parlor, the window overlooking the manicured lawn, the man in the suit so very sorry for our loss, the casket models with the discreet price tags, all added to the horror of our first experience with the business of disposing of a body. We bolted out of there—both of us agreeing that it didn't make any difference what she was buried in, and opting for the cheapest box we could find.

Of course the cemetery affiliated with the fancy death salesman didn't allow for that kind of a coffin. They didn't allow a lot of things, including real flowers on the graves. We didn't know where to bury her; it wasn't as if there was a family plot. Any of Gogo's ancestors who had passed on were probably in quaint church graveyards in England. George and I finally settled on an old Catholic graveyard, still semi-maintained, in Half Moon Bay. At least she would be close to us, even though she would be alone.

Eight of us stood around the gaping hole that had been dug earlier, in the chill but clear late December afternoon, the shadows of dusk coming earlier under the heavy cypress trees. George was white and holding on to Beba for support. I was in jeans, and so was Cathy. Ray said we should have dressed up a little to show respect, but I didn't get the point, I wasn't sure who we were supposed to show respect *to*. Gogo didn't know. It wasn't as if any of us believed in God at the time, or any kind of continuity of spirit, except for Beba. Ken, I wasn't really sure about.

Ken was Cathy's new husband of less than a couple of years. She had only lasted living with me a few months after my mom and Ray moved before she found someone to take care of her. At seventeen, Cathy was far too young to have her mother leave her. Gogo got to see one of us get married before she died, even though at nineteen, Cathy was far too young to get married. I had told her so, dangling the box of addressed invitations over a garbage can, telling her that it wasn't too late to change her mind. Gogo had designed and sewed Cathy's elaborate antique-colored wedding dress, fitting it perfectly to Cathy's busty figure, hand-stitching the details of the many hooks and eyes and snaps and buttons, and using coffee to dye the lace to match the cloth.

If Gogo could have hung on for another three years or so, she could have made my wedding dress too, but instead I bought mine for thirty-nine dollars at a Gunne Sax outlet. Although, she did get to meet my future husband Breen at her last Thanksgiving, only a month or so before.

It had taken a lot of convincing on my part to get a very reluctant Breen to go up to Hopland to meet the family. Even though at thirty-three he was eight years older than me, he was less inclined to want any semblance of a committed relationship, since he was still bruised from his divorce and missed living with his son. After the semi-uncomfortable turkey and pumpkin pie, I was relieved when George started up the projector to watch some home movies, but instead of images of Cathy, George, and me opening Christmas presents or parading around in Halloween costumes, the tripod projector screen displayed a graphic, glistening close-up of a woman giving a man a blow job, the switcheroo of the movie being Ray's idea of a Thanksgiving joke.

The seconds of stunned silence as the projector ticked on felt like an agonizing eternity to me, me being the girl who was introducing her boyfriend to her family and desperately hoping they wouldn't be too weird for him. The silence and tension was broken when Gogo quietly said, "Well, *I* shall never eat sausage again!" Breen laughed so hard he was doubled over. He said that Gogo's joke was the moment he knew he'd be okay with my family.

The eight people who would bury Gogo—George, Beba, Cathy, Ken, my mom, Ray, Breen, and me—chattered nervously around the pit in front of us, hands in our pockets to keep warm, until the nondescript pick up with a camper shell backed up into the driveway of the cemetery. Two men in gray work coveralls jumped out of the cab, followed by the local, more humane funeral director. The workers went around to the back of the truck, opened the camper shell, and started tugging on the box. They clumsily carried the coffin to the hole in the ground and lowered it down.

That's when my breathing became thin and superficial. That's when it all seemed surreal, the way the late, pale winter sun dappled on us through the cypress trees, giving the scene an almost staccato, strobe-light effect as the men grunted a little with the lowering of the box, but simultaneously very real, as I imagined Gogo's body inside the coffin only inches away from me wearing the robe I had just bought her for Christmas.

She was gone. Really gone. All of her hysteria, drama, and manipulation that I had to endure were gone, but so were her qualities of magic, creativity, spirit, and optimism. The contrary feelings running through me, the guilt of my hatred for her, as well as the ferocity of my love, contrasted and collided up against each other with such violence that I felt as if I might swoon and faint.

Cathy read a poem that she had written, and I was grateful for the only bit of ritual that we had. I was also happy with the way the headstone, which wasn't really a stone at all, but a wooden burl, had turned out. I had hand-painted it with flowers and the often-repeated quote from Gogo, uttered during that Sunday drive long ago: "I thought I saw a buttercup... oooh, look at the Pansies!"

When Cathy had finished reading her poem, none of which I heard since my ears were blocked by unexpected roiling emotion, she tossed the paper she had scribbled it on onto the top of the coffin. We each tossed in a flower we had picked.

After this mini-funeral, we all went and got drunk, downing martini after martini in the nearest bar, our way of dealing with the complex and intricate layers of emotion and reaction that desperately needed sorting but instead got drowned in a tidal wave of gin.

Gogo's body was gone, but her spirit lived on. She was the matriarch of our family, the one that tied us all together using The Secret as binding, but more than that she was a force, and when that force was gone it left a void, a vacuum that not only screamed to be filled, but actually sucked us all down into it, one by one. None of the elephant that she had created was buried that December afternoon, not even one ivory tusk. The elephant lived on in us, and would show itself when we least expected it.

* * *

Perhaps the least noticeably affected by Gogo's departure was my mother. Just as she always showed great restraint when interacting with Gogo in life, she took the same controlled reaction when it came to her death, outwardly showing little or no emotion. Six months after the funeral, when I asked if she had been on a diet—she looked so thin— my mother confided to me that she hadn't had a period since Gogo had died, and that she'd found she'd also had very little appetite.

At first, George appeared to take everything in stride, but I had the strange feeling that he was operating on autopilot. I was amazed at how calmly he told me about The Talk he had with Beba, and how he had told Beba that it didn't matter *who* his biological father was, that Beba would always be his Tat, his Dad. George stoically and methodically went through all of Gogo's carefully saved belongings, her scraps of papers with inspirational quotes, her boxes of salvaged buttons and zippers, her shelves of prescription drugs. Cathy, my mom, and I helped to finish the job of clearing out that small Millbrae apartment in one day, laughing and crying over pictures and notes that we found. George took care of all the paperwork, answering mail addressed to Gogo, paying off the many creditors who demanded money for her debts. After the boxes were donated or stored, after the many sacks of garbage were towed away, after the last physical remnants of Gogo's life were sorted, disposed, and dispersed, George moved in with Cathy and Ken, temporarily, so that he could be close to all of us on the coast, but especially so he could be close to Shannon, who continued to be his on-again off-again, love-of-his-life girlfriend.

I would never have guessed that Shannon would be the catalyst that exposed George's already crumbled heart. I didn't know yet that we humans untangle the most difficult conundrums in our souls by using an innocent lover, as if *they* caused the heartbreak, instead of a wound from long ago, which is always the culprit. Even though George was a Thousand Volts, and George Could Fix Anything (two of his more enduring mottos) George did not have the strength to keep a shattered heart whole, not with a newly blasted hole—and although his hole wasn't as inherent or permanent as mine, it was a hole as big as Texas. Before he had much time to digest the fact that his mother was actually his grandmother, and all the implications that had on their relationship, she died. He luckily did not inherit our mother's ability to keep it all inside, although at the time, I thought that trait would be more desirable than the humiliation of having your personal world witness the wind blowing through the window in your heart, which is what happened.

On a fateful January weekend, in the hot rosy desert, with the turquoise sky a winter pale but still bearing down, George finally lost it. What I thought would be a fun, two-day getaway from our mundane jobs instead came to be known as the PSI or Palm Springs Incident, forever etched in our family lore, an event so significant that it needed an acronym for ease of referral.

I could tell the weekend was going to read like a poorly written ballad from the beginning, right from when I was flying down on PSA with two of my best girlfriends, Janet and T, that Friday night, and the guys behind us poked a lit joint through the crack between our seats. The stoner boys were from Oregon, one of them named Dean. The flight down to Palm Springs became a hazy high chant about Dean being from Eugene. We were laughing and drunk, and I already felt off-kilter, and we told Dean from Eugene we were going to our roommate's wedding at the Gene Autry hotel. When I got out of the plane, I smacked straight into a wall of blasting hot desert air, Dean from Eu*gene* and *Gene* Autry swirling around my stoned head, the rhythm of the weekend's narrative already off a beat.

It wasn't long before I was sprawled out in a lawn chair in shorts and a tank top, with a vodka-grape in hand, joining the already-in-progress pool party at the hotel. I could feel the electricity in the air. Part of the energy was the pre-wedding excitement, but there was also an underlying eel-current that put me on edge, the kind of electricity you might feel if you dropped a plugged-in hair dryer in the bathtub. Everyone's face was cast with an eerie, shimmering aqua-green reflection from the pool that was lit up from below, and the effect gave everyone a Frankenstein pallor that increased, in my stoned mind, as the sky turned a salmon color and then settled on a darker blue.

Friends and family trickled in, each making their own mini-entrance. Cathy and George had driven down together, and arrived laughing from whatever jokes they had told each other on the long car ride. Shannon flew in separately, and entered the scene, I half-noticed, with an air of self-importance. She went straight up to her room, and reemerged transformed, wearing a short dress, pearls, and pumps. She positioned herself in a darkened corner, away from the crowd. The thought that she looked awfully dressed up wafted through my head, but I paid little attention to her.

And then…*crash!* I jumped, but was hardly surprised, because of the tenseness in the air, when I heard the distinctive sound of breaking glass, and a collective gasp whooshing through the crowd. Someone had cut their hand badly; was there a doctor in the house? Luckily the groom for the wedding happened to be a doctor, and I saw him pushing his way through the crowd toward the bleeding guest. Soon the chatter around the pool elevated again, until the full moon was high in the clear dark sky, but the moon couldn't compete with the pink and blue neon of the motel's sign, and the turquoise squiggles radiating from the pool. People wandered off to bed early, without saying good night, gearing up for the next day.

The next day, I was a little mortified that the entire contingent from Half Moon Bay made the Palm Springs fashion faux pas of wearing all black to a wedding, making us stand out like sore — no, more like bruised— thumbs, but my slight anxiety over my dress as well as the lingering feeling of foreboding from the night before was quelled in the serenity of the synagogue. I closed my eyes and let the reverberating chants of the cantors wash over and soothe me, but my often longed-for (and rarely attained in those days) serenity was short-lived as I left the temple and was thrown into the fury of wedding reception back at the Gene Autry, dancing wildly along with everyone else in the center of a room bordered with pink tablecloths, rosebud centerpieces, white folding chairs, and clouds of Baby's-breath.

It was during one of the slow songs, from where I sat at our table recovering from a spate of dancing, that I saw George stride purposefully over to where Shannon was standing, surrounded by a group of guys. She was looking particularly put-together that weekend, I thought for a second time, and I could see she was enjoying the attention she was getting. George smiled at Shannon's admirers, and then took her by the elbow and guided her out to the dance floor, where I saw him earnestly talking while looking into Shannon's eyes. He tilted her chin up with one finger, and kissed her on her red lipsticked lips.

It was after the reception, and on the way to the Post Party, as our Black-Clad group crunched down the gravel pathway, wobbly from heels and alcohol, that George suddenly stopped in his tracks and announced, "Well, I did it. I asked Shannon to marry me."

There was a group *Whoop*! and I felt my heart stop with the surprise of the revelation, and then soar with the possibilities. I tuned out as everyone was wowing and congratulating. We needed more beginnings in our family, I'd thought— this was perfect after the Big Ending we'd all still been feeling after Gogo died. My mind started racing ahead to the next wedding, this time George and Shannon's, and then lurched forward to babies. Unlike Cathy, who said she didn't want kids, George always said that he did. I was getting a strong urge to have a baby myself, although

I would have to take care of the little problem of finding a husband first. But Shannon and George had found each other! They had been together for years now; I reasoned in my mind it would be okay. Sure it had been on-again off-again as of late, but I thought that they loved each other, and now that they were getting married...

"I didn't say yes yet, you know." This jarring statement from Shannon cut into my fantasizing like a needle scratching over a record.

The group went silent, and looked to Shannon for explanation. George broke the tension by saying softly, but confidently, "That's okay, babe. You take your time," while putting his arm over her shoulder.

Shannon shrugged him off, saying, "I can't believe you dropped this cold fish in my lap."

Even though I thought this was a very odd thing to say and I wasn't exactly sure what it meant, it sent an icy tingle down my spine. It wasn't just the way she sort of spat it, but more to do with the fact that I knew how much she hated fish. Shannon obsessed over fish; she had a love-hate relationship with them—she drew and painted pictures of them and screamed if she saw them. Mostly Shannon feared fish, or more accurately, she projected all of her fear inside onto fish. If she would have used any other choice of words I might have remained optimistic, but as it was, my hopeful elated heart dropped with a thud.

The evening whirled on in alcoholic fuzz. One particularly drunk guy, an old boyfriend of the bride, kept wobbling up to us, hitting on all of us girls, and asking us one by one if we would meet him at the hot tub at midnight. We were laughing and swapping stories about him—"He asked *me* to meet him there too!" T squealed as we ran into each other in the rambling house of the bride's parents. We instantly dubbed the guy Ichabod Crane because of his tall, lanky appearance, or sometimes we called him Adam, because of his protruding Adam's apple, even though we knew by then his name was Keenan. Each of us was outraged at his audacity, so at one point we ambushed him out in the driveway. We held him down against the hood of a car and laughingly taunted and tickled him. "Loosen that tie will ya? It looks painful!" Janet said, as she took off his tie and unbuttoned his shirt. "Meet me at the hot tub, huh?" Cathy said, as we all tickled him mercilessly, T and I holding him down with one arm each. We laughed and tortured him until we were tired of him, and then the four of us girls walked away, leaving him sprawled on the car hood.

Ichabod. Ick. Ichthyology. Ick. The offbeat Narrative of the Night wore on.

I walked back with Cathy, T, and Janet to the aquamarine hotel pool, and we took off our shoes and swished our tired feet in the water. Men dribbled in with ties loosened, women with heels in hand, and sat in the lawn furniture in the warm desert air, spent from a day of partying. When George showed up he looked more than a little agitated.

"Have you guys seen Shannon? It's past midnight."

We looked at each other and shrugged. I hadn't seen her in quite a while. Then our eyes widened as the same thought simultaneously darted through our heads.

"I'm going to see if she's in the hot tub—be right back!" T called over her shoulder as she ran across the lawn barefoot. She returned walking slowly and shaking her head. I let out a sigh of relief right along with Cathy and Janet.

"Well, I'm going to look for her... see you guys later." George said, walking off into the night.

The day was done, or so we thought. We all straggled up to our rooms. We had rented three or four, but we'd squeezed four to six people in each room to save money, some people sneaking in to sleep on the floor.

Cathy, Janet, T, and I laughed and giggled, reviewing the day when we got into bed, going over the Ichabod story and other gossip of the wedding. I didn't give a second thought about George and Shannon as I closed my eyes— I figured he must've found her and they were sleeping in one of the other rooms.

I was awakened by the sound of the hotel room door crashing open, followed by an anguished, primal, blood-curdling scream.

I bolted straight up in bed, my heart pounding wildly in my chest. In the moonlit room, I saw that everyone else had sat up too. We were staring at the shadowy figure in the doorway. I knew it was George, but I wasn't completely sure—his body and voice, the very essence of his being—was transformed by grief. This alien George was pulling on his own hair with his fist and then punching the wall with another animal howl.

"George, please, George. What's wrong? What happened?"

I was the only one talking. I was terrified of seeing George like this. Never before had I witnessed such a raw outpouring of emotion coming from him. I had felt that feeling I was witnessing, and when I did, it was so powerful that

I thought if I actually experienced the emotion instead of trying to stop it or cover it up, I would literally die. I was shocked to discover that I was saying a silent prayer over and over in my head, I'm not sure to who, but I was repeating 'don't let him die, don't let him die, don't let him die.'

* * *

I didn't know that a part of him had already died.

"She's in there.... *fucking*..." here George pounded the wall three times, "that *asshole*!!" This last word was screamed in a very high octave, and drawn out like the word had four or five syllables. It rang in my ears long after George vomited it up. He stared at this word he had produced, almost apologetically, at this thing that took on a life of its own and hung in the moonlit hotel room, sticking to us like napalm. With that he slammed the door and left.

It was a very long, icky night.

The four of us girls stayed awake and talked and talked in the dark. That Shannon actually went and had sex with that guy on the day George asked her to marry him, right in front of him, was unfathomable. We stayed off the subject; it was too scary. We laughed to the point of hysteria about nonsensical jokes. Sometimes we would be quiet for a while, and start to doze off, when George would come bursting in again, pacing, crying, sobbing, screaming rhetorical questions that couldn't be answered, like *why, why, why*. Then he would leave again.

I had not felt that scared in a very long time. Maybe not since Papa said he was leaving. Now that Fear, that thing I was becoming adept at hiding or sedating, was Back, just like it had never left, like it was waiting, waiting, waiting, in dormancy, for the opening, for the chance to jump up and inhabit my body. George had snapped. I feared he was gone. There was one small lily pad of truth in the conclusions I was jumping to, like a frenzied frog in a pond full of illusions, and that was that a part of him *was* gone. Most people wouldn't even notice, but I did. I don't want to be trite and call it innocence, I think a better name would be defenselessness, a disarming charm that George held was gone from that night forth—or rather hidden behind an armor he started building that very night, an armor that has yet to be penetrated to this day.

I was surprised when I woke up to the sun streaming into the dusty hotel room, the particles dancing through the shaft of light. I didn't think I would ever fall asleep that night. As I scanned the room, I saw that the other girls were still asleep in their various positions and that George was back, slumped on the floor against the wall, his knees drawn up, his hair sweaty, and his head hidden in his arms. He still had on his wedding clothes, the shirt unbuttoned and filthy. I knew he was alive, but I had to check.

"George?"

His curly head snapped up and he looked at me with tragic bloodshot eyes.

The thing about that Fear is that sometimes it turns to anger, which feels safer and more powerful, but actually only helps the Fear to grow by spreading it around. Everyone chose to buoy George up with the anger. The anger spilled out of our hotel room, and infiltrated all the other rooms full of our friends. *How dare she? How dare they?* Indignant, self-righteous anger bound a dozen or so of us together to form a troop, each of us armed with a lawn chair we took from the pool. We formed a semi-circle around the hotel room door where the tryst allegedly occurred between Ichabod, or rather Keenan, and Shannon. They had to come out sometime. We were prepared to wait until they did, arms crossed, and eyes shielded by sunglasses, not only for protection from the sun, but as not to reveal any unwanted emotion.

The door opened a crack, and then Lynnette and Jerry, two of our married friends walked out. The energy went through us with out speaking: they did it front of them? Twenty minutes later, Shannon finally walked out, head held high, sunglasses protecting her, suitcase in hand. Keenan followed her. They faced us like a showdown, but when George started crying, a loud, unselfconscious sobbing, the wall of anger was broken, and they picked their way through the opening to a waiting taxi. This was the final curtain of the weekend called the PSI.

* * *

George moved out of Cathy and Ken's when he got home, and never came over to the coast anymore because he said it reminded him too much of Shannon. He immediately got a rebound girl-pal that he moved in with, but was never exclusive with.

Not that it really matters to my story, but Keenan and Shannon ended up getting married and having a baby. What matters to me is that George was never quite the same. He never let me, or anyone else, get close to him again. He became secretive. He never was completely honest again, embracing the deceit he grew up with instead of rejecting it. George has many endearing gestures that I love, but my favorite was the way he would spread his hands wide open, palms up, when he was being especially sincere. After the PSI, (or the Big Lie, or Gogo dying, it's hard to pinpoint) he didn't do that anymore.

* * *

If I had to summarize that lengthy PSI story, and explain George's response to Gogo's legacy and death in one word, that word would be 'meltdown.' For my story, I'll give you the one-word summary of my response in advance: 'baby.'

At that young, impatient age, I thought the tangles and knots that comprised my life story were so convoluted that there was no unraveling them. I could temporarily *forget* about them through drugs or alcohol, but that was getting tiring because after the fuzzy high was the reality of the low, when the loops in my head were even harder to untangle. The only solution, I reasoned, would be to start over. Since I didn't know how to crawl back into another random womb and try it again, I thought I would have to do it vicariously through a new person with a blank slate. A baby. *My* baby.

I can vouch that the ticking of the proverbial clock is very real. In my case, it was more like the gonging of Big Ben—it drowned out almost every other obsessive thought that I regularly entertained. *I wanted a baby*. God was still elusive to me at that point in my life, and I felt like if I didn't find meaning soon, I was sure to Exit. A baby would surely fill that hole in my heart.

And deep down, in a place I couldn't see, I thought a baby could also fix our family. George would be healed; my parents would step up as grandparents where they never could as parents, Toni and I could form a deeper bond in our new and shy relationship, and maybe the baby would be so irresistible that Cathy and Ken would have one of their own after all. Even though none of them were admitted, even in my own head, I had an awful lot of expectations for a person who wasn't even born yet.

When I met Breen (by being pushed by a friend into the back of a car with him after a wedding) I held off from sleeping with him right away. Someone had told me that a guy would tell you everything you need to know right at the beginning, if you listen. You also had to believe him, and not hope that he would change. So I decided to go against the norm of the day and not have my listening muffled by sex. I would wait. And listen. I held off in spite of the tempting facts that I was drawn to the green eyes that were reluctant to meet mine, and that I thought his skinny body and wavy hair were very cute. I didn't tell him—hell, I didn't even tell myself—that this uncharacteristic prudence was because I was looking for someone to be the father of my baby.

I listened. I listened to the places in between the bantering and flirting, underneath the joking and drunken midnight calls, and I gleaned three important revelations.

The first disclosure took place as he and I were doing what we normally did, sitting on bar stools in the San Benito having a drink. He asked me, once again, why I wouldn't sleep with him, and I dropped the coyness and said, "Because I'm afraid you're going to hurt my feelings."

He gave me a rare look in the eyes and repeated my fear in the negative: "I'm not going to hurt your feelings." Something about the frank, matter-of-fact way he said it made me choose to believe him. First disclosure down, and so far, so good.

The second confession came outside in my driveway, when he was kissing me goodnight. Like the first time, I made the opening by being truthful first. After a fun date and a long goodnight kiss, I told him I loved him. He drew back with seriousness, and said, "I'm not a good person to love." A little ding went off in my head. A statement like this could have been a red flag big enough to smother any embryonic flames of love, but not for me. If anything the unattainable love felt familiar and comfortable, and I cozied down into it.

I was back to the same two bar stools, for the third and most swaying nugget of certainty from Breen. He was rambling on, as he tended to do after a couple of drinks, about his son, Breen Jr., when he looked at me and said, "For me, my son is the sun coming up." A giant, glowing exclamation mark appeared over my head. Bingo! This guy loved being a Dad. At that moment, although it didn't happen for a while, I knew he would be the father of the baby I had wanted to bring into this world.

I didn't want him to know though. I was sure it would scare him away.

But it was as if Breen could read my thoughts. Not long after the exclamation mark faded from above my head (it had lasted a couple of weeks) he said, "I know you. You want to get married and have babies." I could feel the blood rising up into my neck and face, and worried that it might burst out of the top of my head in the form of a fresh exclamation mark that only he could see.

"Oh, sure, maybe someday," I said coolly. "Doesn't every girl want that?"

We clung together for a couple of rocky, tumultuous years, both of us trying to build something, when neither of us had a foundation, but the clock ticking in my head, that sounded like a literal *ba*-by, *ba*-by, kept me holding on. Our relationship was fueled by alcohol and tears, but interspersed with romantic vacations.

It was on one of our road trips, this one up to the wine country, that I experienced another Knowing, like the Knowing I had in second grade that I was going to be a teacher, which still hadn't come to fruition at this point. We were in Boonville, and Breen went into a little store so we could continue one of our favorite activities that we called Eating Our Way Across America. I opted to wait in the car and listen to the music, while he went in and bought us snacks. I sat with my bare feet on the dashboard, spitting sunflower seeds out the window while I absentmindedly watched a young mother play with her daughter on the rustic wooden front porch of the old store. Then the Knowing, which feels a little like a gauzy curtain is lifted so that I see the same scene except more clearly, came over me and I thought, "Oh! That's me! I'm going to have one little blonde daughter."

It was that Knowing that sustained me, and that loud *ba*by ticking that propelled me through eight months of missed periods; pink stripe after pink stripe on the pregnancy tests proving false: no embryo, only desire. The Baby Beat was the only forward moving momentum in my life, and it had me dancing a dance I didn't know I knew until I heard the music. I pushed through Breen's over-drinking, his DUI, and drugs (*ba*by, *ba*by); I didn't turn away when he gave me a blanket for Christmas instead of the ring I had been expecting. Breen moved in with me, and then moved out again to take care of his son. I was devastated, but rather than dump him, I put new linoleum in his kitchen. Oh baby.

The Baby made a temporary appearance (!) but, no, not yet; Breen talked me into an obviously unwanted abortion that left me empty and forlorn, but still I clung on for the love of the baby I knew was To Be, and also for the love for her father, a love that proved to be true long after we were divorced. When The Baby appeared for the second time, we decided, not by proposal on bended knee, but by a series of tearful, fearful, love-infused conversations to get married.

What followed was a rushed whirlwind of wedding plans, made by the three-months-pregnant me, in between answering calls at the phone company. There would be a reception by the sea, a not-too-religious ceremony in the little stained-glassed church, and a solo trombone performance by George who would play *Obla di Obla da* when we exited as husband and wife. We would make the bridesmaid dresses out of maroon sateen and make do with the two thousand dollars each that Toni and my parents were going to give us. Plenty for the important things like champagne and the band, and enough left over to cater the hors d'oeurvres.

I didn't feel like choosing between Ray and Toni as to who should walk me down the aisle; neither of them felt right to me, and I didn't want to cause rifts with either of them, so I asked my mom's Dad, Archibald, who was going to be visiting us from England, to do the honors.

The baby was working already to bring our family together, I thought. After years of seething resentment against Toni for leaving her, my mother was actually talking to him again, if only minimally, to discuss my upcoming wedding. In fact, I had talked the two of them into coming to my house for dinner on the very night that I started bleeding.

I was sitting at my desk at work, my headset on, staring at the little black computer screen with the green uni-font, looking up business phone systems as an Account Representative. As I had been doing for weeks, I would put a customer on hold, and with the light on the six-button touch-tone phone flashing extra guilt into me, would call the caterer or the florist, also putting them on hold for another call. On this afternoon, I juggled a third and fourth button, giving Toni the time to meet for dinner, and reassuring my very nervous mother that I would try to be home before Toni got there.

It was somewhere in between a "Pacific Bell, can I help you?" and a "I thought you said we could have six items for that price. Okay, forget the egg rolls then," and a "Yes, Mom, I talked to him, he said he'll be there at *six*, I'll be home at five-thirty," that I felt a ping, and then a warm gush in my underwear.

My heart started pounding hard in my chest, but I finished up the calls I was on, and then yanked the plug to my microphone out of the socket, and threw my headset on my desk, telling my annoyed supervisor that I needed an emergency bathroom break.

As soon as I sat down on the toilet, I knew. My stomach was cramping as if my intestines were being tied in a knot, and a fast dribble of blood was coming out of me. I felt resigned and sad and alone in the stall of the office bathroom. I felt what I knew must be the embryo pass out of me, and I stood up and looked in the toilet, and saw what looked like a large semi-transparent grape, a small blob that only hours ago had the potential to be a human being, now floating around, already devoid of any life force.

I was too much in shock to cry, or really even think past the thought that I needed to go home. I flushed the baby that was not-to-be away, and had to put my hand against the stall to steady myself as I felt another wave of pain and nausea go through me. I grabbed a Kotex from the supply bin, and watched my supervisor's face change from her usual disapproving frown to concern, as I told her that I was leaving because I was having a miscarriage.

As I drove over the curvy road home, I could feel what was left of the baby's cushioning flowing out of me. I didn't think so much about the wedding, or Breen, or my bio parents coming together that night for dinner, or the loss of the baby, or if or when there would be another one, but rather put every bit of my concentration onto the double yellow line ahead, squeezing my thighs together, and making it home before what felt like my entire insides would come out.

When I got there, my anxious mother was waiting at the door. I pushed past her calling out that I was having a miscarriage, and ran to my bathroom, where I thankfully sat down and locked the door.

My mother's voice was calling through immediately.

"Chris? Are you alright?"

"No!" I called back. I really wanted to be alone as I felt the contractions pushing mini gushes of liquid out of my body.

There was quiet for a minute or two, but I knew she was out there.
"Darling, Toni is going to be here any minute."
"Yeah, I know. What do you want me to do?"

* * *

Now I have to stop this story for a minute, while I'm looking at this anguished girl, who used to be me, sitting on the toilet losing the baby that she really wanted. That girl is telling me not to reveal this next part of the story, because I may be unfairly putting my mother in a disparaging light, when actually she had so many wonderful, nurturing qualities. That girl had no idea that her mother was being self-centered; in fact, that girl felt the guilt her mother should have been feeling, and took it on herself as she sat there expelling her (now-ex) child-to-be. After all, her mother had driven all that way to visit with her hated ex-husband, under the insistence of the old (young) me; and now I was not only ruining everything, but also losing the only leverage I had, the baby, that could make my parents be civil to each other and pay attention to me.

It wasn't until years later, when there was this other Chris, in between that girl on the toilet, and the one typing tonight, that it dawned on her/me that, *Wow, my mother is so fucking narcissistic.*

And now me, the author here, feels compassion for her mother that suffered with such horrible anxiety that she could never be present with me, could never see past her own worrying, who did her best to love me. And I know, that every one of us, every human alive, can go to that place of blinding self-centeredness if they're not diligent and aware. That evening, as many evenings, my mother was lost in her own neurosis, her own fear; she hardly noticed that I was there. I didn't know that someday she would actually go lose her mind, but it might have helped that night.

* * *

Five minutes later she was at the bathroom door again.
"Chris? Can you come out now? Toni is here."
"Mom, I'm having a miscarriage! Do you get it?"

"Yes, I know, but can you come out? I have a drink for you."

I sat with my chin in the palm of my hands, staring at the Mardi Gras poster on the opposite wall. It seemed like I had ejected most of it by now, although the last thing I wanted to do was to come out and socialize. As I tended to do, I sucked it up, grabbed a new Kotex, and slowly stood up, flushing the toilet, shaking all over. When I opened the door, my mother was standing there with a Screwdriver in each hand, and she pushed the one in her left hand out towards me.

* * *

The wedding meeting with my parents went forward as planned, in spite of the miscarriage that was hardly mentioned. When I called Breen and told him the news, he was saddened and said that of course we were getting married anyway, not to worry, the next baby, my third pregnancy, would actually be planned, and being the third, would be the charm, and his prediction was right, it was. But her arrival in our family was not the panacea I hoped it would be, because her birth was overshadowed by something even more dramatic, more attention-getting in our family.

While George withdrew and snuck around, and I was trying to get married and have a baby, Cathy upstaged us both with her response to our dysfunctional family. I could sum it in one word, like I did 'meltdown' for George, and 'baby' for me, but that word has such ugly connotations in our society that perhaps it is more appropriate at the end of the story, after the word has been softened by circumstance.

There had been plenty of clues, and if I hadn't been in the habit of stuffing everything down before I could feel it, I might have had the appropriate suspicion; may have digested the hints and signs, instead of swallowing them whole, without tasting them. Then I wouldn't have been caught offguard the way I was.

There was the time, for instance, a sunny Saturday morning, when I dropped in at Ken and Cathy's house on a whim, during my bike ride. I was surprised to see Marco and Laura when I got there, and even more surprised that they had obviously spent the night. A small coil of jealousy penetrated me, wound through me, and then snaked back out leaving it's bitter trail, the one emotion I *did* allow myself to feel that day. I wondered how Cathy had become so close to our new half-brother and sister, when I felt like I was still barely getting to know them, and couldn't imagine asking them to sleep over.

The three of them were fooling around on the floor in their pajamas, the atmosphere buzzing with a post slumber party vibe, sleeping bags on the floor, a half-empty bowl of popcorn on the table, a few beer bottles strewn about. Ken was nowhere in sight.

Then there was that moment, that one freeze-frame filed carefully away in an obscure part of my brain, before I could take a look at it. The morning sun was slanting through the small, paned windows, the clean autumn air was coming through the front door I had left open, mixing with, and clearing out, the heavy, sleepy ambience inside; I could see the bright orange pumpkins outside in the patch beyond. A nervous but familiar laughter amongst my siblings wafted through the room, adding to my feeling of alienation, like I wasn't in on the joke. The snap came in the second it took for Marco, who was still in his sleeping bag, to roll over onto his back, and for Cathy to pounce on him, straddling him, wrestling with him in a playful way, her knees pinning down his arms, his feet in the bag rendering him helpless. She brought her face a few inches from his, laughing, looking directly into his eyes, her wild curly hair hanging down, partially concealing her face. In that moment, I could see that they shared knowledge, an intimacy that I wasn't privy to, and didn't want to be.

There was that other time, half a year later, on the Fourth of July, a day that was still a little creepy and surreal for me since the Robot thing with my mother, and this Fourth proved to be no different. The dusk that year was the purpley kind, and a bunch of us walked through it, dark silhouettes of three and four laughingly singing patriotic songs, leaving an afternoon party put on by T and Ed to walk down to the beach and set off the fireworks, real ones like M80s, to drop off of the pier; Piccolo Pete's were already whistling in the background.

I walked with T, and ahead of us were Cathy, Ken, and Marco. Cathy and Marco were talking animatedly, exaggerating the gestures of their hands, hitting each other on the butt, and laughing loud, as if they were the only ones that knew the inside jokes. Ken walked a few paces behind them in the shuffling way he had, his hands in the pockets of his cords, his head bent forward looking down at his feet. A boom, and then a big firework exploded in the deepening sky, and in the eerie shade of green that was cast as the sparkles trickled down, I saw Cathy and Marco play-wrestling each other with their hands, and Ken falling further behind them until he joined with another group. That green glow, and the reverberating *ka-BOOM* shot a weird feeling through me. T immediately sensed it, and nudged me in the arm. She raised her eyebrows, and jerked her head towards the scene between Cathy and Marco being played out in front of us. She had seen that snapshot too. I couldn't completely deny the existence of that one.

So really, if I had been completely honest and acknowledged those two pictures, the one of Cathy pinning Marco down on the floor, and the one of them play-fighting with their hands, the latter one perhaps underexposed but lit up by the green sparkles in the background, if I would have paid a little more attention to all the eyebrow twitching Cathy was doing those days, avoiding looking me directly in the eye, then I wouldn't have acted as shocked and outraged as I did that night that Cathy told me.

"I'm in love," is how she first put it that night when she walked in, sitting on a stool at my kitchen counter where I had been having a glass of wine with my friend Lori.

Now I knew that she had already had several 'affairs' on Ken, since she didn't think that their sex life was satisfactory. She justified her behavior by saying it was the only way she could save her marriage and not go crazy. It was just sex. She had never mentioned love.

"You're in *love*?" I repeated, with more than a hint of sarcasm, the aforementioned snapshots neatly pasted away and out of sight in a large album I kept in my head labeled 'Denial.' "Oh please. Cathy, it's not the first time you've had an affair, don't let sex cloud your judgment."

"No, it's way more than affair, and it really wouldn't be so much of a problem except for who it is…"

"You're in love with Marco, aren't you?" Lori said, softly but abruptly.

The words hung there above the kitchen counter. I looked at Cathy, hunched over, an expression of relief and gratitude on her face, but mixed in with a slight smirk of defiance.

I stared at her. I was in shock, until the Denial Album fell open, revealing the two telling snaps, and other unexamined pictures as well. I slammed the book shut in anger, needing to fuel my self-righteousness. *This was the last straw! The bottom!* (Or so I thought—I didn't know the half of it at that point.) My shock changed to horror as all the ramifications of the situation started oozing into my brain, with a little background rhythm I tried to ignore but finally recognized as the word *incest, incest*, thrumming over and over.

"What!?" I screamed at Cathy, pissed off both at her behavior and my own denial of it.

* * *

That word still sounded very bad to me back then, nasty, profane, and unspeakable, like 'cunt' or 'nigger. Later, it became just a word, an almost meaningless word, trying to define another behavior on the wide spectrum that humans exhibit. For those years I had to explain it, there was softening that could be done: *Oh they didn't grow up together, it wasn't as if they were really brother and sister, actually they were only half, and did you know that they allow half-siblings to marry in France?* But mostly I didn't try to explain it at all; I just became incestuous myself, by only hanging around our tight circle of friends who knew—I was too ashamed to explain it to anyone else, as if by hanging around with my siblings, I condoned what they were doing.

* * *

My initial reaction of shock and disdain burned bright the night of Cathy's revelation, but only a cold nugget of anger was left by the next morning. This nugget deposited itself in my stomach, and attached itself to the lining to feed and grow, taking up the space in my abdomen that was reserved for babies and the joy they were sure to bring. Here I was, I reasoned to myself, trying to put our broken Humpty Dumpty family back together again with babies and marriages, and Cathy came behind me and stomped on each piece of shell I carefully tried to glue. I didn't know back then that this job I had taken on, this job of Family Fixer, of course was not mine. Hell, if all the King's horses and all the King's men couldn't do it, what made me think that I had the special power, and what kind of expectations was I putting on my still-to-be-conceived kid? Nonetheless, I still took it as my responsibility. My mom rarely backed me up when it came to boundaries and Cathy, but this time I was sure I could get her on my side to put a stop to this outrageous behavior. I called her first thing, and spilled out the story in half-sentences and false starts. She didn't say much, except for her standard answer of "I'll have to discuss it with Dad." I was surprised when she called me back only a few minutes later to tell me she was coming over that very evening "to take care of things".

Unlike the Denial Album, that I usually kept shut tight until it burst open, spilling out ugly snapshots, I had another book, my book of Magical Thinking, a colorful fantasy book that I used so often it was worn and frayed along the edges. I lovingly opened it the afternoon I was waiting for my mother to arrive from Ukiah. There was a picture of my mother, an air of caring authority on her face, explaining to Cathy about morals. I looked at this page in my Fantasy Book often, especially after that time I caught Cathy kissing Geno, and I turned to it now, with an unrealistic optimism that always lifted me artificially and temporarily, only to drop me down hard with a thud when reality interceded. The reality of that gray afternoon proved to be a display of raw, uncensored emotions, and my perception of it over time has changed from obscenely ugly to unfortunately necessary.

I saw my mother's face through the sliding glass door, pinched and nervous.

"Do you have anything to drink, darling?" she asked me by way of greeting, sniffing, pushing past me, putting her handbag on the counter and already digging inside for her cigarette case. Armed with a martini glass in one hand, a lit Virginia Slim in the other, she sat down and said, "Get Cathy on the phone."

Cathy had told me she was having dinner at the Sottile's that night. Toni and Regina did not know about the romance between Cathy and Marco, and Cathy and Marco had no intention of telling them, but rather expected those of us who knew to shield them, covering up the new Secret, as we were brought up to do. I dialed the number on the wall phone.

"Oh, hi, Regina, this is Chris. I was wondering if I could speak to Cathy? Oh, I'm sorry you're in the middle of dinner," I repeated for my mother's benefit, "but can you put her on the phone a sec?"

I handed the phone to my mother, who stood up, inhaling deeply, her face simultaneously filled with fear and determination.

"Cathy. This is your mother." Her British accent always became stronger when she was being authoritative. "I'm here at Chris's house. Yes. I know what is going on, and I demand that you and Marco come over this instant to discuss it." She rolled her eyes and took another drag of her cigarette. "It doesn't matter what your plans are, if you're not here in an hour, I'm calling Toni and telling him the situation myself!" She hung up the phone with a sense of satisfaction. "She's coming."

I looked at my mother with hopeful admiration for having a limit on her tolerance, for making a stand, even though I knew Ray had probably told her to come.

Even though George had been distant and absent since the PSI, when I called him and told him the situation, he said he'd be right over.

An hour later, our little dysfunctional Family Summit had commenced. My mother sat on my living room couch, her cigarette held high at an angle, I sat on the green rug cross-legged; a crying, defiant Cathy and a nervous, ashen-faced Marco sat across the room, and George paced restlessly back and forth between the two doors. All of us were drinking gin, my mother telling me to "be a dear" any time anyone's glass was empty. The living room was oddly silent. All the big talk of what we were going to do, what we were going to say, all the energy of the anger that had been roiling only moments before was diffused when we came face to face with these people we loved. Finally, my mother took the lead and broke the silence.

"Cathy, we are gathered here this evening because your father and I are deeply concerned and shocked by the news of your behavior." British accent very pronounced now. "You simply must put a stop to it immediately—I won't hear of such a thing." She looked at Cathy pointedly, virtually ignoring Marco, who was rubbing the thighs of his jeans repeatedly with both hands and staring at the floor.

"Mom! All you guys! You don't *know*!" Cathy's mascara was smeared all over her face, and she was gulping on her martini. Her cigarette shook in her hand. "We're in *love*!" She said this as if there was no repudiation.

"Uh, Cathy, do you remember that you are *married*? Forget the minor detail that the guy you're fooling around with is your *brother,* but what about Ken?" I hated the sound of the sarcasm I heard in my voice—my usual defense when I'm scared or hurt.

"Well, he's obviously going to find out." Cathy mumbled this, looking down, talking quickly as she did when she didn't want to belabor a point.

"Yeah? Who is going to tell him? Us? Or are you going to wait 'til he hears it through the grapevine?" I was always worried about the one left in the dark.

This last point struck a nerve in George, the one who was left in the dark the longest. "Cathy, this is fucking *incest*!" He screamed the so far unspoken taboo word. The word instantly permeated the room with a raw, metallic ugliness. George's face was a tomato, the veins in his neck pronounced. I idly thought how easy it was for him to go back to this place of hysteria since he had crossed the barrier at the PSI. "Marco, you are my *brother*," George appealed to Marco, dramatically getting down on his knees and taking Marco's hands. "What kind of a man are you, *fucking your sister?*" He screamed the last part two inches from Marco's nose, but Marco hardly flinched.

Then, to my horror, George started punching himself in the stomach. I jumped up and tried to put my arms around him to calm him, but he shook me off. The floodgate of emotion had been unleashed. I felt the family imploding, the years of anger and pent up emotion, encouraged and fed with alcohol, coming together with such velocity that it was almost visible, like a mushroom cloud in the middle of the room that floated up, up, to the high-vaulted ceiling of my living room, and I went with it, looking down on the scene with detachment. I saw a family in pain, a family who loved each other, all the members yelling at once, everyone spilling passion, and hurtling insults, no one listening, no one seeing beyond their own wounds. I was down there too, crying and gesticulating like the rest of them, caught up in the vortex or the hurricane of energy.

Then George stood on the coffee table.

"People! People! Could everyone please *shut the fuck*...!" George screamed louder than anyone else, his voice cracking.

"Up." The last syllable was a defeated, quiet sob, as George stepped off the coffee table, and crumbled on to the floor, his shoulders heaving, his desperate crying demanding a remedy, suddenly the only sound in the room.

CHAPTER 14

Fixing a Hole (Where the Rain Came in) Whole Again

With the sun streaming through the hospital room window on that hot September Saturday, I held her in my arms for the first time. We looked at each other in the eyes, strangers who had never met on the physical plane. What she conveyed to me with her surprisingly blue (I thought they'd be brown) eyes was clear: "Oh, so *you're* the Mama," as if she had been wondering who had been carrying her around. I said to her softly, "I'm so glad to finally meet you, Reyna May."

And she was born, the only offspring ever to be of our five siblings. She was the only hope to heal a family that had been hurting for generations. Her life was destiny, and I had glimpsed providence when I saw that mother with the little blonde girl and had known that I was seeing my future.

She was probably conceived sometime on our honeymoon, as was meant to be, only about four months after the miscarriage, in spite of the fact that the doctor had advised me to "wait a year" to give my body time to recover. The soul that had been a part of mine since the Beginning, and for eternity, entered at exactly the moment she was fated.

It was difficult for me to accept, and to be happy about, getting what I truly wanted. I wasn't used to it. During my pregnancy, I whined about gaining sixty-five pounds, about feet and ankles so swollen that I could only wear flip-flops, about the insatiable thirst that only Big Gulps could quench, about burning indigestion, about getting out of my waterbed, about the heat of that long summer, about having to go to the beach in order to dig a hole so I could lay on my stomach, and everything else I could think to complain about. At one point I called my mother, crazy, crying, "What have I done?" over and over again, when really the delight and wonder of the life growing inside of me was so overwhelming, so much of a miracle, so much of a dream come true, that I couldn't allow myself to feel it.

I dreamed I was pregnant with a snake. My crazy, abusive mind told me I was kidding myself as I folded the miniature t-shirts to go in the tiny dresser. I felt like a fraud accepting gifts for the baby. I feared if there *were* a baby, surely something would be wrong with it, at least it would be ugly. Not until I saw the sonogram did I quell some of that neurosis, when I saw in the small black-and-white picture in the shape a windshield wiper makes, a perfectly formed little skeleton, and the crude outline of the little skull that already looked adorable to me. The sonogram picture did not reveal the sex however.

I didn't want to jinx what I Knew to be true; my faith was still only incubating like the baby, so the entire pregnancy I said it was a boy. It had to be a boy because I was so big. It had to be a boy because I was so round, because I held it high, because the crystal moved in that direction, because Breen had a boy before. I was doing my best to protect myself, to circumvent a crushing disappointment. *Boy*, *boy*, *boy;* it was a boy goddamn it; the punishing mantra in my head never let up. Then there was that day I came home and found the Hershey's chocolate bar wrapper on the counter, cleverly cut and pasted to say "It's a she."

My heart beat fast, and I felt lightheaded. It was a Sign, as if God was talking to me, but I didn't talk to God back then. I felt exquisite relief that what I Knew to be true simply was. Because of that birth announcement that someone had left on the counter, another obsessive worry stopped, but I still lied and said I thought it was a boy if anyone asked.

During the difficult birth, in hindsight made difficult by my own anxiety, I watched the monitor attached to the head of the baby inside of me, and at one point yelled out to the doctor, "*Don't hurt her*!" The relief of being honest after lying for so long flooded my body in spite of the contractions, the first time I had ever said out loud that I knew it as a girl. I still didn't trust myself completely though, because I *still* had to ask the sex when the baby was born.

The doctor decided on a cesarean, since my angst-ridden cervix refused to dilate in spite of the Pitocin they were dripping in my vein. Breen could see over the sheet they had put up bisecting me at the waist, (I guess to shield me from seeing myself cut open) and when I heard that first loud, lusty, healthy wail of a cry coming from the lower, numbed, seemingly detached part of my body, the first thing I said is, "What is it?"

And Breen's muffled answered through the mask he was wearing was, "I dunno, it's a head."

Minutes later the operating team passed her over me, and I only got a glimpse, maybe a second, of seeing her, but it was enough time to burn the image in my mind, and to memorize every inch of what I could see was a perfect, beautiful, rosy, noisy baby girl.

Now asking a new little person, only minutes old, to help nurse a family back to health, was a high expectation to have of someone who was only beginning to nurse herself. In some ways I could feel it happening before she was born. George seemed a lot better, so much so that his long hiatus from the Coastside ended, and he moved back over, in with me and Breen and his son, so a solid family unit awaited the arrival of the newborn.

Even though my mom and Ray didn't come to the hospital, they seemed genuinely excited about the new baby, and called the hospital several times. My mom came and stayed with me for a week, helping me with the baby and the cooking and all the visitors. I could feel my relationship with them improve almost immediately. I was a parent now; I was, in some respects, their peer.

Breen was the father I knew he would be, falling in love with his first daughter at first sight. He woke up in the night to change Reyna's diaper, when I would sleep right though her crying. Sometimes he would put her on my breast to nurse, without me ever waking up.

Some things have to get worse before they got better. In spite of the ugly confrontation, or maybe because of it, Cathy and Marco stayed together. Cathy moved out of Ken's house, taking almost nothing except for her clothes. For weeks I didn't hear from her. When I had my baby shower, she didn't come, but sent along a gift of a teddy bear like her own Wowo, appropriately wrapped in paper with a pattern of white sheep, with only one black one. Later someone told me that she was telling people that I had forced her to sleep on the beach. Eventually she found a very small studio in

Mill Valley, to be near Marco, who continued to be home for dinner every night with Toni and Regina.

I had been guardedly allowing the relationship between Toni and me to grow, mostly due to his initiative. He was seemingly trying to make up for lost time. When I became pregnant, he reveled in the prospect of having his first (he didn't know that it would be last and only) grandchild. This newly found-again bio-father, who I called Toni, and his wife Regina, (technically my step-mother) had been to a few functions with the family I had lived with most of my life, including Ray, my stepfather who I called Dad, my mom, Toni's ex, and even with Beba, my step-grandfather who had been married to my grandmother Gogo. These functions had been attended with all five of us siblings present, the first one being my wedding. I won't say that there wasn't tension when both sides of my family got together, but not enough for any outward friction, or for any behavior besides reserved politeness and nervous laughter.

That all changed when one of the worst possible scenarios that could occur between our newly forming blend of families happened: Cathy and Marco got together. Toni and Regina were the last to know, and took it worse than anyone else. It was decided by everyone that the two of them were not to be invited to functions together. I agreed that their relationship should not be acknowledged, but I was furious how their selfishness fucked everything up.

Toni made an effort to come over and see Reyna a few times after she was born, but then he started calling less than he had been since we had reunited. So far in our new relationship I had been playing almost hard to get, acting standoffish and refusing to call him Papa or return his *Te amo*s. Now I was feeling the tables turn, and the sick feeling I got when someone was about to dump me, the sickness that started all the way back from the original shocking dump in Chicago when Toni told the four-year-old me that he was moving to California while looking at himself shave in the bathroom mirror. The anxiety was starting to consume me. I called Toni a few times, taking the initiative, trying to reassure myself that he still cared. Toni was always polite enough, but didn't make any extra effort to see me. One day, I decided to go see him.

I crossed the Golden Gate Bridge in my orange bug singing along to KFRC. The late, mellow autumn sun streaming through the passenger-side of the car, shining on the empty car seat, gave me a mixed feeling of separation anxiety, and emancipation at having an afternoon to myself without the baby. I felt happy to take some action against the dread inside of me that something was wrong between Toni and me. I was going to surprise him at his ski shop. He was always complaining that I didn't drop in on him enough. This visit was sure to set things right.

I pulled up to the shingled A-frame nestled in the redwoods. I decided to arrive nonchalantly on the ruse of needing a new ski sweater for the trip to Yosemite I was planning with Breen and Reyna. I walked across all the crinkly fall leaves, in the deep shade, and through the door with huge triangular plate glass windows. The shop was quiet and serene inside, and was permeated with the distinct scent of new Patagonia fleece. I spotted Toni in the corner, helping the only customer in the store, a skinny guy that, as I got closer, sounded as if he had a Russian accent. Toni had heard me come in because the *clangle-clangle* of the door, and he acknowledged me by looking at me, his one inquisitive eyebrow arched. I gave him a little half-wave by wiggling my fingers and smiling. Toni returned my silent greeting with his characteristic frown, and turned his attention back to talking to the customer.

My heart sank a little at the less-than-warm greeting, but I wandered up and down the carpeted aisles looking at the Nordic style sweaters and fleecy shirts. Holding up one sweater at the end of the aisle, I glanced over the top of it to see what progress he had made with the Russian, who had put a new pair of skis on the counter. Toni rang up the sale, but then started talking in earnest to the customer, never once looking in my direction, giving the guy an awful lot of instruction about how to use the skis, about how to get in and out of the bindings, about how often they should be tuned up. The Russian picked up the skis several times and put them over his shoulder, as if he were ready to leave, but then put them back down as Toni went on and on. Finally he turned to walk out, nodding to me on the way.

"Hi Toni!" I said brightly, approaching the counter.

"Oh, hello, Christina." He was frowning at the receipt he had just printed from the cash register.

"How are you?" I pressed on, but he didn't answer. "Is everything okay?" I asked the question that summed up everything I had been feeling for months. I fiddled with the ski wax on the counter, suddenly afraid to look into my father's face.

"How am I?" Toni asked almost rhetorically, but more as if to say, 'Do you have enough time to listen to the answer?' "I am fine, I suppose,

Christina, as fine as I can be under the circumstances that my son is now making love to my daughter."

I nodded my head in sympathy and agreement, but I thought that this was not considered news anymore. I waited for him to ask me how Reyna was—I still didn't necessarily expect him to ask about me, but I didn't even get that.

"What is it you want?" He said it like the whoosh of a fly swatter. It smashed me, took my breath away, my heart pounding in the old terror. *Don't go to California.* I dared to look in his face, just as I had looked in the bathroom mirror at him so many years before when I was standing on the toilet, searching for some understanding. His face had gone dark; it was in more shadow than the dwindling sun setting in the trees warranted. I babbled on out of nervousness.

"Uh, well, Breen said he'd watch Reyna, so I thought I'd drive over... we're going to the snow next weekend... and the baby, too." I tripped and stumbled over my words, losing concentration, feeling the blood in my face. "So then, well, I was wondering if maybe I could get a sweater to take... my other one...it's kind of tight since the baby..." I kept mentioning Reyna. The cure to make it better. I was used to being rejected, but no one was going to reject her.

"What, they do not have ski shops nearer to where you live?" He saw me squirming. He didn't care.

"Well, yeah, they do...but I thought, well, I hadn't talked to you for a while and... I thought you might be wondering how the baby was doing and..."

"Christina, can we go outside for a little walk? I need some air, I am suffocating in here." Toni walked quickly for the door, holding it open for me. I walked out before him, into the cold October air. The sky was that deep red that happens at that time of year, and we walked out past the dark silhouetted trees to the jogger's path by an inlet of water. Toni started walking at a very fast pace, and I kept up with him in perfect synch.

Slightly out of breath, partly from the speed we were walking, and partly because of the deep Fear that hadn't been around in a while, I said, "Toni, what's wrong? Are you mad at me for something?" My mind started making a list of what I could have possibly done wrong. Was it because I didn't visit sooner? Because I asked him for a sweater? Because I came without letting him know first? I was back in confession, making up things I had done wrong, because I couldn't think of any.

"Actually I *AM* mad," he barked finally.

My heart was pounding. I glanced over and saw that same displeased look on his face that he gave me when I was four, when I cried because he threw me in the lake. Panic. Don't leave. God.

"What? Why? Not at me?" I did little skips to keep up with him.

"Why? I told you why. All this business. The Cathy, the Marco. I don't understand this, *merda*, this kind of thing." He was starting to pepper his sentences with Italian.

"Well, I don't like it either, Toni, but what does this have to do with me?"

"What does it have to do with you? Hmmm. What does it have to do with you."

He said it like a statement, not a question. I didn't understand the sarcasm in his voice. His thin hair blew up with a gust of wind, and he looked at me sideways through squinted eyes as if to see exactly what it did have to do with me.

"I don't know Christina, when I see your face I see Cathy. You look like her. You remind me of all the ugly business that's going on, the Cathy, the Marco. Now Regina is hardly speaking to me. Sometimes I wonder if..." Here he stopped himself, shaking his head.

"But I haven't done anything wrong!" I cried out, surprised at the pitch of my voice, the velocity that it came out of me. This got Toni's attention, and he stopped abruptly on the path, causing a cyclist to veer around us. He rubbed his chin as if he really needed to think this one over.

"No, no I don't suppose you have," he finally said, giving me a second of relief. "But I cannot help the way I feel. I am sorry. I just cannot look at you right now; it brings me too much pain. You remind me of Cathy." He dug his hands into his windbreaker, and started walking again, a little slower now.

The cold wind blew the tears out the sides of my eyes. We were back at the shop. I actually considered trying to go in for a sweater, just to buy more time, like I tried to get one more day before he left for California. My face and hands were cold from the late afternoon air, but I was freezing on the inside.

"I'm going to go," I said, my teeth chattering like crazy.

"Yes, goodbye, Christina." He turned and walked into the store.

This time Toni watched me go from inside the window. I ignored him for eight years; only half the time he ignored me.

* * *

It was an unseasonably warm June day sixteen years later, when the air that swirled through the open pavilion was scented with California golden hay for the first time that year. From my vantage point, sitting next to Cathy at the elevated table of honor, I gazed down at the sea of large round tables covered in white, and the contingents of people, the tables separating them like ethnic New York neighborhoods, whose diversity, when put together, make up the flavor of the city as a whole. One table was chatting in Polish, another talking loudly in Italian, a quiet table with clipped British accents were scattered among the tables of rowdy Americans of all ages. The talking and laughter within these enclaves had ratcheted up a notch after the hushed silence and subsequent wild applause that erupted when a smiling George and his beautiful new wife Laurie floated into the room like a cliché of the slow-mo in a romantic movie, their wedding finery rippling out behind them like a gentle wind machine had been turned on them. At forty-five, George had surprised us all by ending his confirmed bachelor status. As I looked down on the tables below me, I saw no hint of animosity, no vibes of hostility; no evidence was apparent of the turmoil that preceded this monumental event. On this day the crowd was sweet and accepting of one another; the only emotion I could feel snaking through the tables was love.

From one corner of the roofed pavilion, the dozen or so who made up Beba's family, the Polish contingent, stood up. Each was holding a tiny shot of cherry liqueur called Wisniuwka, (you say it *vish-noof-ka*) and started singing a song in slow, deliberate unison, their pale blue eyes wide and sincere: *"Sto lat, sto lat, nie zyje zyje nam!"* a popular song meaning *Good luck, good cheer, may you live a hundred years!* I thought I detected the slightest hint of defiance, or maybe it was more like possessiveness, as if they wanted to make sure that people knew George, or Jurek as they called him, was part of their family. After a momentary pause, the crowd burst out in a fresh round of applause.

As if not to be outdone, the Italians stood up. I looked over to see Toni, Regina, Marco, Laura, and various cousins, uncles, and aunts stand up with their glasses of red wine, cheering, *"Evviva gli sposi! Salute!"*

I looked over to the table where some of my mother's family had flown in from England. My cousin Lucille looked fetching in her gigantic green flowery hat, like something only Princess Di could have pulled off, and her daughter Ami looked quite SoHo in her tight, skinny black pants and metallic tunic.

My gaze wandered over to the table where Breen sat with his family. He was now my ex-husband, and had been for about ten years due to his drinking, but now he was sober, and he and I remained the best of friends. He sat with his new wife Lori, his brother Mark, and girlfriend Alicia, along with the now seventeen-year-old Reyna May, and her stepsiblings Val and Jason.

* * *

We had been there the day before, practicing, when the pavilion was quiet and peaceful, instead of crackling with excitement as it was now. There had been a moment of tension when the Wedding Coordinator could not place all the round and other odd-shaped pegs of our family members into the square family box she had in mind.

"Who is ushering the parents to the front row?" The coiffed coordinator asked Laurie. The planning lady seemed more nervous than the bride, to me. "Rather, I should say your parents, Laurie. George said not to worry about his parents, there were too many," she said, and then in a lower tone, "We have dealt with blended families before."

Laurie responded with a quick arch of one eyebrow.

"Absolutely not," Laurie said with certainty. "*All* of the parents will be ushered to the front."

"How many parents does George have?" The woman was struggling to maintain her serene in-control face.

"He has, uh..." her eyes rolled up while she counted, "...six. Six attending the wedding, but since Johnny is the best man, we'll only need five seats up front."

Johnny was her name for Beba, after the English name he adopted for himself, John. Beba had already seen his eightieth birthday, and was a little frail. I had had a moment with him earlier as he stood on the lawn looking forlorn. I had taken his arm and guided him to the practice area, and was walking slowly when suddenly I was overwhelmed by a feeling of love and gratitude for this man who had taken the time to take me on Sunday drives, and to church, and doughnuts afterward, where no one else had paid that kind of attention to me.

I liked the way Laurie gave the wedding coordinator the number of parents without a hint of embarrassment, where I always stumbled and faltered over the explanations of my family red-faced, trying to change the subject. This girl, who was about to enter our family, had parents that had been married over fifty years, yet saw no irony in saying George had six parents. I thought that he would actually have seven if Gogo was still alive, but as it was, Beba was in the wedding, and his wife Eva, Toni and Regina, and my mom and Ray would be escorted to the front as the groom's, my brother's, parents. My parents. This was my family.

* * *

As I said in the beginning, before I started showing selected slices of my life's cake, the Agreement I made in *this* particular life, in *this* journey through the world, was to fix the one dark hole in my heart. Not a literal hole in my cardiac muscle, but rather the large, yet gauzy and elusive, hole in my soul heart. The hole I promised to take on, with as much humor and grace as possible, and then fill, in time to tell about it.

At the time I made this contract with the Universe, before Toni's sperm had ever danced around and finally penetrated my mother's egg, sparking me into this plane of consciousness, I had no idea how to fulfill the mission. I didn't know whether the hole should be closed up, filled, cauterized, or simply eradicated as if it never existed. I took on the task anyway, and allowed myself to be born after those two days of indecision that caused my mom that extra agony of labor, as well as missing her Christmas dinner, and began my task of healing this mysterious cavity that I had no idea how to restore.

The hole was a deep one that had passed on through generations, this much I knew at the start. What I didn't know was that as I healed my own soul, I was simultaneously healing the hearts and souls of all the ancestors that came before me, and all the descendants yet to come, which would have to funnel through the narrow one-person channel of Reyna. I knew that I had to have Reyna to help heal the family, but what I didn't know was why. I thought the reason was that the family would step up; be awed and inspired by an innocent one, which was partially true, but more importantly, and why I felt the need to procreate so urgently, I believe, was that without her, the family would not be able to continue to grow and reconcile. Through Reyna and her offspring-to-be, the seed of our family, planted millenniums ago, would ripen, and eventually reach its proper fruition. The limited, mortal part of me, of course, has no idea when, and in what generation, this fruit will eventually appear, but I imagine it to be gloriously orange and juicy, and when completely ripe, purple and luscious.

* * *

Some psychologists and spiritual teachers suggest that you have to go back at least three generations to look for reasons or explanations when untangling the emotional legacy of a family's history. After trying to unravel some of the knots by writing this tale, I believe you may have to go a lot farther back than that. As I asked myself why, one why would lead to another, until there were so many *whys* zinging through my head and bouncing off the pages I wrote that I started to believe that the question of the hole couldn't be answered. I felt like Hercules trying to slay the Hydra, the many-headed monster. Every time I tried to cut off one of the ugly heads, two more would grow in their place. A dysfunctional family, which I have, (and it seems that the majority of us have) is a Hydra. The problem is almost always multifaceted and can't be eliminated in a single effort or by single person, unless maybe you're a half-God like Hercules, because the problem is persistent, the problem is pervasive, and the problem is attributed not to one, but to many people.

* * *

On my mother's side, back in England, my great-grandfather Charles left my great-grandmother May, to run away with his Canadian mistress who supposedly ended up taking all his money, leaving none for his five children, one of them being my grandmother Gogo. Gogo never really talked about her dad, either kindly or unkindly, as though he never existed.

Gogo left her husband, my grandfather, Archibald to move to Canada with her young Polish lover. My mother followed her there and obeyed Gogo's instructions not to write to or contact her father in any way, causing her to lose touch with him for many years.

My mother had a baby for her mother, after much coercing by my grandmother, with the agreement to lie about the arrangement, causing her husband to leave her.

* * *

On my father's side, my great-grandfather Michele killed a man. He had left the extortionists of Sicily, had taken refuge in the great hope of America, and settled in Boston where my grandmother Michaela was born. While shaving one morning, he saw a man with a gun in the mirror. He may have wondered briefly how the Mafia had followed him to America, and then, on instinct, he whirled around and slashed the intruder's throat with a long old-fashioned razor. Shots rang out from the backup thug. My great-grandfather Michele was shot in the chest, missing his heart, but widening the hole. My great-grandmother was shot in the knee.

The family fled back to Sicily, where my eleven-year-old grandmother Michela couldn't keep up with the reading and writing in Italian, and was sent to the first grade. After only a few years in school, she dropped out to help her mom. My grandfather, Giuseppe, was a chauffer for a baron and drove the only car in town. He courted my grandmother by serenading her outside of her window, singing relentlessly day after day until he saw the response he wanted: she slightly opened the curtain. With this pane glass-separated courtship as their only dating experience, they married and had five children, my father, Antonino, being the oldest.

When Toni was of age, he couldn't date either, he could only ride his bike by girls' houses while on ruse of doing errands. One day during the war, he was on one such bike ride when he saw his friends lying in a nearby field of tall grass. They appeared to be asleep in the noontime sun. Puzzled, my father approached his buddies to see what they were doing, but before he reached them he knew they were dead. He tried to pick one of them up, but his hand went right through a Hole in his gut. Toni pulled his hand out and absentmindedly wiped the blood and entrails on his pants, unaware of how the phantom Hole shot in his grandfather's heart by the extortionist had lain dormant in Toni's soul and was now shot open as he saw his friends that had been killed by the allied invaders.

Toni fled to Canada after the war, waiting to get into this America he had heard so much about from his mother. He and my mother married in Canada, and immigrated to Chicago, my mother insisting in retrospect that Toni used her to get in the country. After agreeing to give away his first son, Toni left my mother to marry Regina on the other side of the country, abandoning my siblings and me.

* * *

Three generations of divorced women before me. I was the third generation of fatherless women. I had to divorce Breen before he would stop drinking. Cathy divorced Ken.

* * *

It seemed this hole was so many generations old that it would be impossible to fill. I tried all the usual methods: pouring alcohol down the hole, camouflaging it with a cigarette smoke screen. Making love, the hole was filled temporarily, and sometimes a new romance would let me forget the hole ever existed, but after the glow wore off, more than once I fell into the hole, drowning, almost swallowed up whole.

I never fell down in the hole after I divorced Breen, like I did with Kevin, because he really never left, breaking the pattern by always being there for Reyna, as I knew he would before I had her. But after Breen, I quickly filled up the hole with a passionate, inappropriate, consuming, drama and drug-filled relationship with Tom, twelve years my junior. When that ended two and a half years later, I fell in, the hole bigger than it had ever been.

It was during this period of gurgling around in the hole, trying to cling to the rim of it so I could at least catch my breath that a laser-pen beam of enlightenment shined on me. Not a golden glow with angel voices, just a thin, blue, LED moonbeam between the eyes. It happened one afternoon when I was lying on my bedroom floor in a fetal position, as I had every afternoon for months, sobbing, rocking back and forth, and wallowing in my perceived pain, when suddenly I had my moment of Providence. I think this moment may only come once in a lifetime, sometimes not at all; it sits in dormancy waiting for the drowning person to hit the bottom of the well. It's tricky to catch that moment, because if it is a second too late, I think it is lost forever; I've seen it happen. Luckily, I had my moment, and I listened to it, instead of thinking I had imagined it, or boo-hooing louder than the patient wisdom that was trying to get through. I heard a clear voice; the voice sounded a lot like mine, but it wasn't in my head, it was distinctly external and speaking to me. It said simply, "It doesn't have to be this way."

That was the first time I heard my inner voice. The first time I knew God in this way. What the voice had said made startling sense to me: there was no gain in wallowing in this anguish. I had never before considered that I had a choice. That is all that healing is, I think. It is far simpler than some people make it out to be. There's really no need for pilgrimages, Holy Waters, or Shamans, though they can't hurt; it really only takes a decision. I think that the healing is accomplished the instant the sufferer no longer sees the value in pain. That afternoon when I was crying on the floor of my bedroom was my moment to begin. Soon after that came the journaling, meditation, Buddhism, yoga, and lots more therapy, but all that was just icing; that beautiful moment on the floor of my room was the cake.

Just as I see the patterns running through generations, I see the patterns that also exist in individual lives, changing, if at all, over decades, rather than centuries, as in our family heritage. Many patterns in my family continued, and some still continue. Cathy continued being a part of dramatic events, stealing away her gay friend's husband, ending her fifteen-year relationship with Marco. My mother continued to be absent and in denial of reality, increasing this tendency with alarming alacrity, until she no longer identified with this world at all, dissolving into a babbling dementia the doctors diagnosed as Alzheimer's, for lack of any deeper understanding. Toni's pattern of flight rather than fight is still present but improving as it becomes more intermittent. Ray's pattern of selfishness and control had an apex, that when reached, began to reverse as his heart softened and opened with each advancing year. Gogo's pattern of secrecy was handed off to George when she died, and he hasn't been able to completely escape it yet.

My pattern, of trying to change everyone else around me instead of the only person I *could* change, myself, comes to me slowly but vividly, humbling me for my former audacity. Like a kaleidoscope, I change one little pebble of color within myself, and the entire pattern completely changes, the many mirrors, my family and friends, reflecting back to me in myriad of ways I never expected.

I knew in second grade I was going to be a teacher, but what I didn't know was that I was born into a family of teachers. Every member, Gogo, Beba, my mother, Toni, Cathy, George, Reyna, the rest of the family, my friends and loves; every one of them was and is there for a reason, to teach me lessons I needed to learn in order to fulfill this Agreement I made at the beginning: How to fix the hole in my heart, in time to tell the story.

And now I know. The Hole is put there for a reason, and though it might not be apparent at first, the bigger the hole, the luckier that soul actually is. Where before I thought of the pain and struggle that created my hole as a sort of failure to hide, I now see it as a right of passage to celebrate. I notice that people, who make it through the dark tunnel of the hole to the other side, are often the people I am most in awe of, not only for surviving, but also for sometimes turning their sorrow into something else. My misunderstanding was that I had to fill the hole up with stuff, but now I know that only clogs it. The hole needs to be left alone, yet not avoided for fear of falling in, just watched, observed, and tended to; then Spirit can breathe through it, through me, through you, and instead of fear, love can, and will, eventually swirl out that dark place.

Made in the USA
San Bernardino, CA
13 January 2013